SOPHIE TREADWELL

Sophie Treadwell was born in California in 1885. She went to
High School in San Francisco and then to the University of
California, from which she graduated in 1906 and became a
reporter on the San Francisco Bulletin. The highlights of
her career as a journalist included an investigative series
on homeless women, an exclusive interview with Mexican
revolutionary Pancho Villa, and a spell in Europe as one of the
first women foreign correspondents covering the 1914-18 War.
She wrote four novels and more than thirty plays, including
O Nightingale (1922), *Gringo* (1922), *Machinal* (1928),
Ladies Leave (1929), *Lusita* (1931), *Plumes in the Dust* (1936),
For Saxophone (1939-41) and *Hope for a Harvest* (1941), after
which she gave up writing for the stage. She died in 1970.

A Selection of Other Volumes in this Series

*Published by Theatre Communications Group, distributed by Nick Hern Books

SOPHIE TREADWELL

MACHINAL

ROYAL NATIONAL THEATRE
London

NICK HERN BOOKS
London

A Nick Hern Book

Machinal first published in this edition
in Great Britain in 1993 as a paperback original
jointly by the Royal National Theatre, London
and Nick Hern Books Limited,
14 Larden Road, London W3 7ST

Reprinted 1998, 1999

Machinal copyright © 1993 by the Roman Catholic Church of the
Diocese of Tucson

Front cover photo of Fiona Shaw in the 1993
Royal National Theatre production by Mark Douet

Typeset by Country Setting, Woodchurch, Kent TN26 3TB
Printed and bound in Great Britain by Cox & Wyman Ltd,
Reading, Berkshire

A CIP catalogue record for this book is available from the
British Library

ISBN 1 85459 211 4

Produced off-Broadway by the New York Shakespeare Festival:
Joseph Papp, producer

Machinal was first performed in Great Britain as *The Life Machine* in 1931. It was first performed in Britain under its original title in 1993 on the Lyttelton stage of the Royal National Theatre with the following cast and production team. Previews from 9 October. Press night: 15 October.

EPISODE ONE: TO BUSINESS

Adding Clerk	Bill Wallis
Filing Clerk	James Duke
Stenographer	Lynn Farleigh
Telephone Girl	Matilda Ziegler
George H. Jones	John Woodvine
Young Woman	Fiona Shaw

EPISODE TWO: AT HOME

Young Woman	Fiona Shaw
Mother	June Watson
Garbage Man	Alec Wallis
Woman	Yvonne Nicholson
Boy	Timothy Matthews
Young Man	David Bark-Jones
Girl	Juliette Gruber
Woman	Rachel Power
Man	Michael Brogan
Wife	Cate Hamer
Husband	Michael Bott
Singer	Sara Griffiths

EPISODE THREE: HONEYMOON

George H. Jones	John Woodvine
Bellboy	Timothy Matthews
Young Woman	Fiona Shaw

EPISODE FOUR: MATERNAL

Nurse	Lynn Farleigh
Young Woman	Fiona Shaw
George H. Jones	John Woodvine
Doctor	Christopher Rozycki

EPISODE FIVE: PROHIBITED

First Man	Ciaran Hinds
Second Man	Colin Stinton
Man at Bar	Roger Sloman
Boy at Bar	Timothy Matthews

Man at Bar	Michael Brogan
Woman at Bar	Rachel Power
Telephone Girl	Matilda Ziegler
Young Woman	Fiona Shaw
Man Behind Bar	Marcus Heath
Girl	Harriet Harrison
Man	Michael Bott

EPISODE SIX: INTIMATE

| Man | Ciaran Hinds |
| Young Woman | Fiona Shaw |

EPISODE SEVEN: DOMESTIC

| George H Jones | John Woodvine |
| Young Woman | Fiona Shaw |

EPISODE EIGHT: THE LAW

Bailiff	Alec Wallis
Clerk	David Holdaway
Court Reporter	Christopher Rozycki
Judge	Bill Wallis
Defense Lawyer	Roger Sloman
First Reporter	James Duke
Second Reporter	Michael Brogan
Young Woman	Fiona Shaw
Prosecution Lawyer	Colin Stinton
Third Reporter	David Bark-Jones

EPISODE NINE: A MACHINE

Priest	Allan Mitchell
Singer	Marcus Heath
Jailer	Paul Benzing
Young Woman	Fiona Shaw
Matron	Lynn Farleigh
Barber 1	Bill Wallis
Barber 2	David Holdaway
First Guard	Alec Wallis
Second Guard	Christopher Rozycki

Director	Stephen Daldry
Settings	Ian MacNeil
Costumes	Clare Mitchell
Lighting	Rick Fisher
Music	Stephen Warbeck
Movement	Quinny Sacks
Dialect Coach	Joan Washington
Company Voice Work	Patsy Rodenburg

Introduction

Machinal is the most famous work of Sophie Treadwell, a playwright, journalist, novelist, producer and sometime actor and director who was born and raised in California. She began writing plays and acting at the University of California, from which she graduated in 1906. Treadwell hoped to be a performer but her onstage career was limited to a brief stint in vaudeville and occasional dramatic roles, usually in her own works. Like many American women playwrights of her generation she was trained as a reporter, and in her early years she covered everything from theatrical premieres to baseball games for the *San Francisco Bulletin*. Treadwell soon became a respected journalist whose accomplishments included an 'undercover' series on homeless women, an exclusive interview with Mexican revolutionary Pancho Villa, a European tour as a war reporter during World War One, and a year as a special correspondent in Mexico during World War Two.

As Nancy Wynn records in her dissertation on Treadwell, the playwright had a long and extraordinary life. Although she suffered from debilitating illnesses (with symptoms resembling those attributed to Helen in *Machinal*) she was an indefatigable worker and traveler. Her journeys throughout the world were sometimes the inspiration for her plays, whose settings extend from Moscow to Mexico. Treadwell was married for two decades until his death to journalist William O. McGeehan, but she retained her own name and career and often maintained a residence separate from his. A member of the feminist Lucy Stone League, she marched in favor of women's suffrage and wrote about society's oppression of women. She occasionally produced and even directed her own work, a rare accomplishment in the male-dominated world of the American commercial theater. In the course of her career Treadwell – who died in 1970 at the age of 84 – completed hundreds of newspaper stories, four novels and more than thirty plays, seven of which appeared on New York stages.

Treadwell's early works include *Gringo*, based on her experiences in Mexico, and *O Nightingale*, a comedy about a stage-struck young woman that Treadwell herself co-produced. She wrote *Machinal* (the term is French for 'mechanical' or 'automatic'), the play for which she is best remembered today, in 1928. Loosely based on the sensational murder trial of Ruth Snyder and Judd Gray, *Machinal* was a critical success, ran for

91 performances in New York, and was chosen by Burns Mantle for his volume *The Best Plays of 1928-29*. Reviewers compared the work favorably to Theodore Dreiser's *An American Tragedy* in theme and Elmer Rice's *The Adding Machine* in technique. Brooks Atkinson of *The New York Times* – who was so intrigued by *Machinal* that he reviewed the production twice – called it 'a triumph of individual distinction, gleaming with intangible beauty . . . an illuminating, measured drama such as we are not likely to see again.' *Machinal* was even lauded in a *Times* editorial as a play that 'in a hundred years . . . should still be vital and vivid.' In 1931 the drama premiered in London under the title *The Life Machine*. Although some reviewers were offended by the play's sexual content, the London *Times* critic had no such problem and considered all but the last scene 'expressive and beautifully clean-cut.' *Machinal* had its greatest triumph in Russia, where it enjoyed a long run at Moscow's Kamerny Theatre before touring the provinces. A television adaptation was aired in the United States in 1954, and a revival with choreography by Sophie Maslow was performed a few years later.

Machinal uses expressionist techniques to create a parable about 'an ordinary young woman' who lives in a mechanized, materialistic world. Treadwell takes Helen through the stages of a kind of modern Everywoman: work in a boring office, marriage to a boss who offers her financial security ('he's a Vice-President – of course he's decent' her mother insists), a motherhood that oppresses her and a lover who abandons her. The expressionist form – flat characters, repetitive dialogue and action, numerous short scenes, harsh audio effects, confusion of inner and outer reality – is the perfect medium for presenting the life of a young woman who asks an impersonal society 'Is nothing mine?'

Treadwell attacks capitalism for putting even intimate relationships on an economic footing, but her critique extends to technology, medicine, law, motherhood, the press, romance (including a speakeasy that closely resembles a contemporary singles bar) and even religion. It is a recognizably feminist critique as well: the audience looks through Helen's eyes, understands the events from her perspective. Throughout the nine scenes – perhaps echoing the nine months of gestation – Treadwell shows her protagonist confronting a phalanx of male characters with the power to determine her life. Again and again Helen complains of claustrophobia, a motif of entrapment that runs as a common thread through the plays of such female contemporaries of Treadwell as Susan Glaspell, Zona Gale, Georgia Douglas Johnson and Lillian Hellman.

Sophie Treadwell never had another success comparable to *Machinal*, although she continued writing novels and plays for many years. Closest in theme and style to *Machinal* is the expressionist *For Saxophone* which relies heavily on music, dance and the voices of unseen characters to tell the story of another young woman trapped in a marriage of convenience. Her works also include *Plumes in the Dust*, based on the life of writer Edgar Allan Poe; *Rights*, an unproduced drama about eighteenth-century feminist Mary Wollstonecraft; and *Hope for a Harvest*, an autobiographical play exposing prejudice and environmental destruction in her native California. Embittered by the lukewarm reception of *Harvest*, Treadwell presented no more plays on the New York stage. In 1941, the very same year *Hope for a Harvest* appeared, the eminent critic George Jean Nathan sneered that 'even the best of our [American] women playwrights falls immeasurably short of the mark of our best masculine' because women 'by nature' lack 'complete objectivity' and the emotional control enjoyed by their male counterparts. It was in such an atmosphere of condescension that Sophie Treadwell strove to make her mark as a dramatist.

Unfortunately, most of the standard histories of drama in the United States reveal similar attitudes, and Treadwell rarely rates more than a line or two if she is acknowledged at all. Even granted that *Machinal* is her only outstanding work, the obscurity into which she and her play fell obviously has much to do with her gender (her sister playwrights suffered a similar fate) and to *Machinal*'s biting indictment of a world ruled by men. The current scholarly and theatrical interest in Treadwell and *Machinal* in the United States is partly due to feminist efforts to write women back into the theatrical history from which they have been erased, but it also stems from the fact that *Machinal*'s universe is uncomfortably like our own. The cacophony of urban sounds that underlies each scene is remarkably similar, while *Machinal*'s repetitive dialogue, woven of clichés, foreshadows the work of playwrights like Samuel Beckett, Harold Pinter and, as critic Frank Rich recently observed, David Mamet. As our lives become ever more mechanized and standardized, the story of one lone individual seeking to make her voice heard grows in relevance. Just as timely is the way Helen – like Treadwell herself – tries to find financial security without sacrificing her dreams, to control her own body and shape her own future, in a world in which women's power to do so remains severely limited.

Judith E. Barlow
State University of New York at Albany

Characters

YOUNG WOMAN
TELEPHONE GIRL
STENOGRAPHER
FILING CLERK
ADDING CLERK
MOTHER
HUSBAND
BELLBOY
NURSE
DOCTOR
YOUNG MAN
GIRL
MAN
BOY
MAN
ANOTHER MAN
WAITER
JUDGE
LAWYER FOR DEFENSE
LAWYER FOR PROSECUTION
COURT REPORTER
BAILIFF
REPORTER
SECOND REPORTER
THIRD REPORTER
JAILER
MATRON
PRIEST

The Plot is the story of a woman who murders her husband – an ordinary young woman, any woman.

The Plan is to tell this story by showing the different phases of life that the woman comes in contact with, and in none of which she finds any place, any peace. The woman is essentially soft, tender, and the life around her is essentially hard, mechanized. Business, home, marriage, having a child, seeking pleasure – all are difficult for her – mechanical, nerve nagging. Only in an illicit love does she find anything with life in it for her, and when she loses this, the desperate effort to win free to it again is her undoing.

The story is told in nine scenes. In the dialogue of these scenes there is the attempt to catch the rhythm of our common city speech, its brassy sound, its trick of repetition, etc.

Then there is, also, the use of many different sounds chosen primarily for their inherent emotional effect (steel riveting, a priest chanting, a Negro singing, jazz band, etc.), but contributing also to the creation of a background, an atmosphere.

The Hope is to create a stage production that will have 'style,' and at the same time, by the story's own innate drama, by the directness of its telling, by the variety and quick changingness of its scenes, and the excitement of its sounds, to create an interesting play.

Scenically this play is planned to be handled in two basic sets (or in one set with two backs)

The first division – the first Four Episodes – needs an entrance at one side, and a back having a door and a large window. The door gives, in

Episode 1 – to Vice President's office.

Episode 2 – to hall.

Episode 3 – to bathroom.

Episode 4 – to corridor.

And the window shows, in

Episode 1 – An opposite office.

Episode 2 – An inner apartment court.

Episode 3 – Window of a dance casino opposite.

Episode 4 – Steel girders. (Of these, only the casino window is important. Sky could be used for the others.)

The second division – the last Five Episodes – has the same side entrance, but the back has only one opening – for a small window (barred).

Episode 5, window is masked by electric piano.
Episode 6, window is disclosed (sidewalk outside).
Episode 7, window is curtained.
Episode 8, window is masked by Judge's bench.
Episode 9, window is disclosed (sky outside).

There is a change of furniture, and props for each episode – only essential things, full of character. For Episode 9, the room is closed in from the sides, and there is a place with bars and a door in it, put straight across stage down front (back far enough to leave a clear passageway in front of it).

Lighting concentrated and intense. – Light and shadow – bright light and darkness. – This darkness, already in the scene, grows and blacks out the light for dark stage when the scene changes are made.

Offstage Voices: Characters in the Background Heard, but Unseen:
A Janitor
A Baby
A Boy and a Girl
A Husband and Wife
A Husband and Wife
A Radio Announcer
A Negro Singer

Mechanical Offstage Sounds
A small jazz band
A hand organ
Steel riveting
Telegraph instruments
Aeroplane engine

Mechanical Onstage Sounds
Office Machines (typewriters, telephones, etc.)
Electric piano.

Characters: in the Background Seen, Not Heard
(Seen, off the main set; i.e., through a window or door)
Couples of men and women dancing
A Woman in a bathrobe
A Woman in a wheel chair
A Nurse with a covered basin
A Nurse with a tray
The feet of men and women passing in the street .

EPISODE ONE

To Business

Scene: an office: a switchboard, filing cabinet, adding machine, typewriter and table, manifold machine.

Sounds: office machines: typewriters, adding machine, manifold, telephone bells, buzzers.

Characters and their machines
 A YOUNG WOMAN *(typewriter)*
 A STENOGRAPHER *(typewriter)*
 A FILING CLERK *(filing cabinet and manifold)*
 AN ADDING CLERK *(adding machine)*
 TELEPHONE OPERATOR *(switchboard)*
 JONES

Before the curtain
 Sounds of machines going. They continue throughout the scene, and accompany the YOUNG WOMAN'*s thoughts after the scene is blacked out.*

At the rise of the curtain
 All the machines are disclosed, and all the characters with the exception of the YOUNG WOMAN.

 Of these characters, the YOUNG WOMAN, *going any day to any business. Ordinary. The confusion of her own inner thoughts, emotions, desires, dreams cuts her off from any actual adjustment to the routine of work. She gets through this routine with a very small surface of her consciousness. She is not homely and she is not pretty. She is preoccupied with herself – with her person. She has well kept hands, and a trick of constantly arranging her hair over her ears.*

 The STENOGRAPHER *is the faded, efficient woman office worker. Drying, dried.*

 The ADDING CLERK *is her male counterpart.*

 The FILING CLERK *is a boy not grown, callow adolescence.*

 The TELEPHONE GIRL, *young, cheap and amorous.*

 Lights come up on office scene. Two desks right and left.

Telephone booth back right center. Filing cabinet back of center. Adding machine back left center.

ADDING CLERK (*in the monotonous voice of his monotonous thoughts; at his adding machine*). 2490, 28, 76, 123, 36842, 1, 1/4, 37, 804, 23 1/2, 982.

FILING CLERK (*in the same way – at his filing desk*). Accounts – A. Bonds – B. Contracts – C. Data – D. Earnings – E.

STENOGRAPHER (*in the same way – left*). Dear Sir – in re – your letter – recent date – will state –

TELEPHONE GIRL. Hello – Hello – George H. Jones Company good morning – hello hello – George H. Jones Company good morning – hello.

FILING CLERK. Market – M. Notes – N. Output – O. Profits – P. – ! (*Suddenly.*) What's the matter with Q?

TELEPHONE GIRL. Matter with it – Mr. J. – Mr. K. wants you – What you mean matter? Matter with what?

FILING CLERK. Matter with Q.

TELEPHONE GIRL. Well – what is? Spring 1726?

FILING CLERK. I'm asking yuh –

TELEPHONE GIRL. WELL?

FILING CLERK. Nothing filed with it –

TELEPHONE GIRL. Well?

FILING CLERK. Look at A. Look at B. What's the matter with Q?

TELEPHONE GIRL. Ain't popular. Hello – Hello – George H. Jones Company.

FILING CLERK. Hot dog! Why ain't it?

ADDING CLERK. Has it personality?

STENOGRAPHER. Has it Halitosis?

TELEPHONE GIRL. Has it got it?

FILING CLERK. Hot dog!

TELEPHONE GIRL. What number do you want? (*Recognizing but not pleased.*). Oh – hello – sure I know who it is – tonight? Uh, uh – (*Negative, but each with a different inflection.*) You heard me – No!

FILING CLERK. Don't you like him?

STENOGRAPHER. She likes 'em all.

TELEPHONE GIRL. I do not!

STENOGRAPHER. Well – pretty near all!

TELEPHONE GIRL. What number do you want? Wrong number. Hello – hello – George H. Jones Company. Hello, hello –

STENOGRAPHER. Memorandum – attention Mr. Smith – at a conference of –

ADDING CLERK. 125 – 83 3/4 – 22 – 908 – 34 – 1/4 – 28593.

FILING CLERK. Report – R, Sales – S, Trade – T.

TELEPHONE GIRL. Shh – ! Yes, Mr. J. – ? No – Miss A. ain't in yet – I'll tell her, Mr. J. – just the minute she gets in.

STENOGRAPHER. She's late again, huh?

TELEPHONE GIRL. Out with her sweetie last night, huh?

FILING CLERK. Hot dog.

ADDING CLERK. She ain't got a sweetie.

STENOGRAPHER. How do you know?

ADDING CLERK. I know.

FILING CLERK. Hot dog.

ADDING CLERK. She lives alone with her mother.

TELEPHONE GIRL. Spring 1876? Hello – Spring 1876. Spring! Hello, Spring 1876? 1876! Wrong number! Hello! Hello!

STENOGRAPHER. Director's meeting semi-annual report card.

FILING CLERK. Shipments – Sales – Schedules – S.

ADDING CLERK. She doesn't belong in an office.

TELEPHONE GIRL. Who does?

STENOGRAPHER. I do!

ADDING CLERK. You said it!

FILING CLERK. Hot dog!

TELEPHONE GIRL. Hello – hello – George H. Jones Company – hello – hello –

STENOGRAPHER. I'm efficient. She's inefficient.

FILING CLERK. She's inefficient.

TELEPHONE GIRL. She's got J. going.

STENOGRAPHER. Going?

TELEPHONE GIRL. Going and coming.

FILING CLERK. Hot dog.

Enter JONES.

JONES. Good morning, everybody.

TELEPHONE GIRL. Good morning.

FILING CLERK. Good morning.

ADDING CLERK. Good morning.

STENOGRAPHER. Good morning, Mr. J.

JONES. Miss A. isn't in yet?

TELEPHONE GIRL. Not yet, Mr. J.

FILING CLERK. Not yet.

ADDING CLERK. Not yet.

STENOGRAPHER. She's late.

JONES. I just wanted her to take a letter.

STENOGRAPHER. I'll take the letter.

JONES. One thing at a time and that done well.

ADDING CLERK (*yessing*). Done well.

STENOGRAPHER. I'll finish it later.

JONES. Hew to the line.

ADDING CLERK. Hew to the line.

STENOGRAPHER. Then I'll hurry.

JONES. Haste makes waste.

ADDING CLERK. Waste.

STENOGRAPHER. But if you're in a hurry.

JONES. I'm never in a hurry – That's how I get ahead! (*Laughs. They all laugh.*) First know you're right – then go ahead.

ADDING CLERK. Ahead.

JONES (*to* TELEPHONE GIRL). When Miss A. comes in tell her I want her to take a letter. (*Turns to go in – then.*) It's important.

TELEPHONE GIRL (*making a note*). Miss A. – important.

JONES (*starts up – then*). And I don't want to be disturbed.

TELEPHONE GIRL. You're in conference?

JONES. I'm in conference. (*Turns – then.*) Unless its A.B. – of course.

TELEPHONE GIRL. Of course – A.B.

JONES (*starts – turns again; attempts to be facetious*). Tell Miss
A. the early bird catches the worm.

Exit JONES.

TELEPHONE GIRL. The early worm gets caught.

ADDING CLERK. He's caught.

TELEPHONE GIRL. Hooked.

ADDING CLERK. In the pan.

FILING CLERK. Hot dog.

STENOGRAPHER. We beg leave to announce –

Enter YOUNG WOMAN. *Goes behind telephone booth to
desk right.*

STENOGRAPHER. You're late!

FILING CLERK. You're late.

ADDING CLERK. You're late.

STENOGRAPHER. And yesterday!

FILING CLERK. The day before.

ADDING CLERK. And the day before.

STENOGRAPHER. You'll lose your job.

YOUNG WOMAN. No!

STENOGRAPHER. No?

Workers exchange glances.

YOUNG WOMAN. I can't!

STENOGRAPHER. Can't?

Same business.

FILING CLERK. Rent – bills – installments – miscellaneous.

ADDING CLERK. A dollar ten – ninety-five – 3.40 – 35 – 12.60.

STENOGRAPHER. Then why are you late?

YOUNG WOMAN. Why?

STENOGRAPHER. Excuse!

ADDING CLERK. Excuse!

FILING CLERK. Excuse.

TELEPHONE GIRL. Excuse it, please.

STENOGRAPHER. Why?

YOUNG WOMAN. The subway?

TELEPHONE GIRL. Long distance?

FILING CLERK. Old stuff!

ADDING CLERK. That stall!

STENOGRAPHER. Stalled?

YOUNG WOMAN. No –

STENOGRAPHER. What?

YOUNG WOMAN. I had to get out!

ADDING CLERK. Out!

FILING CLERK. Out?

STENOGRAPHER. Out where?

YOUNG WOMAN. In the air!

STENOGRAPHER. Air?

YOUNG WOMAN. All those bodies pressing.

FILING CLERK. Hot dog!

YOUNG WOMAN. I thought I would faint! I had to get out in the air!

FILING CLERK. Give her the air.

ADDING CLERK. Free air –

STENOGRAPHER. Hot air.

YOUNG WOMAN. Like I'm dying.

STENOGRAPHER. Same thing yesterday. (*Pause.*) And the day before.

YOUNG WOMAN. Yes – what am I going to do?

ADDING CLERK. Take a taxi! (*They laugh.*)

FILING CLERK. Call a cop!

TELEPHONE GIRL. Mr. J. wants you.

YOUNG WOMAN. Me?

TELEPHONE GIRL. You!

YOUNG WOMAN (*rises*). Mr. J.!

STENOGRAPHER. Mr. J.

TELEPHONE GIRL. He's bellowing for you!

YOUNG WOMAN *gives last pat to her hair – goes off into door – back.*

STENOGRAPHER (*after her*). Get it just right.

FILING CLERK. She's always doing that to her hair.

TELEPHONE GIRL. It gives a line – it gives a line –

FILING CLERK. Hot dog.

ADDING CLERK. She's artistic.

STENOGRAPHER. She's inefficient.

FILING CLERK. She's inefficient.

STENOGRAPHER. Mr. J. knows she's inefficient.

ADDING CLERK. 46 – 23 – 84 – 2 – 2 – 2 – 1,492 – 678.

TELEPHONE GIRL. Hello – hello – George H. Jones Company – hello – Mr. Jones? He's in conference.

STENOGRAPHER (*sarcastic*). Conference!

ADDING CLERK. Conference.

FILING CLERK. Hot dog!

TELEPHONE GIRL. Do you think he'll marry her?

ADDING CLERK. If she'll have him.

STENOGRAPHER. If she'll have him!

FILING CLERK. Do you think she'll have him?

TELEPHONE GIRL. How much does he get?

ADDING CLERK. Plenty – 5,000 – 10,000 – 15,000 – 20,000 – 25,000.

STENOGRAPHER. And plenty put away.

ADDING CLERK. Gas Preferred – 4's – steel – 5's – oil – 6's.

FILING CLERK. Hot dog.

STENOGRAPHER. Will she have him? Will she have him? This agreement entered into – party of the first part – party of the second part – will he have her?

TELEPHONE GIRL. Well, I'd hate to get into bed with him. (*Familiar melting voice.*) Hello – humhum – hum – hum – hold the line a minute – will you – hum hum. (*Professional voice.*) Hell, hello – A.B., just a minute, Mr. A.B. – Mr. J.? Mr. A.B. – go ahead, Mr. A.B. (*Melting voice.*) We were interrupted – huh – huh – huh – huhuh – hum – hum.

Enter YOUNG WOMAN – *she goes to her chair, sits with folded hands.*

FILING CLERK. That's all you ever say to a guy –

STENOGRAPHER. Hum – hum – or uh huh – (*Negative.*)

TELEPHONE GIRL. That's all you have to. (*To phone.*) Hum – hum – hum hum – hum hum –

STENOGRAPHER. Mostly hum hum.

ADDING CLERK. You've said it!

FILING CLERK. Hot dog.

TELEPHONE GIRL. Hum hum huh hum humhumhum – tonight? She's got a date – she told me last night – humhumhuh – hum – all right. (*Disconnects.*) Too bad – my boy friend's got a friend – but my girl friend's got a date.

YOUNG WOMAN. You have a good time.

TELEPHONE GIRL. Big time.

STENOGRAPHER. Small time.

ADDING CLERK. A big time on the small time.

TELEPHONE GIRL. I'd ask you, kid, but you'd be up to your neck!

STENOGRAPHER. Neckers!

ADDING CLERK. Petters!

FILING CLERK. Sweet papas.

TELEPHONE GIRL. Want to come?

YOUNG WOMAN. Can't.

TELEPHONE GIRL. Date?

YOUNG WOMAN. My mother.

STENOGRAPHER. Worries?

TELEPHONE GIRL. Nags – hello – George H. Jones Company – Oh hello –

YOUNG WOMAN *sits before her machine – hands in lap, looking at them.*

STENOGRAPHER. Why don't you get to work?

YOUNG WOMAN (*dreaming*). What?

ADDING CLERK. Work!

YOUNG WOMAN. Can't.

STENOGRAPHER. Can't?

YOUNG WOMAN. My machine's out of order.

STENOGRAPHER. Well, fix it!

YOUNG WOMAN. I can't – got to get somebody.

STENOGRAPHER. Somebody! Somebody! Always somebody! Here, sort the mail, then!

YOUNG WOMAN (*rises*). All right.

STENOGRAPHER. And hurry! You're late.

YOUNG WOMAN (*sorting letters*). George H. Jones and Company – George H. Jones Inc. George H. Jones –

STENOGRAPHER. You're always late.

ADDING CLERK. You'll lose your job.

YOUNG WOMAN (*hurrying*). George H. Jones – George H. Jones Personal –

TELEPHONE GIRL. Don't let 'em get your goat, kid – tell 'em where to get off.

YOUNG WOMAN. What?

TELEPHONE GIRL. Ain't it all set?

YOUNG WOMAN. What?

TELEPHONE GIRL. You and Mr. J.

STENOGRAPHER. You and the boss.

FILING CLERK. You and the big chief.

ADDING CLERK. You and the big cheese.

YOUNG WOMAN. Did he tell you?

TELEPHONE GIRL. I told you!

ADDING CLERK. I told you!

STENOGRAPHER. I don't believe it.

ADDING CLERK. 5,000 – 10,000 – 15,000.

FILING CLERK. Hot dog.

YOUNG WOMAN. No – it isn't so.

STENOGRAPHER. Isn't it?

YOUNG WOMAN. No.

TELEPHONE GIRL. Not yet.

ADDING CLERK. But soon.

FILING CLERK. Hot dog.

Enter JONES.

TELEPHONE GIRL (*busy*). George H. Jones Company – Hello – Hello.

STENOGRAPHER. Awaiting your answer –

ADDING CLERK. 5,000 – 10,000 – 15,000 –

JONES (*crossing to* YOUNG WOMAN – *puts hand on her shoulder, all stop and stare*). That letter done?

YOUNG WOMAN. No. (*She pulls away.*)

JONES. What's the matter?

STENOGRAPHER. She hasn't started.

JONES. O.K. – want to make some changes.

YOUNG WOMAN. My machine's out of order.

JONES. O.K. – use the one in my room.

YOUNG WOMAN. I'm sorting the mail.

STENOGRAPHER (*sarcastic*). One thing at a time!

JONES (*retreating – goes back center*). O.K. (*To* YOUNG WOMAN.) When you're finished. (*Starts back to his room.*)

STENOGRAPHER. Haste makes waste.

JONES (*at door*). O.K. – don't hurry.

Exits.

STENOGRAPHER. Hew to the line!

TELEPHONE GIRL. He's hewing.

FILING CLERK. Hot dog.

TELEPHONE GIRL. Why did you flinch, kid?

YOUNG WOMAN. Flinch?

TELEPHONE GIRL. Did he pinch?

YOUNG WOMAN. No!

TELEPHONE GIRL. Then what?

YOUNG WOMAN. Nothing! – Just his hand.

TELEPHONE GIRL. Oh – just his hand – (*Shakes her head thoughtfully.*) Uhhuh. (*Negative.*) Uhhuh. (*Decisively.*) No! Tell him no.

STENOGRAPHER. If she does she'll lose her job.

ADDING CLERK. Fired.

FILING CLERK. The sack!

TELEPHONE GIRL (*on the defensive*). And if she doesn't?

ADDING CLERK. She'll come to work in a taxi!

TELEPHONE GIRL. Work?

FILING CLERK. No work.

STENOGRAPHER. No worry.

ADDING CLERK. Breakfast in bed.

STENOGRAPHER (*sarcastic*). Did Madame ring?

FILING CLERK. Lunch in bed!

TELEPHONE GIRL. A double bed! (*In phone.*) Yes, Mr. J. (*To YOUNG WOMAN.*) J. wants you.

YOUNG WOMAN (*starts to get to her feet – but doesn't*). I can't – I'm not ready – In a minute. (*Sits staring ahead of her.*)

ADDING CLERK. 5,000 – 10,000 – 15,000 –

FILING CLERK. Profits – plans – purchase –

STENOGRAPHER. Call your attention our prices are fixed.

TELEPHONE GIRL. Hello – hello – George H. Jones Company – hello – hello –

YOUNG WOMAN (*thinking her thoughts aloud – to the subdued accompaniment of the office sounds and voices*). Marry me – wants to marry me – George H. Jones – George H. Jones and Company – Mrs. George H. Jones – Mrs. George H. Jones. Dear Madame – marry – do you take this man to be your wedded husband – I do – to love honor and to love – kisses – no – I can't – George H. Jones – How would you like to marry me – What do you say – Why Mr. Jones I – let me look at your little hands – you have such pretty little hands – let me hold your pretty little hands – George H. Jones – Fat hands – flabby hands – don't touch me – please – fat hands are never weary – please don't – married – all girls – most girls – married – babies – a baby – curls – little curls all over its head – George H. Jones – straight – thin – bald – don't touch me – please – no – can't – must – somebody – something – no rest – must rest – no rest – must rest – no rest – late today – yesterday – before – late – subway – air – pressing – bodies pressing – bodies – trembling – air – stop – air – late – job – no job – fired – late – alarm clock – alarm clock – alarm clock – hurry – job – ma – nag – nag – nag – ma – hurry – job – no job – no money – installments due – no money – money – George H. Jones –

money – Mrs. George H. Jones – money – no work – no worry – free! – rest – sleep till nine – sleep till ten – sleep till noon – now you take a good rest this morning – don't get up till you want to – thank you – oh thank you – oh don't! – please don't touch me – I want to rest – no rest – earn – got to earn – married – earn – no – yes – earn – all girls – most girls – ma – pa – ma – all women – most women – I can't – must – maybe – must – somebody – something – ma – pa – ma – can I, ma? Tell me, ma – something – somebody.

The scene blacks out. The sounds of the office machines continue until the scene lights into Episode Two – and the office sounds become the sound of a   radio, offstage.

EPISODE TWO

At Home

Scene: a kitchen: table, chairs, plates and food, garbage can, a pair of rubber gloves. The door at the back now opens on a hall – the window, on an apartment house court.

Sounds: buzzer, radio (voice of announcer; music and singer).

Characters
    YOUNG WOMAN
    MOTHER

Outside voices: characters heard, but not seen
    A JANITOR
    A BABY
    A MOTHER *and a* SMALL BOY
    A YOUNG BOY *and* YOUNG GIRL
    A HUSBAND *and a* WIFE
    ANOTHER HUSBAND *and a* WIFE

At rise: YOUNG WOMAN *and* MOTHER *eating – radio offstage – radio stops.*

YOUNG WOMAN. Ma – I want to talk to you.

MOTHER. Aren't you eating a potato?

YOUNG WOMAN. No.

MOTHER. Why not?

YOUNG WOMAN. I don't want one.

MOTHER. That's no reason. Here! Take one.

YOUNG WOMAN. I don't want it.

MOTHER. Potatoes go with stew – here!

YOUNG WOMAN. Ma, I don't want it!

MOTHER. Want it! Take it!

YOUNG WOMAN. But I – oh, all right. (*Takes it – then.*) Ma, I want to ask you something.

MOTHER. Eat your potato.

YOUNG WOMAN (*takes a bite – then*). Ma, there's something I want to ask you – something important.

MOTHER. Is it mealy?

YOUNG WOMAN. S'all right. Ma – tell me.

MOTHER. Three pounds for a quarter.

YOUNG WOMAN. Ma – tell me – (*Buzzer.*)

MOTHER (*her dull voice brightening*). There's the garbage. (*Goes to door – or dumbwaiter – opens it. Stop radio.*)

JANITOR'S VOICE (*offstage*). Garbage.

MOTHER (*pleased – busy*). All right. (*Gets garbage can – puts it out.* YOUNG WOMAN *walks up and down.*)What's the matter now?

YOUNG WOMAN. Nothing.

MOTHER. That jumping up from the table every night the garbage is collected! You act like you're crazy.

YOUNG WOMAN. Ma, do all women –

MOTHER. I suppose you think you're too nice for anything so common! Well, let me tell you, my lady, that it's a very important part of life.

YOUNG WOMAN. I know, but, Ma, if you –

MOTHER. If it weren't for garbage cans where would we be? Where would we all be? Living in filth – that's what! Filth! I should think you'd be glad! I should think you'd be grateful!

YOUNG WOMAN. Oh, Ma!

MOTHER. Well, are you?

YOUNG WOMAN. Am I what?

MOTHER. Glad! Grateful.

YOUNG WOMAN. Yes!

MOTHER. You don't act like it!

YOUNG WOMAN. Oh, Ma, don't talk!

MOTHER. You just said you wanted to talk.

YOUNG WOMAN. Well now – I want to think. I got to think.

MOTHER. Aren't you going to finish your potato?

YOUNG WOMAN. Oh, Ma!

MOTHER. Is there anything the matter with it?

YOUNG WOMAN. No –

MOTHER. Then why don't you finish it?

YOUNG WOMAN. Because I don't want it.

MOTHER. Why don't you?

YOUNG WOMAN. Oh, Ma! Let me alone!

MOTHER. Well, you've got to eat! If you don't eat –

YOUNG WOMAN. Ma! Don't nag!

MOTHER. Nag! Just because I try to look out for you – nag! Just because I try to care for you – nag! Why, you haven't sense enough to eat! What would become of you I'd like to know – if I didn't nag!

Offstage – a sound of window opening – all these offstage sounds come in through the court window at the back.

WOMAN'S VOICE. Johnny – Johnny – come in now!

A SMALL BOY'S VOICE. Oh, Ma!

WOMAN'S VOICE. It's getting cold.

A SMALL BOY'S VOICE. Oh, Ma!

WOMAN'S VOICE. You heard me! (*Sound of window slamming.*)

YOUNG WOMAN. I'm grown up, Ma.

MOTHER. Grown up! What do you mean by that?

YOUNG WOMAN. Nothing much – I guess. (*Offstage sound of baby crying.* MOTHER *rises, clatters dishes.*) Let's not do the dishes right away, Ma. Let's talk – I gotta.

MOTHER. Well, I can't talk with dirty dishes around – you may be able to but – (*Clattering – clattering.*)

YOUNG WOMAN. Ma! Listen! Listen! – There's a man wants to marry me.

MOTHER (*stops clattering – sits*). What man?

YOUNG WOMAN. He says he fell in love with my hands.

MOTHER. In love! Is that beginning again! I thought you were over that!

Offstage BOY's *voice – whistles – * GIRL's *voice answers.*

BOY'S VOICE. Come on out.

GIRL'S VOICE. Can't.

BOY'S VOICE. Nobody'll see you.

GIRL'S VOICE. I can't.

BOY'S VOICE. It's dark now – come on.

GIRL'S VOICE. Well – just for a minute.

BOY'S VOICE. Meet you round the corner.

YOUNG WOMAN. I got to get married, Ma.

MOTHER. What do you mean?

YOUNG WOMAN. I gotta.

MOTHER. You haven't got in trouble, have you?

YOUNG WOMAN. Don't talk like that!

MOTHER. Well, you say you got to get married – what do you mean?

YOUNG WOMAN. Nothing.

MOTHER. Answer me!

YOUNG WOMAN. All women get married, don't they?

MOTHER. Nonsense!

YOUNG WOMAN. You got married, didn't you?

MOTHER. Yes, I did!

Offstage voices.

WOMAN'S VOICE. Where you going?

MAN'S VOICE. Out.

WOMAN'S VOICE. You were out last night.

MAN'S VOICE. Was I?

WOMAN'S VOICE. You're always going out.

MAN'S VOICE. Am I?

WOMAN'S VOICE. Where you going?

MAN'S VOICE. Out.

End of offstage voices.

MOTHER. Who is he? Where did you come to know him?

YOUNG WOMAN. In the office.

MOTHER. In the office!

YOUNG WOMAN. It's Mr. J.

MOTHER. Mr. J.?

YOUNG WOMAN. The Vice-President.

MOTHER. Vice-President! His income must be – Does he know you've got a mother to support?

YOUNG WOMAN. Yes.

MOTHER. What does he say?

YOUNG WOMAN. All right.

MOTHER. How soon you going to marry him?

YOUNG WOMAN. I'm not going to.

MOTHER. Not going to!

YOUNG WOMAN. No! I'm not going to.

MOTHER. But you just said –

YOUNG WOMAN. I'm not going to.

MOTHER. Are you crazy?

YOUNG WOMAN. I can't, Ma! I can't!

MOTHER. Why can't you?

YOUNG WOMAN. I don't love him.

MOTHER. Love! – what does that amount to! Will it clothe you? Will it feed you? Will it pay the bills?

YOUNG WOMAN. No! But it's real just the same!

MOTHER. Real!

YOUNG WOMAN. If it isn't – what can you count on in life?

MOTHER. I'll tell you what you can count on! You can count that you've got to eat and sleep and get up and put clothes on your back and take 'em off again – that you got to get old – and that you got to die. That's what you can count on! All the rest is in your head!

YOUNG WOMAN. But Ma – didn't you love Pa?

MOTHER. I suppose I did – I don't know – I've forgotten – what difference does it make – now?

YOUNG WOMAN. But then! – oh Ma, tell me!

MOTHER. Tell you what?

YOUNG WOMAN. About all that – love!

Offstage voices.

WIFE'S VOICE. Don't.

HUSBAND'S VOICE. What's the matter – don't you want me to kiss you?

WIFE'S VOICE. Not like that.

HUSBAND'S VOICE. Like what?

WIFE'S VOICE. That silly kiss!

HUSBAND'S VOICE. Silly kiss?

WIFE'S VOICE. You look so silly – oh I know what's coming when you look like that – and kiss me like that – don't – go away –

End of offstage voices.

MOTHER. He's a decent man, isn't he?

YOUNG WOMAN. I don't know. How should I know – yet.

MOTHER. He's a Vice-President – of course he's decent.

YOUNG WOMAN. I don't care whether he's decent or not. I won't marry him.

MOTHER. But you just said you wanted to marry –

YOUNG WOMAN. Not him.

MOTHER. Who?

YOUNG WOMAN. I don't know – I don't know – I haven't found him yet!

MOTHER. You talk like you're crazy!

YOUNG WOMAN. Oh, Ma – tell me!

MOTHER. Tell you what?

YOUNG WOMAN. Tell me – (*Words suddenly pouring out.*) Your skin oughtn't to curl – ought it – when he just comes near you – ought it? That's wrong, ain't it? You don't get over that, do you – ever, do you or do you? How is it, Ma – do you?

MOTHER. Do you what?

YOUNG WOMAN. Do you get used to, it – so after a while it doesn't matter? Or don't you? Does it always matter? You ought to be in love, oughtn't you, Ma? You must be in love, mustn't you, Ma? That changes everything, doesn't it – or does it? Maybe if you just like a person it's all right – is it? When he puts a hand on me, my blood turns cold. But your blood oughtn't to run cold, ought it? His hands are – his hands are fat, Ma – don't you see – his hands are fat – and they sort of press – and they're fat – don't you see? – Don't you see?

MOTHER (*stares at her bewildered*). See what?

YOUNG WOMAN (*rushing on*). I've always thought I'd find somebody – somebody young – and – and attractive – with wavy hair – wavy hair – I always think of children with curls – little curls all over their head – somebody young – and attractive – that I'd like – that I'd love – But I haven't found anybody like that yet – I haven't found anybody – I've hardly known anybody – you'd never let me go with anybody and –

MOTHER. Are you throwing it up to me that –

YOUNG WOMAN. No – let me finish, Ma! No – let me finish! I just mean I've never found anybody – anybody – nobody's ever asked me – till now – he's the only man that's ever asked me – And I suppose I got to marry somebody – all girls do –

MOTHER. Nonsense.

YOUNG WOMAN. But, I can't go on like this, Ma – I don't know why – but I can't – it's like I'm all tight inside – sometimes I feel like I'm stifling! – You don't know – stifling. (*Walks up and down.*) I can't go on like this much longer – going to work – coming home – going to work – coming home – I can't – Sometimes in the subway I think I'm going to die – sometimes even in the office if something don't happen – I got to do something – I don't know – it's like I'm all tight inside.

MOTHER. You're crazy.

YOUNG WOMAN. Oh, Ma!

MOTHER. You're crazy!

YOUNG WOMAN. Ma – if you tell me that again I'll kill you! I'll kill you!

MOTHER. If that isn't crazy!

YOUNG WOMAN. I'll kill you – Maybe I am crazy – I don't know. Sometimes I think I am – the thoughts that go on in my mind – sometimes I think I am – I can't help it if I am – I do the best I can – I do the best I can and I'm nearly crazy! (MOTHER *rises and sits.*) Go away! Go away! You don't know anything about anything! And you haven't got any pity – no pity – you just take it for granted that I go to work every day – and come home every night and bring my money every week – you just take it for granted – you'd let me go on forever – and never feel any pity –

Offstage radio – a voice singing a sentimental mother song or popular home song. MOTHER *begins to cry – crosses to chair left – sits.*

Oh Ma – forgive me! Forgive me!

MOTHER. My own child! To be spoken to like that by my own child!

YOUNG WOMAN. I didn't mean it, Ma – I didn't mean it! (*She goes to her mother – crosses to left.*)

MOTHER (*clinging to her hand*). You're all I've got in the world – and you don't want me – you want to kill me.

YOUNG WOMAN. No – no, I don't, Ma! I just said that!

MOTHER. I've worked for you and slaved for you!

YOUNG WOMAN. I know, Ma.

MOTHER. I brought you into the world.

YOUNG WOMAN. I know, Ma.

MOTHER. You're flesh of my flesh and –

YOUNG WOMAN. I know, Ma, I know.

MOTHER. And –

YOUNG WOMAN. You rest, now, Ma – you rest –

MOTHER (*struggling*). I got to do the dishes.

YOUNG WOMAN. I'll do the dishes – You listen to the music, Ma – I'll do the dishes.

MA *sits.* YOUNG WOMAN *crosses to behind screen. Takes a pair of rubber gloves and begins to put them on. The* MOTHER *sees them – they irritate her – there is a return of her characteristic mood.*

MOTHER. Those gloves! I've been washing dishes for forty years and I never wore gloves! But my lady's hands! My lady's hands!

YOUNG WOMAN. Sometimes you talk to me like you're jealous, Ma.

MOTHER. Jealous?

YOUNG WOMAN. It's my hands got me a husband.

MOTHER. A husband? So you're going to marry him now!

YOUNG WOMAN. I suppose so.

MOTHER. If you ain't the craziest –

The scene blacks out. In the darkness, the mother song goes into jazz – very faint – as the scene lights into

EPISODE THREE

Honeymoon

Scene: hotel bedroom: bed, chair, mirror. The door at the back now opens on a bathroom; the window, on a dancing casino opposite.

Sounds: a small jazz band (violin, piano, saxophone – very dim, at first, then louder).

Characters
YOUNG WOMAN
HUSBAND
BELLBOY

Offstage: seen but not heard, MEN *and* WOMEN *dancing in couples.*

At rise: set dark. BELLBOY, HUSBAND, *and* YOUNG WOMAN *enter.* BELLBOY *carries luggage. He switches on light by door. Stop music.*

HUSBAND: Well, here we are. (*Throws hat on bed;* BELLBOY *puts luggage down, crosses to window; raises shade three inches. Opens window three inches. Sounds of jazz music louder. Offstage.*)

BELLBOY (*comes to man for tip*). Anything else, Sir? (*Receives tip. Exits.*)

HUSBAND. Well, here we are.

YOUNG WOMAN. Yes, here we are.

HUSBAND. Aren't you going to take your hat off – stay a while? (YOUNG WOMAN *looks around as though looking for a way out, then takes off her hat, pulls the hair automatically around her ears.*) This is all right, isn't it? Huh? Huh?

YOUNG WOMAN. It's very nice.

HUSBAND. Twelve bucks a day! They know how to soak you in these pleasure resorts. Twelve bucks! (*Music.*) Well – we'll get our money's worth out of it all right. (*Goes toward bathroom.*)

I'm going to wash up. (*Stops at door.*) Don't you want to wash up?

YOUNG WOMAN *shakes head 'No'.*

I do! It was a long trip! I want to wash up!

Goes off – closes door; sings in bathroom. YOUNG WOMAN *goes to window – raises shade – sees the dancers going round and round in couples. Music is louder. Re-enter* HUSBAND.

Say, pull that blind down! They can see in!

YOUNG WOMAN. I thought you said there'd be a view of the ocean!

HUSBAND. Sure there is.

YOUNG WOMAN. I just see people – dancing.

HUSBAND. The ocean's beyond.

YOUNG WOMAN (*desperately*). I was counting on seeing it!

HUSBAND. You'll see it tomorrow – what's eating you? We'll take in the boardwalk – Don't you want to wash up?

YOUNG WOMAN. No!

HUSBAND. It was a long trip. Sure you don't? (YOUNG WOMAN *shakes her head 'No'.* HUSBAND *takes off his coat – puts it over chair.*) Better make yourself at home. I'm going to. (*She stares at him – moves away from the window.*) Say, pull down that blind! (*Crosses to chair down left – sits.*)

YOUNG WOMAN. It's close – don't you think it's close?

HUSBAND. Well – you don't want people looking in, do you? (*Laughs.*) Huh – huh?

YOUNG WOMAN. No.

HUSBAND (*laughs*). I guess not. Huh? (*Takes off shoes.* YOUNG WOMAN *leaves the window, and crosses down to the bed.*) Say – you look a little white around the gills! What's the matter?

YOUNG WOMAN. Nothing.

HUSBAND. You look like you're scared.

YOUNG WOMAN. No.

HUSBAND. Nothing to be scared of. You're with your husband, you know. (*Takes her to chair, left.*)

YOUNG WOMAN. I know.

HUSBAND. Happy?

YOUNG WOMAN. Yes.

HUSBAND (*sitting*). Then come here and give us a kiss. (*He puts her on his knee.*) That's the girlie. (*He bends her head down, and kisses her along the back of her neck.*) Like that? (*She tries to get to her feet.*) Say – stay there! What you moving for? – You know – you got to learn to relax, little girl – (*Dancers go off. Dim lights. Pinches her above knee.*) Say, what you got under there?

YOUNG WOMAN. Nothing.

HUSBAND. Nothing! (*Laughs.*) That's a good one! Nothing, huh? Huh? That reminds me of the story of the pullman porter and the – what's the matter – did I tell you that one? (*Music dims off and out.*)

YOUNG WOMAN. I don't know.

HUSBAND. The pullman porter and the tart?

YOUNG WOMAN. No.

HUSBAND. It's a good one – well – the train was just pulling out and the tart –

YOUNG WOMAN. You did tell that one!

HUSBAND. About the –

YOUNG WOMAN. Yes! Yes! I remember now!

HUSBAND. About the –

YOUNG WOMAN. Yes!

HUSBAND. All right – if I did. You're sure it was the one about the –

YOUNG WOMAN. I'm sure.

HUSBAND. When he asked her what she had underneath her seat and she said –

YOUNG WOMAN. Yes! Yes! That one!

HUSBAND. All right – But I don't believe I did. (*She tries to get up again, as he holds her.*) You know you have got something under there – what is it?

YOUNG WOMAN. Nothing – just – just my garter.

HUSBAND. Your garter! Your garter! Say did I tell you the one about –

YOUNG WOMAN. Yes! Yes!

HUSBAND (*with dignity*). How do you know which one I meant?

YOUNG WOMAN. You told me them all!

HUSBAND (*pulling her back to his knee*). No, I didn't! Not by a jugful! I got a lot of 'em up my sleeve yet – that's part of what I owe my success to – my ability to spring a good story – You know – you got to learn to relax, little girl – haven't you?

YOUNG WOMAN. Yes.

HUSBAND. That's one of the biggest things to learn in life. That's part of what I owe my success to. Now you go and get those heavy things off – and relax.

YOUNG WOMAN. They're not heavy.

HUSBAND. You haven't got much on – have you? But you'll feel better with 'em off. (*Gets up.*) Want me to help you?

YOUNG WOMAN. No.

HUSBAND. I'm your husband, you know.

YOUNG WOMAN. I know.

HUSBAND. You aren't afraid of your husband, are you?

YOUNG WOMAN. No – of course not – but I thought maybe – can't we go out for a little while?

HUSBAND. Out? What for?

YOUNG WOMAN. Fresh air – walk – talk.

HUSBAND. We can talk here – I'll tell you all about myself. Go along now. (YOUNG WOMAN *goes toward bathroom door. Gets bag.*) Where are you going?

YOUNG WOMAN. In here.

HUSBAND. I thought you'd want to wash up.

YOUNG WOMAN. I just want to – get ready.

HUSBAND. You don't have to go in there to take your clothes off!

YOUNG WOMAN. I want to.

HUSBAND. What for?

YOUNG WOMAN. I always do.

HUSBAND. What?

YOUNG WOMAN. Undress by myself.

HUSBAND. You've never been married till now – have you? (*Laughs.*) Or have you been putting something over on me?

YOUNG WOMAN. No.

HUSBAND. I understand – kind of modest – huh? Huh?

YOUNG WOMAN. Yes.

HUSBAND. I understand women – (*Indulgently*.) Go along.

She goes off – starts to close door. YOUNG WOMAN *exits.*

Don't close the door – thought you wanted to talk.

He looks around the room with satisfaction – after a pause – rises – takes off his collar.

You're awful quiet – what are you doing in there?

YOUNG WOMAN. Just – getting ready –

HUSBAND (*still in his mood of satisfaction*). I'm going to enjoy life from now on – I haven't had such an easy time of it. I got where I am by hard work and self denial – now I'm going to enjoy life – I'm going to make up for all I missed – aren't you about ready?

YOUNG WOMAN. Not yet.

HUSBAND. Next year maybe we'll go to Paris. You can buy a lot of that French underwear – and Switzerland – all my life I've wanted a Swiss watch – that I bought right there – I coulda' got a Swiss watch here, but I always wanted one that I bought right there – Isn't that funny – huh? Isn't it? Huh? Huh?

YOUNG WOMAN. Yes.

HUSBAND. All my life I've wanted a Swiss watch that I bought right there. All my life I've counted on having that some day – more than anything – except one thing – you know what?

YOUNG WOMAN. No.

HUSBAND. Guess.

YOUNG WOMAN. I can't.

HUSBAND. Then I'm coming in and tell you.

YOUNG WOMAN. No! Please! Please don't.

HUSBAND. Well hurry up then! I thought you women didn't wear much of anything these days – huh? Huh? I'm coming in!

YOUNG WOMAN. No – no! Just a minute!

HUSBAND. All right. Just a minute. (YOUNG WOMAN *is silent.* HUSBAND *laughs and takes out watch.*) 13 – 14 – I'm counting the seconds on you – that's what you said, didn't you – just a minute! – 49 – 50 – 51 – 52 – 53 –

Enter YOUNG WOMAN.

YOUNG WOMAN (*at the door*). Here I am. (*She wears a little white gown that hangs very straight. She is very still, but her eyes are wide with a curious, helpless, animal terror.*)

HUSBAND (*starts toward her – stops. The room is in shadow except for one dim light by the bed. Sound of girl weeping*). You crying? (*Sound of weeping.*) What you crying for? (*Crosses to her.*)

YOUNG WOMAN (*crying out*). Ma! Ma! I want my mother!

HUSBAND. I thought you were glad to get away from her.

YOUNG WOMAN. I want her now – I want somebody.

HUSBAND. You got me, haven't you?

YOUNG WOMAN. Somebody – somebody –

HUSBAND. There's nothing to cry about. There's nothing to cry about.

The scene blacks out. The music continues until the lights go up for Episode Four. Rhythm of the music is gradually replaced by the sound of steel riveting for Episode Four.

EPISODE FOUR

Maternal

Scene: a room in a hospital: bed, chair. The door in the back now opens on a corridor; the window on a tall building going up.

Sounds: outside window – riveting.

Characters in the scene
    YOUNG WOMAN
    DOCTORS
    NURSES
    HUSBAND

Characters seen but not heard
    WOMAN IN WHEEL CHAIR
    WOMAN IN BATHROBE
    STRETCHER WAGON
    NURSE WITH TRAY
    NURSE WITH COVERED BASIN

At rise YOUNG WOMAN *lies still in bed. The door is open. In the corridor, a stretcher wagon goes by. Enter* NURSE.

NURSE: How are you feeling today? (*No response from* YOUNG WOMAN.) Better? (*No response.*) No pain? (*No response.* NURSE *takes her watch in one hand,* YOUNG WOMAN's *wrist in the other – stands, then goes to chart at foot of bed – writes.*) You're getting along fine. (*No response.*) Such a sweet baby you have, too. (*No response.*) Aren't you glad it's a girl? (YOUNG WOMAN *makes sign with her head 'No'.*) You're not! Oh, my! That's no way to talk! Men want boys – women ought to want girls. (*No response.*) Maybe you didn't want either, eh? (YOUNG WOMAN *signs 'No'. Riveting machine.*) You'll feel different when it begins to nurse. You'll just love it then. Your milk hasn't come yet – has it? (*Sign – 'No'.*) It will! (*Sign – 'No'.*) Oh, you don't know Doctor! (*Goes to door – turns.*) Anything else you want? (YOUNG WOMAN *points to window.*) Draft? (*Sign – 'No'.*) The noise? (YOUNG WOMAN *signs 'Yes'.*) Oh, that can't be helped. Hospital's got to have a new wing. We're the biggest Maternity Hospital in the world.

I'll close the window, though. (YOUNG WOMAN *signs 'No'*.) No?

YOUNG WOMAN (*whispers*). I smell everything then.

NURSE (*starting out the door – riveting machine.*) Here's your man!

Enter HUSBAND with large bouquet. Crosses to bed.

HUSBAND. Well, how are we today? (YOUNG WOMAN – *no response.*)

NURSE. She's getting stronger!

HUSBAND. Of course she is!

NURSE (*taking flowers*). See what your husband brought you.

HUSBAND. Better put 'em in water right away. (*Exit* NURSE.) Everything O.K.? (YOUNG WOMAN *signs 'No'.*) Now see here, my dear, you've got to brace up, you know! And – and face things! Everybody's got to brace up and face things! That's what makes the world go round. I know all you've been through but – (YOUNG WOMAN *signs 'No'.*) Oh, yes I do! I know all about it! I was right outside all the time! (YOUNG WOMAN *makes violent gestures of 'No'. Ignoring.*) Oh yes! But you've got to brace up now! Make an effort! Pull yourself together! Start the up-hill climb! Oh I've been down – but I haven't stayed down. I've been licked but I haven't stayed licked! I've pulled myself up by my own bootstraps, and that's what you've got to do! Will power! That's what conquers! Look at me! Now you've got to brace up! Face the music! Stand the gaff! Take life by the horns! Look it in the face! – Having a baby's natural! Perfectly natural thing – why should –

YOUNG WOMAN *chokes – points wildly to door. Enter* NURSE *with flowers in a vase.*

NURSE. What's the matter?

HUSBAND. She's got that gagging again – like she had the last time I was here.

YOUNG WOMAN *gestures him out.*

NURSE. Better go, sir.

HUSBAND (*at door*). I'll be back.

YOUNG WOMAN *gasping and gesturing.*

NURSE. She needs rest.

HUSBAND. Tomorrow then. I'll be back tomorrow – tomorrow and every day – goodbye. (*Exits.*)

NURSE. You got a mighty nice husband, I guess you know that? (*Writes on chart.*) Gagging.

Corridor life – WOMAN IN BATHROBE *passes door. Enter* DOCTOR, YOUNG DOCTOR, NURSE, *wheeling surgeon's wagon with bottles, instruments, etc.*

DOCTOR. How's the little lady today? (*Crosses to bed.*)

NURSE. She's better, Doctor.

DOCTOR. Of course she's better! She's all right – aren't you? (YOUNG WOMAN *does not respond.*) What's the matter? Can't you talk? (*Drops her hand. Takes chart.*)

NURSE. She's a little weak yet, Doctor.

DOCTOR (*at chart*). Milk hasn't come yet?

NURSE. No, Doctor.

DOCTOR. Put the child to breast. (YOUNG WOMAN – *'No – no'! – Riveting machine.*) No? Don't you want to nurse your baby? (YOUNG WOMAN *signs 'No'.*) Why not? (*No response.*) These modern neurotic women, eh, Doctor? What are we going to do with 'em? (YOUNG DOCTOR *laughs.* NURSE *smiles.*) Bring the baby!

YOUNG WOMAN. No!

DOCTOR. Well – that's strong enough. I thought you were too weak to talk – that's better. You don't want your baby?

YOUNG WOMAN. No.

DOCTOR. What do you want?

YOUNG WOMAN. Let alone – let alone.

DOCTOR. Bring the baby.

NURSE. Yes, Doctor – she's behaved very badly every time, Doctor – very upset – maybe we better not.

DOCTOR. I decide what we better and better not here, Nurse!

NURSE. Yes, Doctor.

DOCTOR. Bring the baby.

NURSE. Yes, Doctor.

DOCTOR (*with chart*). Gagging – you mean nausea.

NURSE. Yes, Doctor, but –

DOCTOR. No buts, nurse.

NURSE. Yes, Doctor.

DOCTOR. Nausea! – Change the diet! – What is her diet?

NURSE. Liquids.

DOCTOR. Give her solids.

NURSE. Yes, Doctor. She says she can't swallow solids.

DOCTOR. Give her solids.

NURSE. Yes, Doctor. (*Starts to go – riveting machine.*)

DOCTOR. Wait – I'll change her medicine. (*Takes pad and writes prescription in Latin. Hands it to* NURSE.) After meals. (*To door.*) Bring her baby.

Exit DOCTOR, *followed by* YOUNG DOCTOR *and* NURSE *with surgeon's wagon.*

NURSE. Yes, Doctor.

Exits.

YOUNG WOMAN (*alone*). Let me alone – let me alone – let me alone – I've submitted to enough – I won't submit to any more – crawl off – crawl off in the dark – Vixen crawled under the bed – way back in the corner under the bed – they were all drowned – puppies don't go to heaven – heaven – golden stairs – long stairs – long – too long – long golden stairs – climb those golden stairs – stairs – stairs – climb – tired – too tired – dead – no matter – nothing matters – dead – stairs – long stairs – all the dead going up – going up – to be in heaven – heaven – golden stairs – all the children coming down – coming down to be born – dead going up – children coming down – going up – coming down – going up – coming down – going up – coming down – going up – stop – stop – no – no traffic cop – no – no traffic cop in heaven – traffic cop – traffic cop – can't you give us a smile – tired – too tired – no matter – it doesn't matter – St. Peter – St. Peter at the gate – you can't come in – no matter – it doesn't matter – I'll rest – I'll lie down – down – all written down – down in a big book – no matter – it doesn't matter – I'll lie down – it weighs me – it's over me – it weighs – weighs – it's heavy – it's a heavy book – no matter – lie still – don't move – can't move – rest – forget – they say you forget – a girl – aren't you glad it's a girl – a little girl – with no hair – none – little curls all over his head – a little bald girl – curls – curls all over his head – what kind of hair had God? no matter – it doesn't matter – everybody loves God – they've got to – got to – got to love God – God is love – even if he's bad they got to love him – even if he's got fat hands – fat hands – no no – he wouldn't be God – His hands make you well – He lays on his hands – well – and happy – no matter – doesn't matter – far – too far – tired – too tired Vixen crawled off under bed – eight –

there were eight – a woman crawled off under the bed – a
woman has one – two three four – one two three four – one two
three four – two plus two is four – two times two is four – two
times four is eight Vixen had eight – one two three four five six
seven eight – eight – Puffie had eight – all drowned – drowned
– drowned in blood – blood – oh God! God – God never had
one – Mary had one – in a manger – the lowly manger – God's
on a high throne – far – too far – no matter – it doesn't matter –
God Mary Mary God Mary – Virgin Mary – Mary had one –
the Holy Ghost – the Holy Ghost – George H. Jones – oh
don't – please don't! Let me rest – now I can rest – the weight
is gone – inside the weight is gone – it's only outside – outside – all around – weight – I'm under it – Vixen crawled under
the bed – there were eight – I'll not submit any more – I'll not
submit – I'll not submit –

*The scene blacks out. The sound of riveting continues until it
goes into the sound of an electric piano and the scene lights up
for Episode Five.*

EPISODE FIVE
Prohibited

Scene: bar: bottles, tables, chairs, electric piano.

Sound: electric piano.

Characters
  MAN *behind the bar*
  POLICEMAN *at bar*
  WAITER
  At Table 1: a MAN *and a* WOMAN
  At Table 2: a MAN *and a* BOY
  At Table 3: TWO MEN *waiting for* TWO GIRLS, *who are*
  TELEPHONE GIRL *of Episode One and* YOUNG WOMAN.

At rise: everyone except the GIRLS *on. Of the characters, the*
  MAN *and* WOMAN *at Table 1 are an ordinary man and*
  woman. THE MAN *at Table 2 is a middle-aged fairy; the* BOY
  is young, untouched. At Table 3, FIRST MAN *is pleasing,*
  common, vigorous. He has coarse wavy hair. SECOND MAN
  is an ordinary salesman type.

  At Table 3.

FIRST MAN. I'm going to beat it.

SECOND MAN. Oh, for the love of Mike.

FIRST MAN. They ain't going to show.

SECOND MAN. Sure they'll show.

FIRST MAN. How do you know they'll show?

SECOND MAN. I tell you you can't keep that baby away from
  me – just got to – (*Snaps fingers.*) – She comes running.

FIRST MAN. Looks like it.

SECOND MAN (*to* WAITER *makes sign '2' with his fingers*).
  The same. (WAITER *goes to the bar.*)

At Table 2.

MAN. Oh, I'm sorry I brought you here.

BOY. Why?

MAN. This Purgatory of noise! I brought you here to give you
pleasure – let you taste pleasure. This sherry they have here is
bottled – heaven. Wait till you taste it.

BOY. But I don't drink.

MAN. Drink! This isn't drink! Real amontillado is sunshine and
orange groves – it's the Mediterranean and blue moonlight
and – love? Have you ever been in love?

BOY. No.

MAN. Never in love with – a woman?

BOY. No – not really.

MAN. What do you mean really?

BOY. Just – that.

MAN. Ah! (*Makes sign to* WAITER.) Two – you know what I
want – Two. (WAITER *goes to the bar.*)

At Table 1.

MAN. Well, are you going through with it, or ain't you?

WOMAN. That's what I want to do – go through with it.

MAN. But you can't.

WOMAN. Why can't I?

MAN. How can yuh? (*Silence.*) It's nothing – most women don't
think anything about it – they just – Bert told me a doctor to go
to – gave me the address –

WOMAN. Don't talk about it!

MAN. Got to talk about it – you got to get out of this. (*Silence –*
MAN *makes sign to* WAITER.) What you having?

WOMAN. Nothing – I don't want anything. I had enough.

MAN. Do you good. The same?

WOMAN. I suppose so.

MAN (*makes sign '2' to* WAITER). The same. (WAITER *goes to
the bar.*)

At Table 3.

FIRST MAN. I'm going to beat it.

SECOND MAN. Oh say, listen! I'm counting on you to take the other one off my hands.

FIRST MAN. I'm going to beat it.

SECOND MAN. For the love of Mike have a heart! Listen – as a favor to me – I got to be home by six – I promised my wife – sure. That don't leave me no time at all if we got to hang around – entertain some dame. You got to take her off my hands.

FIRST MAN. Maybe she won't fall for me.

SECOND MAN. Sure she'll fall for you! They all fall for you – even my wife likes you – tries to kid herself it's your brave exploits, but I know what it is – sure she'll fall for you.

Enter two girls – TELEPHONE GIRL *and* YOUNG WOMAN.

GIRL (*coming to table*). Hello –

SECOND MAN (*grouch*). Good night.

GIRL. Good night? What's eatin' yuh?

SECOND MAN (*same*). Nothin's eatin' me – thought somethin' musta swallowed you.

GIRL. Why?

SECOND MAN. You're late!

GIRL (*unimpressed*). Oh – (*Brushing it aside.*) Mrs. Jones – Mr. Smith.

SECOND MAN. Meet my friend, Mr. Roe. (*They all sit. To the* WAITER.) The same and two more. (WAITER *goes.*)

GIRL. So we kept you waiting, did we?

SECOND MAN. Only about an hour.

YOUNG WOMAN. Was it that long?

SECOND MAN. We been here that long – ain't we Dick?

FIRST MAN. Just about, Harry.

SECOND MAN. For the love of God what delayed yuh?

GIRL. Tell Helen that one.

SECOND MAN (*to* YOUNG WOMAN). The old Irish woman that went to her first race? Bet on the skate that came in last – she went up to the jockey and asked him, 'For the love of God, what delayed yuh'.

All laugh.

YOUNG WOMAN. Why, that's kinda funny!

SECOND MAN. Kinda! – What do you mean kinda?

YOUNG WOMAN. I just mean there are not many of 'em that are funny at all.

SECOND MAN. Not if you haven't heard the funny ones.

YOUNG WOMAN. Oh I've heard 'em all.

FIRST MAN. Not a laugh in a carload, eh?

GIRL. Got a cigarette?

SECOND MAN (*with package*). One of these?

GIRL (*taking one*). Uhhuh.

He offers the package to YOUNG WOMAN.

YOUNG WOMAN (*taking one*). Uhhuh.

SECOND MAN (*to* FIRST MAN). One of these?

FIRST MAN (*showing his own package*). Thanks – I like these.

He lights YOUNG WOMAN'*s cigarette.*

SECOND MAN (*lighting* GIRL'*s cigarette*). Well – baby – how they comin', huh?

GIRL. Couldn't be better.

SECOND MAN. How's every little thing?

GIRL. Just great.

SECOND MAN. Miss me?

GIRL. I'll say so – when did you get in?

SECOND MAN. Just a coupla hours ago.

GIRL. Miss me?

SECOND MAN. Did I? You don't know the half of it.

YOUNG WOMAN (*interrupting restlessly*). Can we dance here?

SECOND MAN. Not here.

YOUNG WOMAN. Where do we go from here?

SECOND MAN. Where do we go from here! You just got here!

FIRST MAN. What's the hurry?

SECOND MAN. What's the rush?

YOUNG WOMAN. I don't know.

GIRL. Helen wants to dance.

YOUNG WOMAN. I just want to keep moving.

FIRST MAN (*smiling*). You want to keep moving, huh?

SECOND MAN. You must be one of those restless babies! Where do we go from here!

YOUNG WOMAN. It's only some days – I want to keep moving.

FIRST MAN. You want to keep moving, huh? (*He is staring at her smilingly.*)

YOUNG WOMAN (*nods*). Uhhuh.

FIRST MAN (*quietly*). Stick around a while.

SECOND MAN. Where do we go from here! Say, what kind of a crowd do you run with, anyway?

GIRL. Helen don't run with any crowd – do you, Helen?

YOUNG WOMAN (*embarrassed*). No.

FIRST MAN. Well, I'm not a crowd – run with me.

SECOND MAN (*gratified*). All set, huh? – Dick was about ready to beat it.

FIRST MAN. That's before I met the little lady.

WAITER *serves drinks.*

FIRST MAN. Here's how.

SECOND MAN. Here's to you.

GIRL. Here's looking at you.

YOUNG WOMAN. Here's – happy days.

They all drink.

FIRST MAN. That's good stuff!

SECOND MAN. Off a boat.

FIRST MAN. Off a boat?

SECOND MAN. They get all their stuff here – off a boat.

GIRL. That's what *they* say.

SECOND MAN. No! Sure! Sure they do! Sure!

GIRL. It's all right with me.

SECOND MAN. But they do! Sure!

GIRL. I believe you, darling!

SECOND MAN. Did you miss me?

GIRL. Uhhuh. (*Affirmative.*)

SECOND MAN. Any other daddies?

GIRL. Uhhuh. (*Negative.*)

SECOND MAN. Love any daddy but daddy?

GIRL. Uhhuh. (*Negative.*)

SECOND MAN. Let's beat it!

GIRL (*a little self-conscious before* YOUNG WOMAN). We just got here.

SECOND MAN. Don't I know it – Come on!

GIRL. But – (*Indicates* YOUNG WOMAN.)

SECOND MAN (*not understanding*). They're all set – aren't you?

FIRST MAN (*to* YOUNG WOMAN). Are we? (*She doesn't answer.*)

SECOND MAN. I got to be out to the house by six – come on – (*Rising – to* GIRL.) Come on, kid – let's us beat it! (GIRL *indicates* YOUNG WOMAN. *Now understanding – very elaborate.*) Business is business, you know! I got a lot to do yet this afternoon – thought you might go along with me – help me out – how about it?

GIRL (*rising, her dignity preserved*). Sure – I'll go along with you – help you out. (*Both rise.*)

SECOND MAN. All right with you folks?

FIRST MAN. All right with me.

SECOND MAN. All right with you? (*To* YOUNG WOMAN.)

YOUNG WOMAN. All right with me.

SECOND MAN. Come on, kid. (*They rise.*) Where's the damage?

FIRST MAN. Go on!

SECOND MAN. No!

FIRST MAN. Go on!

SECOND MAN. I'll match you.

YOUNG WOMAN. Heads win!

GIRL. Heads I win – tails you lose.

SECOND MAN (*impatiently*). He's matching me.

FIRST MAN. Am I matching you or you matching me?

SECOND MAN. I'm matching you. (*They match.*)You're stung!

FIRST MAN (*contentedly*). Not so you can notice it. (*Smiles at* YOUNG WOMAN.)

GIRL. That's for you, Helen.

SECOND MAN. She ain't dumb! Come on.

GIRL (*to* FIRST MAN). You be nice to her now. She's very fastidious. – Goodbye.

Exit SECOND MAN *and* GIRL.

YOUNG WOMAN. I know what business is like.

FIRST MAN. You do – do yuh?

YOUNG WOMAN. I used to be a business girl myself before –

FIRST MAN. Before what?

YOUNG WOMAN. Before I quit.

FIRST MAN. What did you quit for?

YOUNG WOMAN. I just quit.

FIRST MAN. You're married, huh?

YOUNG WOMAN. Yes – I am.

FIRST MAN. All right with me.

YOUNG WOMAN. Some men don't seem to like a woman after she's married –

WAITER *comes to the table*.

FIRST MAN. What's the difference?

YOUNG WOMAN. Depends on the man, I guess.

FIRST MAN. Depends on the woman, I guess. (*To* WAITER, *makes sign of '2'*.) The same. (WAITER *goes to the bar*.)

At Table 1.

MAN. It don't amount to nothing. God! Most women just –

WOMAN. I know – I know – I know.

MAN. They don't think nothing of it. They just –

WOMAN. I know – I know – I know.

Re-enter SECOND MAN *and* GIRL. *They go to Table 3*.

SECOND MAN. Say, I forgot – I want you to do something for me, will yuh?

FIRST MAN. Sure – what is it?

SECOND MAN. I want you to telephone me out home tomorrow – and ask me to come into town – will yuh?

FIRST MAN. Sure – why not?

SECOND MAN. You know – business – get me?

FIRST MAN. I get you.

SECOND MAN. I've worked the telegraph gag to death – and my wife likes you.

FIRST MAN. What's your number?

SECOND MAN. I'll write it down for you. (*Writes*.)

FIRST MAN. How is your wife?

SECOND MAN. She's fine.

FIRST MAN. And the kid?

SECOND MAN. Great. (*Hands him the card. To girl.*) Come on, kid. (*Turns back to* YOUNG WOMAN.) Get this bird to tell you about himself.

GIRL. Keep him from it.

SECOND MAN. Get him to tell you how he killed a couple of spig down in Mexico.

GIRL. You been in Mexico?

SECOND MAN. He just came up from there.

GIRL. Can you teach us the tango?

YOUNG WOMAN. You killed a man?

SECOND MAN. Two of 'em! With a bottle! Get him to tell you – with a bottle. Come on, kid. Goodbye.

Exit SECOND MAN *and* GIRL.

YOUNG WOMAN. Why did you?

FIRST MAN. What?

YOUNG WOMAN. Kill 'em?

FIRST MAN. To get free.

YOUNG WOMAN. Oh.

At Table 2.

MAN. You really must taste this – just taste it. It's a real amontillado, you know.

BOY. Where do they get it here?

MAN. It's always down the side streets one finds the real pleasures, don't you think?

BOY. I don't know.

MAN. Learn. Come, taste this! Amontillado! Or don't you like amontillado?

BOY. I don't know. I never had any before.

MAN. Your first taste! How I envy you! Come, taste it! Taste it! And die.

BOY *tastes wine – finds it disappointing.*

MAN (*gilding it*). Poe was a lover of amontillado. He returns to it continually, you remember – or are you a lover of Poe?

BOY. I've read a lot of him.

MAN. But are you a lover?

At Table 3.

FIRST MAN. There were a bunch of bandidos – bandits, you know, took me into the hills – holding me there – what was I to do? got the two birds that guarded me drunk one night, and then I filled the empty bottle with small stones – and let 'em have it!

YOUNG WOMAN. Oh!

FIRST MAN. I had to get free, didn't I? I let 'em have it –

YOUNG WOMAN. Oh – then what did you do?

FIRST MAN. Then I beat it.

YOUNG WOMAN. Where to – ?

FIRST MAN. Right here. (*Pause.*) Glad?

YOUNG WOMAN (*nods*). Yes.

FIRST MAN (*makes sign to* WAITER *of '2'*). The same. (WAITER *goes to the bar.*)

At Table 1.

MAN. You're just scared because this is the first time and –

WOMAN. I'm not scared.

MAN. Then what are you for Christ's sake?

WOMAN. I'm not scared. I want it – I want to have it – that ain't being scared, is it?

MAN. It's being goofy.

WOMAN. I don't care.

MAN. What about your folks?

WOMAN. I don't care.

MAN. What about your job? (*Silence.*) You got to keep your job, haven't you? (*Silence.*) Haven't you?

WOMAN. I suppose so.

MAN. Well – there you are!

WOMAN (*silence – then*). All right – let's go now – You got the address?

MAN. Now you're coming to.

They get up and go off. Exit MAN and WOMAN.

At Table 3.

YOUNG WOMAN. A bottle like that? (*She picks it up.*)

FIRST MAN. Yeah – filled with pebbles.

YOUNG WOMAN. What kind of pebbles?

FIRST MAN. Pebbles! Off the ground.

YOUNG WOMAN. Oh.

FIRST MAN. Necessity, you know, mother of invention. (*As YOUNG WOMAN handles the bottle.*) Ain't a bad weapon – first you got a sledge hammer – then you got a knife.

YOUNG WOMAN. Oh. (*Puts bottle down.*)

FIRST MAN. Women don't like knives, do they? (*Pours drink.*)

YOUNG WOMAN. No.

FIRST MAN. Don't mind a hammer so much, though, do they?

YOUNG WOMAN. No –

FIRST MAN. I didn't like it myself – any of it – but I had to get free, didn't I? Sure I had to get free, didn't I? (*Drinks*.) Now I'm damn glad I did.

YOUNG WOMAN. Why?

FIRST MAN. You know why. (*He puts his hand over hers*.)

At Table 2.

MAN. Let's go to my rooms – and I'll show them to you – I have a first edition of Verlaine that will simply make your mouth water. (*They stand up*.) Here – there's just a sip at the bottom of my glass –

BOY *takes it.*

That last sip's the sweetest – Wasn't it?

BOY (*laughs*). And I always thought that was dregs. (*Exit* MAN *followed by* BOY.)

At Table 3.

The MAN *is holding her hand across the table.*

YOUNG WOMAN. When you put your hand over mine! When you just touch me!

FIRST MAN. Yeah? (*Pause*.) Come on, kid, let's go!

YOUNG MAN. Where?

FIRST MAN. You haven't been around much, have you, kid?

YOUNG WOMAN. No.

FIRST MAN. I could tell that just to look at you.

YOUNG WOMAN. You could?

FIRST MAN. Sure I could, What are you running around with a girl like that other one for?

YOUNG WOMAN. I don't know. She seems to have a good time.

FIRST MAN. So that's it?

YOUNG WOMAN. Don't she?

FIRST MAN. Don't you?

YOUNG WOMAN. No.

FIRST MAN. Never?

YOUNG WOMAN. Never.

FIRST MAN. What's the matter?

YOUNG WOMAN. Nothing – just me, I guess.

FIRST MAN. You're all right.

YOUNG WOMAN. Am I?

FIRST MAN. Sure. You just haven't met the right guy – that's all – girl like you – you got to meet the right guy.

YOUNG WOMAN. I know.

FIRST MAN. You're different from girls like that other one – any guy'll do her. You're different.

YOUNG WOMAN. I guess I am.

FIRST MAN. You didn't fall for that business gag – did you – when they went off?

YOUNG WOMAN. Well, I thought they wanted to be alone probably, but –

FIRST MAN. And how!

YOUNG WOMAN. Oh – so that's it.

FIRST MAN. That's it. Come along – let's go –

YOUNG WOMAN. Oh, I couldn't! Like this?

FIRST MAN. Don't you like me?

YOUNG WOMAN. Yes.

FIRST MAN. Then what's the matter?

YOUNG WOMAN. Do – you – like me?

FIRST MAN. Like yuh? You don't know the half of it – listen – you know what you seem like to me?

YOUNG WOMAN. What?

FIRST MAN. An angel. Just like an angel.

YOUNG WOMAN. I do?

FIRST MAN. That's what I said! Let's go!

YOUNG WOMAN. Where?

FIRST MAN. Where do you live?

YOUNG WOMAN. Oh, we can't go to my place.

FIRST MAN. Then come to my place.

YOUNG WOMAN. Oh I couldn't – is it far?

FIRST MAN. Just a step – come on –

YOUNG WOMAN. Oh I couldn't – what is it – a room?

FIRST MAN. No – an apartment – a one room apartment.

YOUNG WOMAN. That's different.

FIRST MAN. On the ground floor – no one will see you – coming or going.

YOUNG WOMAN (*getting up*). I couldn't.

FIRST MAN (*rises*). Wait a minute – I got to pay the damage – and I'll get a bottle of something to take along.

YOUNG WOMAN. No – don't.

FIRST MAN. Why not?

YOUNG WOMAN. Well – don't bring any pebbles.

FIRST MAN. Say – forget that! Will you?

YOUNG WOMAN. I just meant I don't think I'll need anything to drink.

FIRST MAN (*leaning to her eagerly*). You like me – don't you, kid?

YOUNG WOMAN. Do you me?

FIRST MAN. Wait!

He goes to the bar. She remains, her hands outstretched on the table, staring ahead. Enter a MAN and a GIRL. They go to one of the empty tables. The WAITER goes to them.

MAN (*to GIRL*). What do you want?

GIRL. Same old thing.

MAN (*to the WAITER*). The usual. (*Makes a sign '2'.*)

The FIRST MAN crosses to YOUNG WOMAN with a wrapped bottle under his arm. She rises and starts out with him. As they pass the piano, he stops and puts in a nickle – the music starts as they exit. The scene blacks out.

The music of the electric piano continues until the lights go up for Episode Six, and the music has become the music of a hand organ, very very faint.

EPISODE SIX

Intimate

Scene: a dark room.

Sounds: a hand organ; footbeats, of passing feet.

Characters
MAN
YOUNG WOMAN

*At rise: darkness. Nothing can be discerned. From the outside
comes the sound of a hand organ, very faint, and the irregular
rhythm of passing feet. The hand organ is playing* Cielito
Lindo, *that Spanish song that has been on every hand organ
lately.*

MAN. You're awful still, honey. What you thinking about?

WOMAN. About sea shells. (*The sound of her voice is beautiful.*)

MAN. Sheshells? Gee! I can't say it!

WOMAN. When I was little my grandmother used to have a big
pink sea shell on the mantle behind the stove. When we'd go to
visit her they'd let me hold it, and listen. That's what I was
thinking about now.

MAN. Yeah?

WOMAN. You can hear the sea in 'em, you know.

MAN. Yeah, I know.

WOMAN. I wonder why that is?

MAN. Search me. (*Pause.*)

WOMAN. You going? (*He has moved.*)

MAN. No. I just want a cigarette.

WOMAN (*glad, relieved*). Oh.

MAN. Want one?

WOMAN. No. (*Taking the match.*) Let me light it for you.

MAN. You got mighty pretty hands, honey. (*The match is out.*)
This little pig went to market. This little pig stayed home. This
little pig went –

WOMAN (*laughs*). Diddle diddle dee. (*Laughs again.*)

MAN. You got awful pretty hands.

WOMAN. I used to have. But I haven't taken much care of them
lately. I will now – (*Pause. The music gets clearer.*) What's
that?

MAN. What?

WOMAN. That music?

MAN. A dago hand organ. I gave him two bits the first day I got
here – so he comes every day.

WOMAN. I mean – what's that he's playing?

MAN. *Cielito Lindo*.

WOMAN. What does that mean?

MAN. Little Heaven.

WOMAN. Little Heaven?

MAN. That's what lovers call each other in Spain.

WOMAN. Spain's where all the castles are, ain't it?

MAN. Yeah.

WOMAN. Little Heaven – sing it!

MAN (*singing to the music of the hand organ*). Da la sierra
morena viene, bajando viene, bajando; un par de ojitos negros –
cielito lindo – da contrabando.

WOMAN. What does it mean?

MAN. From the high dark mountains.

WOMAN. From the high dark mountains – ?

MAN. Oh it doesn't mean anything. It doesn't make sense. It's
love. (*Taking up the song.*) Ay-ay-ay-ay.

WOMAN. I know what that means.

MAN. What?

WOMAN. Ay-ay-ay-ay. (*They laugh.*)

MAN (*taking up the song*). Canta non llores – Sing don't cry –

WOMAN (*taking up song*). La-la-la-la-la-la-la-la-la-la – Little
Heaven!

MAN. You got a nice voice, honey.

WOMAN. Have I? (*Laughs – tickles him.*)

MAN. You bet you have – hey!

WOMAN (*laughing*). You ticklish?

MAN. Sure I am! Hey! (*They laugh.*) Go on, honey, sing something.

WOMAN. I couldn't.

MAN. Go on – you got a fine voice.

WOMAN (*laughs and sings*). Hey, diddle, diddle, the cat and the fiddle, The cow jumped over the moon, The little dog laughed to see the sport, And the dish ran away with the spoon –

Both laugh.

I never thought that had any sense before – now I get it.

MAN. You got me beat.

WOMAN. It's you and me – La-lalalalalala – lalalalalalala – Little Heaven. You're the dish and I'm the spoon.

MAN. You're a little spoon all right.

WOMAN. And I guess I'm the little cow that jumped over the moon. (*A pause.*) Do you believe in sorta guardian angels?

MAN. What?

WOMAN. Guardian angels?

MAN. I don't know. Maybe.

WOMAN. I do. (*Taking up the song again.*) Lalalalala – lalalalala – lalalala – Little Heaven. (*Talking.*) There must be something that looks out for you and brings you your happiness, at last – look at us! How did we both happen to go to that place today if there wasn't something!

MAN. Maybe you're right.

WOMAN. Look at us!

MAN. Everything's us to you, kid – ain't it?

WOMAN. Ain't it?

MAN. All right with me.

WOMAN. We belong together! We belong together! And we're going to stick together, ain't we?

MAN. Sing something else.

WOMAN. I tell you I can't sing!

MAN. Sure you can!

WOMAN. I tell you I hadn't thought of singing since I was a little bit of a girl.

MAN. Well sing anyway.

WOMAN (singing). And every little wavelet had its night cap on – its night cap on – its night cap on – and every little wave had its night cap on – so very early in the morning. (Talking.) Did you used to sing that when you were a little kid?

MAN. Nope.

WOMAN. Didn't you? We used to – in the first grade – little kids – we used to go round and round in a ring – and flop our hands up and down – supposed to be the waves. I remember it used to confuse me – because we did just the same thing to be little angels.

MAN. Yeah?

WOMAN. You know why I came here?

MAN. I can make a good guess.

WOMAN. Because you told me I looked like an angel to you! That's why I came.

MAN. Jeez, honey, all women look like angels to me – all white women. I ain't been seeing nothing but Indians, you know for the last couple a years. Gee, when I got off the boat here the other day – and saw all the women – gee I pretty near went crazy – talk about looking like angels – why –

WOMAN. You've had a lot of women, haven't you?

MAN. Not so many – real ones.

WOMAN. Did you – like any of 'em – better than me?

MAN. Nope – there wasn't one of 'em any sweeter than you, honey – not as sweet – no – not as sweet.

WOMAN. I like to hear you say it. Say it again –

MAN (protesting good humoredly). Oh –

WOMAN. Go on – tell me again!

MAN. Here! (Kisses her.) Does that tell you?

WOMAN. Yes. (Pause.) We're going to stick together – always – aren't we?

MAN (honestly). I'll have to be moving on, kid – some day, you know.

WOMAN. When?

MAN. Quien sabe?

WOMAN. What does that mean?

MAN. Quien sabe? You got to learn that, kid, if you're figuring on coming with me. It's the answer to everything – below the Rio Grande.

WOMAN. What does it mean?

MAN. It means – who knows?

WOMAN. Keen sabe?

MAN. Yep – don't forget it – now.

WOMAN. I'll never forget it!

MAN. Quien sabe?

WOMAN. And I'll never get to use it.

MAN. Quien sabe.

WOMAN. I'll never get – below the Rio Grande – I'll never get out of here.

MAN. Quien sabe.

WOMAN (*change of mood*).That's right! Keen sabe? Who knows?

MAN. That's the stuff.

WOMAN. You must like it down there.

MAN. I can't live anywhere else – for long.

WOMAN. Why not?

MAN. Oh – you're free down there! You're free!

A street light is lit outside. The outlines of a window take form against this light. There are bars across it, and from outside it, the sidewalk cuts across almost at the top. It is a basement room. The constant going and coming of passing feet, mostly feet of couples, can be dimly seen. Inside, on the ledge, there is a lily blooming in a bowl of rocks and water.

WOMAN. What's that?

MAN. Just the street light going on.

WOMAN. Is it as late as that?

MAN. Late as what?

WOMAN. Dark.

MAN. It's been dark for hours – didn't you know that?

WOMAN. No! – I must go! (*Rises.*)

MAN. Wait – the moon will be up in a little while – full moon.

WOMAN. It isn't that! I'm late! I must go!

She comes into the light. She wears a white chemise that might be the tunic of a dancer, and as she comes into the light she fastens about her waist a little skirt. She really wears almost exactly the clothes that women wear now, but the finesse of their cut, and the grace and ease with which she puts them on, must turn this episode of her dressing into a personification, an idealization of a woman clothing herself. All her gestures must be unconscious, innocent, relaxed, sure and full of natural grace. As she sits facing the window pulling on a stocking.

What's that?

MAN. What?

WOMAN. On the window ledge.

MAN. A flower.

WOMAN. Who gave it to you?

MAN. Nobody gave it to me. I bought it.

WOMAN. For yourself?

MAN. Yeah – Why not?

WOMAN. I don't know.

MAN. In Chinatown – made me think of Frisco where I was a kid – so I bought it.

WOMAN. Is that where you were born – Frisco?

MAN. Yep. Twin Peaks.

WOMAN. What's that?

MAN. A couple of hills – together.

WOMAN. One for you and one for me.

MAN. I bet you'd like Frisco.

WOMAN. I know a woman went out there once!

MAN. The bay and the hills! Jeez, that's the life! Every Saturday we used to cross the Bay – get a couple nags and just ride – over the hills. One would have a blanket on the saddle – the other, the grub. At night, we'd make a little fire and eat – and then roll up in the old blanket and –

WOMAN. Who? Who was with you?

MAN (*indifferently*). Anybody. (*Enthusiastically.*) Jeez, that dry old grass out there smells good at night – full of tar weed – you know –

WOMAN. Is that a good smell?

MAN. Tar weed? Didn't you ever smell it? (*She shakes her head 'No'.*) Sure it's a good smell! The Bay and the hills.

She goes to the mirror of the dresser, to finish dressing. She has only a dress to put on that is in one piece – with one fastening on the side. Before slipping it on, she stands before the mirror and stretches. Appreciatively but indifferently.

You look in good shape, kid. A couple of months riding over the mountains with me, you'd be great.

WOMAN. Can I?

MAN. What?

WOMAN. Some day – ride mountains with you?

MAN. Ride mountains? Ride donkeys!

WOMAN. It's the same thing! – with you! – Can I – some day? The high dark mountains?

MAN. Who knows?

WOMAN. It must be great!

MAN. You ever been off like that, kid? – high up? On top of the world?

WOMAN. Yes.

MAN. When?

WOMAN. Today.

MAN. You're pretty sweet.

WOMAN. I never knew anything like this way! I never knew that I could feel like this! So, – so purified! Don't laugh at me!

MAN. I ain't laughing, honey.

WOMAN. Purified.

MAN. It's a hell of a word – but I know what you mean. That's the way it is – sometimes.

WOMAN (*she puts on a little hat, then turns to him*). Well – goodbye.

MAN. Aren't you forgetting something? (*Rises.*)

She looks toward him, then throws her head slowly back, lifts her right arm – this gesture that is in so many statues of women – Volupte. He comes out of the shadow, puts his arm around her, kisses her. Her head and arm go further back – then she brings her arm around with a wide encircling gesture, her hand closes over his head, her fingers spread. Her fingers are protective, clutching. When he releases her, her eyes are shining with tears. She turns away. She looks back at him – and the room – and her eyes fasten on the lily.

WOMAN. Can I have that?

MAN. Sure – why not?

She takes it – goes. As she opens the door, the music is louder. The scene blacks out.

WOMAN. Goodbye. And – (*Hesitates.*) And – thank you.

Curtain

The music continues until the curtain goes up for Episode Seven. It goes up on silence.

EPISODE SEVEN

Domestic

Scene: a sitting room: a divan, a telephone, a window.

Characters
HUSBAND
YOUNG WOMAN

They are seated on opposite ends of the divan. They are both reading papers – to themselves.

HUSBAND. Record production.

YOUNG WOMAN. Girl turns on gas.

HUSBAND. Sale hits a million –

YOUNG WOMAN. Woman leaves all for love –

HUSBAND. Market trend steady –

YOUNG WOMAN. Young wife disappears –

HUSBAND. Owns a life interest –

Phone rings. YOUNG WOMAN *looks toward it.*

That's for me. (*In phone.*) Hello – oh hello, A.B. It's all settled? – Everything signed? Good. Good! Tell R.A. to call me up. (*Hangs up phone – to* YOUNG WOMAN.) Well, it's all settled. They signed! – aren't you interested? Aren't you going to ask me?

YOUNG WOMAN (*by rote*). Did you put it over?

HUSBAND. Sure I put it over.

YOUNG WOMAN. Did you swing it?

HUSBAND. Sure I swung it.

YOUNG WOMAN. Did they come through?

HUSBAND. Sure they came through.

YOUNG WOMAN. Did they sign?

HUSBAND. I'll say they signed.

YOUNG WOMAN. On the dotted line?

HUSBAND. On the dotted line.

YOUNG WOMAN. The property's yours?

HUSBAND. The property's mine. I'll put a first mortgage. I'll put a second mortgage and the property's mine. Happy?

YOUNG WOMAN (*by rote*). Happy.

HUSBAND (*going to her*). The property's mine! It's not all that's mine! (*Pinching her cheek – happy and playful.*) I got a first mortgage on her – I got a second mortgage on her – and she's mine!

YOUNG WOMAN *pulls away swiftly.*

What's the matter?

YOUNG WOMAN. Nothing – what?

HUSBAND. You flinched when I touched you.

YOUNG WOMAN. No.

HUSBAND. You haven't done that in a long time.

YOUNG WOMAN. Haven't I?

HUSBAND. You used to do it every time I touched you .

YOUNG WOMAN. Did I?

HUSBAND. Didn't know that, did you?

YOUNG WOMAN (*unexpectedly*). Yes. Yes, I know it.

HUSBAND. Just purity.

YOUNG WOMAN. No.

HUSBAND. Oh, I liked it. Purity.

YOUNG WOMAN. No.

HUSBAND. You're one of the purest women that ever lived.

YOUNG WOMAN. I'm just like anybody else only – (*Stops.*)

HUSBAND. Only what?

YOUNG WOMAN (*pause*). Nothing.

HUSBAND. It must be something.

Phone rings. She gets up and goes to window.

HUSBAND (*in phone*). Hello – hello, R.A. – well, I put it over – yeah, I swung it – sure they came through – did they sign? On the dotted line! The property's mine. I made the proposition. I sold them the idea. Now watch me. Tell D.D. to call me up.

(*Hangs up.*) That was R.A. What are you looking at?

YOUNG WOMAN. Nothing.

HUSBAND. You must be looking at something.

YOUNG WOMAN. Nothing – the moon.

HUSBAND. The moon's something, isn't it?

YOUNG WOMAN. Yes.

HUSBAND. What's it doing?

YOUNG WOMAN. Nothing.

HUSBAND. It must be doing something.

YOUNG WOMAN. It's moving – moving – (*She comes down restlessly.*)

HUSBAND. Pull down the shade, my dear.

YOUNG WOMAN. Why?

HUSBAND. People can look in.

Phone rings.

Hello – hello D.D. – Yes – I put it over – they came across – I put it over on them – yep – yep – yep – I'll say I am – yep – on the dotted line – Now you watch me – yep. Yep yep. Tell B.M. to phone me. (*Hangs up.*) That was D.D. (*To* YOUNG WOMAN *who has come down to davenport and picked up a paper.*) Aren't you listening?

YOUNG WOMAN. I'm reading.

HUSBAND. What you reading?

YOUNG WOMAN. Nothing.

HUSBAND. Must be something. (*He sits and picks up his paper.*)

YOUNG WOMAN (*reading*). Prisoner escapes – lifer breaks jail – shoots way to freedom –

HUSBAND. Don't read that stuff – listen – here's a first rate editorial. I agree with this. I agree absolutely. Are you listening?

YOUNG WOMAN. I'm listening.

HUSBAND (*importantly*). All men are born free and entitled to the pursuit of happiness. (YOUNG WOMAN *gets up.*) My, you're nervous tonight.

YOUNG WOMAN. I try not to be.

HUSBAND. You inherit that from your mother. She was in the office today.

YOUNG WOMAN. Was she?

HUSBAND. To get her allowance.

YOUNG WOMAN. Oh –

HUSBAND. Don't you know it's the *first*.

YOUNG WOMAN. Poor Ma.

HUSBAND. What would she do without me?

YOUNG WOMAN. I know. You're very good.

HUSBAND. One thing – she's grateful.

YOUNG WOMAN. Poor Ma – poor Ma.

HUSBAND. She's got to have care.

YOUNG WOMAN. Yes. She's got to have care.

HUSBAND. A mother's a very precious thing – a good mother.

YOUNG WOMAN (*excitedly*). I try to be a good mother.

HUSBAND. Of course you're a good mother.

YOUNG WOMAN. I try! I try!

HUSBAND. A mother's a very precious thing – (*Resuming his paper.*) And a child's a very precious thing. Precious jewels.

YOUNG WOMAN (*reading*). Sale of jewels and precious stones.

   YOUNG WOMAN *puts her hand to throat.*

HUSBAND. What's the matter?

YOUNG WOMAN. I feel as though I were drowning.

HUSBAND. Drowning?

YOUNG WOMAN. With stones around my neck.

HUSBAND. You just imagine that.

YOUNG WOMAN. Stifling.

HUSBAND. You don't breathe deep enough – breathe now – look at me. (*He breathes.*) Breath is life. Life is breath.

YOUNG WOMAN (*suddenly*). And what is death?

HUSBAND (*smartly*). Just – no breath!

YOUNG WOMAN (*to herself*). Just no breath.

   Takes up paper.

HUSBAND. All right?

YOUNG WOMAN. All right.

HUSBAND (*reads as she stares at her paper. Looks up after a pause.*) I feel cold air, my dear.

YOUNG WOMAN. Cold air?

HUSBAND. Close the window, will you?

YOUNG WOMAN. It isn't open.

HUSBAND. Don't you feel cold air?

YOUNG WOMAN. No – you just imagine it.

HUSBAND. I never imagine anything. (YOUNG WOMAN *is staring at the paper.*) What are you reading?

YOUNG WOMAN. Nothing.

HUSBAND. You must be reading something.

YOUNG WOMAN. Woman finds husband dead.

HUSBAND (*uninterested*). Oh. (*Interested.*) Here's a man says 'I owe my success to a yeast cake a day – my digestion is good – I sleep very well – and – (*His wife gets up, goes toward door.*) Where you going?

YOUNG WOMAN. No place.

HUSBAND. You must be going some place.

YOUNG WOMAN. Just – to bed.

HUSBAND. It isn't eleven yet. Wait.

YOUNG WOMAN. Wait?

HUSBAND. It's only ten-forty-six – wait! (*Holds out his arms to her.*) Come here!

YOUNG WOMAN (*takes a step toward him – recoils*). Oh – I want to go away!

HUSBAND. Away? Where?

YOUNG WOMAN. Anywhere – away.

HUSBAND. Why, what's the matter?

YOUNG WOMAN. I'm scared.

HUSBAND. What of?

YOUNG WOMAN. I can't sleep – I haven't slept.

HUSBAND. That's nothing.

YOUNG WOMAN. And the moon – when it's full moon.

HUSBAND. That's nothing.

YOUNG WOMAN. I can't sleep.

HUSBAND. Of course not. It's the light.

YOUNG WOMAN. I don't see it! I feel it! I'm afraid.

HUSBAND (*kindly*). Nonsense – come here.

YOUNG WOMAN. I want to go away.

HUSBAND. But I can't get away now.

YOUNG WOMAN. Alone!

HUSBAND. You've never been away alone.

YOUNG WOMAN. I know.

HUSBAND. What would you do?

YOUNG WOMAN. Maybe I'd sleep.

HUSBAND. Now you wait.

YOUNG WOMAN (*desperately*). Wait?

HUSBAND. We'll take a trip – we'll go to Europe – I'll get my watch – I'll get my Swiss watch – I've always wanted a Swiss watch that I bought right there – isn't that funny? Wait – wait. (YOUNG WOMAN *comes down to davenport – sits. Husband resumes his paper.*) Another revolution below the Rio Grande.

YOUNG WOMAN. Below the Rio Grande?

HUSBAND. Yes – another –

YOUNG WOMAN. Anyone – hurt?

HUSBAND. No.

YOUNG WOMAN. Any prisoners?

HUSBAND. No.

YOUNG WOMAN. All free?

HUSBAND. All free.

> *He resumes his paper.* YOUNG WOMAN *sits, staring ahead of her. The music of the hand organ sounds off very dimly, playing* Cielito Lindo. *Voices begin to sing it –* 'Ay-ay-ay-ay' *– and then the words – the music and voices get louder.*

THE VOICE OF HER LOVER. They were a bunch of bandidos – bandits you know – holding me there – what was I to do – I had to get free – didn't I? I had to get free –

VOICES. Free – free – free –

LOVER. I filled an empty bottle with small stones –

VOICES. Stones – stones – precious stones – millstones – stones – stones – millstones

LOVER. Just a bottle with small stones.

VOICES. Stones – stones – small stones –

LOVER. You only need a bottle with small stones.

VOICES. Stones – stones – small stones –

VOICE OF A HUCKSTER. Stones for sale – stones – stones – small stones – precious stones –

VOICES. Stones – stones – precious stones –

LOVER. Had to get free, didn't I? Free?

VOICES. Free? Free?

LOVER. Quien sabe? Who knows? Who knows?

VOICES. Who'd know? Who'd know? Who'd know?

HUCKSTER. Stones – stones – small stones – big stones – millstones – cold stones – head stones –

VOICES. Head stones – head stones – head stones.

The music – the voices – mingle – increase – the YOUNG WOMAN *flies from her chair and cries out in terror.*

YOUNG WOMAN. Oh! Oh!

The scene blacks out – the music and the dim voices, 'Stones – stones – stones,' continue until the scene lights for Episode Eight.

EPISODE EIGHT

The Law

Scene: courtroom.

Sounds: clicking of telegraph instruments offstage.

Characters
    JUDGE
    JURY
    LAWYERS
    SPECTATORS
    REPORTERS
    MESSENGER BOYS
    LAW CLERKS
    BAILIFF
    COURT REPORTER
    YOUNG WOMAN

The words and movements of all these people except the YOUNG
WOMAN *are routine – mechanical. Each is going through the
motions of his own game.*

At rise: all assembled, except JUDGE.

    Enter JUDGE.

BAILIFF (*mumbling*). Hear ye – hear ye – hear ye! (*All rise.
    *JUDGE *sits. All sit.* LAWYER FOR DEFENSE *gets to his feet
    – He is the verbose, 'eloquent' typical criminal defense lawyer.
    *JUDGE *signs to him to wait – turns to* LAW CLERKS,
    grouped at foot of the bench.

FIRST CLERK (*handing up a paper – routine voice*). State versus
    Kling – stay of execution.

JUDGE. Denied.

    FIRST CLERK *goes.*

SECOND CLERK. Bing vs. Ding – demurrer.

    JUDGE *signs.* SECOND CLERK *goes.*

THIRD CLERK. Case of John King – habeas corpus.

JUDGE signs. THIRD CLERK goes. JUDGE signs to
BAILIFF.

BAILIFF (*mumbling*). People of the State of ——— versus Helen
Jones.

JUDGE (*to* LAWYER FOR DEFENSE). Defense ready to
proceed?

LAWYER FOR DEFENSE. We're ready, your Honor.

JUDGE. Proceed.

LAWYER FOR DEFENSE. Helen Jones.

BAILIFF. HELEN JONES!

YOUNG WOMAN rises.

LAWYER FOR DEFENSE. Mrs. Jones, will you take the stand?

YOUNG WOMAN goes to witness stand.

FIRST REPORTER (*writing rapidly*). The defense sprang a
surprise at the opening of court this morning by putting the
accused woman on the stand. The prosecution was swept off
its feet by this daring defense strategy and – (*Instruments get*
louder.)

SECOND REPORTER. Trembling and scarcely able to stand,
Helen Jones, accused murderess, had to be almost carried to
the witness stand this morning when her lawyer –

BAILIFF (*mumbling – with Bible*). Do you swear to tell the truth,
the whole truth and nothing but the truth – so help you God?

YOUNG WOMAN. I do.

JUDGE. You may sit.

She sits in witness chair.

COURT REPORTER. What is your name?

YOUNG WOMAN. Helen Jones.

COURT REPORTER. Your age?

YOUNG WOMAN (*hesitates – then*). Twenty-nine.

COURT REPORTER. Where do you live?

YOUNG WOMAN. In prison.

LAWYER FOR DEFENSE. This is my client's legal address.

Hands a scrap of paper.

LAWYER FOR PROSECUTION (*jumping to his feet*). I object to this insinuation on the part of counsel of any illegality in the holding of this defendant in jail when the law –

LAWYER FOR DEFENSE. I made no such insinuation.

LAWYER FOR PROSECUTION. You implied it –

LAWYER FOR DEFENSE. I did not!

LAWYER FOR PROSECUTION. You're a –

JUDGE. Order!

BAILIFF. Order!

LAWYER FOR DEFENSE. Your Honor, I object to counsel's constant attempt to –

LAWYER FOR PROSECUTION. I protest – I –

JUDGE. Order!

BAILIFF. Order!

JUDGE. Proceed with the witness.

LAWYER FOR DEFENSE. Mrs. Jones, you are the widow of the late George H. Jones, are you not?

YOUNG WOMAN. Yes.

LAWYER FOR DEFENSE. How long were you married to the late George H. Jones before his demise?

YOUNG WOMAN. Six years.

LAWYER FOR DEFENSE. Six years! And it was a happy marriage, was it not? (YOUNG WOMAN *hesitates*.) Did you quarrel?

YOUNG WOMAN. No, sir.

LAWYER FOR DEFENSE. Then it was a happy marriage, wasn't it?

YOUNG WOMAN. Yes, sir.

LAWYER FOR DEFENSE. In those six years of married life with your late husband, the late George H. Jones, did you EVER have a quarrel?

YOUNG WOMAN. No, sir.

LAWYER FOR DEFENSE. Never one quarrel?

LAWYER FOR PROSECUTION. The witness has said –

LAWYER FOR DEFENSE. Six years without one quarrel! Six years! Gentlemen of the jury, I ask you to consider this fact!

Six years of married life without a quarrel. (*The* JURY *grins.*)
I ask you to consider it seriously! Very seriously! Who of us –
and this is not intended as any reflection on the sacred
institution of marriage – no – but!

JUDGE. Proceed with your witness.

LAWYER FOR DEFENSE. You have one child – have you not,
Mrs. Jones?

YOUNG WOMAN. Yes, sir.

LAWYER FOR DEFENSE. A little girl, is it not?

YOUNG WOMAN. Yes, sir.

LAWYER FOR DEFENSE. How old is she?

YOUNG WOMAN. She's five – past five.

LAWYER FOR DEFENSE. A little girl of past five. Since the
demise of the late Mr. Jones you are the only parent she has
living, are you not?

YOUNG WOMAN. Yes, sir.

LAWYER FOR DEFENSE. Before your marriage to the late Mr.
Jones, you worked and supported your mother, did you not?

LAWYER FOR PROSECUTION. I object, your honor! Irrelevant
– immaterial – and –

JUDGE. Objection sustained!

LAWYER FOR DEFENSE. In order to support your mother and
yourself as a girl, you worked, did you not?

YOUNG WOMAN. Yes, sir.

LAWYER FOR DEFENSE. What did you do?

YOUNG WOMAN. I was a stenographer.

LAWYER FOR DEFENSE. And since your marriage you have
continued as her sole support, have you not?

YOUNG WOMAN. Yes, sir.

LAWYER FOR DEFENSE. A devoted daughter, gentlemen of the
jury! As well as a devoted wife and a devoted mother!

LAWYER FOR PROSECUTION. Your Honor!

LAWYER FOR DEFENSE (*quickly*). And now, Mrs. Jones, I will
ask you – the law expects me to ask you – it demands that I ask
you – did you – or did you not – on the night of June 2nd last or
the morning of June 3rd last – kill your husband, the late
George H. Jones – did you, or did you not?

YOUNG WOMAN. I did not.

LAWYER FOR DEFENSE. You did not?

YOUNG WOMAN. I did not.

LAWYER FOR DEFENSE. Now, Mrs. Jones, you have heard the witnesses for the State – They were not many – and they did not have much to say –

LAWYER FOR PROSECUTION. I object.

JUDGE. Sustained.

LAWYER FOR DEFENSE. You have heard some police and you have heard some doctors. None of whom was present! The prosecution could not furnish any witness to the crime – not one witness!

LAWYER FOR PROSECUTION. Your Honor!

LAWYER FOR DEFENSE. Nor one motive.

LAWYER FOR PROSECUTION. Your Honor – I protest! I –

JUDGE. Sustained.

LAWYER FOR DEFENSE. But such as these witnesses were, you have heard them try to accuse you of deliberately murdering your own husband, this husband with whom, by your own statement, you had never had a quarrel – not one quarrel in six years of married life, murdering him, I say, or rather – they say, while he slept, by brutally hitting him over the head with a bottle – a bottle filled with small stones – Did you, I repeat this, or did you not?

YOUNG WOMAN. I did not.

LAWYER FOR DEFENSE. You did not! Of course you did not! (*Quickly.*) Now, Mrs, Jones, will you tell the jury in your own words exactly what happened on the night of June 2nd or the morning of June 3rd last, at the time your husband was killed.

YOUNG WOMAN. I was awakened by hearing somebody – something – in the room, and I saw two men standing by my husband's bed.

LAWYER FOR DEFENSE. Your husband's bed – that was also your bed, was it not, Mrs. Jones?

YOUNG WOMAN. Yes.

LAWYER FOR DEFENSE. You hadn't the modern idea of separate beds, had you, Mrs. Jones?

YOUNG WOMAN. Mr. Jones objected.

LAWYER FOR DEFENSE. I mean you slept in the same bed, did you not?

YOUNG WOMAN. Yes.

LAWYER FOR DEFENSE. Then explain just what you meant by saying 'my husband's bed'.

YOUNG WOMAN. Well – I –

LAWYER FOR DEFENSE. You meant his side of the bed, didn't you?

YOUNG WOMAN. Yes. His side.

LAWYER FOR DEFENSE. That is what I thought, but I wanted the jury to be clear on that point. (*To the* JURY.) Mr. and Mrs. Jones slept in the same bed. (*To her.*) Go on, Mrs. Jones. (*As she is silent.*) You heard a noise and –

YOUNG WOMAN. I heard a noise and I awoke and saw two men standing beside my husband's side of the bed.

LAWYER FOR DEFENSE. Two men?

YOUNG WOMAN. Yes.

LAWYER FOR DEFENSE. Can you describe them?

YOUNG WOMAN. Not very well – I couldn't see them very well.

LAWYER FOR DEFENSE. Could you say whether they were big or small – light or dark, thin or –

YOUNG WOMAN. They were big dark looking men.

LAWYER FOR DEFENSE. Big dark looking men?

YOUNG WOMAN. Yes.

LAWYER FOR DEFENSE. And what did you do, Mrs. Jones, when you suddenly awoke and saw two big dark looking men standing beside your bed?

YOUNG WOMAN. I didn't do anything!

LAWYER FOR DEFENSE. You didn't have time to do anything – did you?

YOUNG WOMAN. No. Before I could do anything – one of them raised – something in his hand and struck Mr. Jones over the head with it.

LAWYER FOR DEFENSE. And what did Mr. Jones do?

SPECTATORS *laugh*.

JUDGE. Silence.

BAILIFF. Silence.

LAWYER FOR DEFENSE. What did Mr. Jones do, Mrs. Jones?

YOUNG WOMAN. He gave a sort of groan and tried to raise up.

LAWYER FOR DEFENSE. Tried to raise up!

YOUNG WOMAN. Yes!

LAWYER FOR DEFENSE. And then what happened?

YOUNG WOMAN. The man struck him again and he fell back.

LAWYER FOR DEFENSE. I see. What did the men do then? The big dark looking men.

YOUNG WOMAN. They turned and ran out of the room.

LAWYER FOR DEFENSE. I see. What did you do then, Mrs. Jones?

YOUNG WOMAN. I saw Mr. Jones was bleeding from the temple. I got towels and tried to stop it, and then I realized he had – passed away

LAWYER FOR DEFENSE. I see. What did you do then?

YOUNG WOMAN. I didn't know what to do. But I thought I'd better call the police. So I went to the telephone and called the police.

LAWYER FOR DEFENSE. What happened then.

YOUNG WOMAN. Nothing. Nothing happened.

LAWYER FOR DEFENSE. The police came, didn't they?

YOUNG WOMAN. Yes – they came.

LAWYER FOR DEFENSE (*quickly*). And that is all you know concerning the death of your husband in the late hours of June 2nd or the early hours of June 3rd last, isn't it?

YOUNG WOMAN. Yes sir.

LAWYER FOR DEFENSE. All?

YOUNG WOMAN. Yes sir.

LAWYER FOR DEFENSE (*to* LAWYER FOR PROSECUTION). Take the witness.

FIRST REPORTER (*writing*). The accused woman told a straightforward story of –

SECOND REPORTER. The accused woman told a rambling, disconnected story of –

LAWYER FOR PROSECUTION. You made no effort to cry out, Mrs. Jones, did you, when you saw those two big dark men standing over your helpless husband, did you?

YOUNG WOMAN. No sir. I didn't. I –

LAWYER FOR PROSECUTION. And when they turned and ran out of the room, you made no effort to follow them or cry out after them, did you?

YOUNG WOMAN. No sir.

LAWYER FOR PROSECUTION. Why didn't you?

YOUNG WOMAN. I saw Mr. Jones was hurt.

LAWYER FOR PROSECUTION. Ah! You saw Mr. Jones was hurt! You saw this – how did you see it?

YOUNG WOMAN. I just saw it.

LAWYER FOR PROSECUTION. Then there was a light in the room?

YOUNG WOMAN. A sort of light.

LAWYER FOR PROSECUTION. What do you mean – a sort of light? A bed light?

YOUNG WOMAN. No. No, there was no light on.

LAWYER FOR PROSECUTION. Then where did it come from – this sort of light?

YOUNG WOMAN. I don't know.

LAWYER FOR PROSECUTION. Perhaps – from the window.

YOUNG WOMAN. Yes – from the window.

LAWYER FOR PROSECUTION. Oh, the shade was up!

YOUNG WOMAN. No – no, the shade was down.

LAWYER FOR PROSECUTION. You're sure of that?

YOUNG WOMAN. Yes. Mr. Jones always wanted the shade down.

LAWYER FOR PROSECUTION. The shade was down – there was no light in the room – but the room was light – how do you explain this?

YOUNG WOMAN. I don't know.

LAWYER FOR PROSECUTION. You don't know!

YOUNG WOMAN. I think where the window was open – under the shade – light came in

LAWYER FOR PROSECUTION. There is a street light there?

YOUNG WOMAN. No – there's no street light.

LAWYER FOR PROSECUTION. Then where did this light come from – that came in under the shade?

YOUNG WOMAN (*desperately*). From the moon!

LAWYER FOR PROSECUTION. The moon!

YOUNG WOMAN. Yes! It was bright moon!

LAWYER FOR PROSECUTION. It was bright moon – you are sure of that!

YOUNG WOMAN. Yes.

LAWYER FOR PROSECUTION. How are you sure?

YOUNG WOMAN. I couldn't sleep – I never can sleep in the bright moon. I never can.

LAWYER FOR PROSECUTION. It was bright moon. Yet you could not see two big dark looking men – but you could see your husband bleeding from the temple.

YOUNG WOMAN. Yes sir.

LAWYER FOR PROSECUTION. And did you call a doctor?

YOUNG WOMAN. No.

LAWYER FOR PROSECUTION. Why didn't you?

YOUNG WOMAN. The police did.

LAWYER FOR PROSECUTION. But you didn't?

YOUNG WOMAN. No.

LAWYER FOR PROSECUTION. Why didn't you? (*No answer.*) Why didn't you?

YOUNG WOMAN (*whispers*). I saw it was – useless.

LAWYER FOR PROSECUTION. Ah! You saw that! You saw that – very clearly.

YOUNG WOMAN. Yes.

LAWYER FOR PROSECUTION. And you didn't call a doctor.

YOUNG WOMAN. It was – useless.

LAWYER FOR PROSECUTION. What did you do?

YOUNG WOMAN. It was useless – there was no use of anything.

LAWYER FOR PROSECUTION. I asked you what you did?

YOUNG WOMAN. Nothing.

LAWYER FOR PROSECUTION. Nothing!

YOUNG WOMAN. I just sat there.

LAWYER FOR PROSECUTION. You sat there! A long while, didn't you?

YOUNG WOMAN. I don't know.

LAWYER FOR PROSECUTION. You don't know? (*Showing her the neck of a broken bottle.*) Mrs. Jones, did you ever see this before?

YOUNG WOMAN. I think so.

LAWYER FOR PROSECUTION. You think so.

YOUNG WOMAN. Yes.

LAWYER FOR PROSECUTION. What do you think it is?

YOUNG WOMAN. I think it's the bottle that was used against Mr. Jones.

LAWYER FOR PROSECUTION. Used against him – yes – that's right. You've guessed right. This neck and these broken pieces and these pebbles were found on the floor and scattered over the bed. There were no fingerprints, Mrs. Jones, on this bottle. None at all. Doesn't that seem strange to you?

YOUNG WOMAN. No.

LAWYER FOR PROSECUTION. It doesn't seem strange to you that this bottle held in the big dark hand of one of those big dark men left no mark! No print! That doesn't seem strange to you?

YOUNG WOMAN. No.

LAWYER FOR PROSECUTION. You are in the habit of wearing rubber gloves at night, Mrs. Jones – are you not? To protect – to soften your hands – are you not?

YOUNG WOMAN. I used to.

LAWYER FOR PROSECUTION. Used to – when was that?

YOUNG WOMAN. Before I was married.

LAWYER FOR PROSECUTION. And after your marriage you gave it up?

YOUNG WOMAN. Yes.

LAWYER FOR PROSECUTION. Why?

YOUNG WOMAN. Mr. Jones did not like the feeling of them.

LAWYER FOR PROSECUTION. You always did everything Mr. Jones wanted?

YOUNG WOMAN. I tried to – Anyway I didn't care any more – so much – about my hands.

LAWYER FOR PROSECUTION. I see – so after your marriage you never wore gloves at night any more?

YOUNG WOMAN. No.

LAWYER FOR PROSECUTION. Mrs. Jones, isn't it true that you began wearing your rubber gloves again – in spite of your husband's expressed dislike – about a year ago – a year ago this spring?

YOUNG WOMAN. No.

LAWYER FOR PROSECUTION. You did not suddenly begin to care particularly for your hands again – about a year ago this spring?

YOUNG WOMAN. No.

LAWYER FOR PROSECUTION. You're quite sure of that?

YOUNG WOMAN. Yes.

LAWYER FOR PROSECUTION. Quite sure?

YOUNG WOMAN. Yes.

LAWYER FOR PROSECUTION. Then you did not have in your possession, on the night of June 2nd last, a pair of rubber gloves?

YOUNG WOMAN (*shakes her head*). No.

LAWYER FOR PROSECUTION (*to* JUDGE). I'd like to introduce these gloves as evidence at this time, your Honor.

JUDGE. Exhibit 24.

LAWYER FOR PROSECUTION. I'll return to them later – now, Mrs. Jones – this nightgown – you recognize it, don't you?

YOUNG WOMAN. Yes.

LAWYER FOR PROSECUTION. Yours, is it not?

YOUNG WOMAN. Yes.

LAWYER FOR PROSECUTION. The one you were wearing the night your husband was murdered, isn't it?

YOUNG WOMAN. The night he died – yes.

LAWYER FOR PROSECUTION. Not the one you wore under your peignoir – I believe that it's what you call it, isn't it? A peignoir? When you received the police – but the one you wore before that – isn't it?

YOUNG WOMAN. Yes.

LAWYER FOR PROSECUTION. This was found – not where the gloves were found – no – but at the bottom of the soiled clothes hamper in the bathroom – rolled up and wet – why was it wet, Mrs. Jones?

YOUNG WOMAN. I had tried to wash it.

LAWYER FOR PROSECUTION. Wash it? I thought you had just sat?

YOUNG WOMAN. First – I tried to make things clean.

LAWYER FOR PROSECUTION. Why did you want to make this – clean – as you say?

YOUNG WOMAN. There was blood on it.

LAWYER FOR PROSECUTION. Spattered on it?

YOUNG WOMAN. Yes.

LAWYER FOR PROSECUTION. How did that happen?

YOUNG WOMAN. The bottle broke – and the sharp edge cut.

LAWYER FOR PROSECUTION. Oh, the bottle broke and the sharp edge cut!

YOUNG WOMAN. Yes. That's what they told me afterwards.

LAWYER FOR PROSECUTION. Who told you ?

YOUNG WOMAN. The police – that's what they say happened.

LAWYER FOR PROSECUTION. Mrs. Jones, why did you try so desperately to wash that blood away – before you called the police?

LAWYER FOR DEFENSE. I object!

JUDGE. Objection overruled.

LAWYER FOR PROSECUTION. Why, Mrs. Jones?

YOUNG WOMAN. I don't know. It's what anyone would have done, wouldn't they?

LAWYER FOR PROSECUTION. That depends, doesn't it? (*Suddenly taking up bottle.*) Mrs. Jones – when did you first see this?

YOUNG WOMAN. The night my husband was – done away with.

LAWYER FOR PROSECUTION. Done away with! You mean killed?

YOUNG WOMAN. Yes.

LAWYER FOR PROSECUTION. Why don't you say killed?

YOUNG WOMAN. It sounds so brutal.

LAWYER FOR PROSECUTION. And you never saw this before then?

YOUNG WOMAN. No sir.

LAWYER FOR PROSECUTION. You're quite sure of that?

YOUNG WOMAN. Yes.

LAWYER FOR PROSECUTION. And these stones – when did you first see them?

YOUNG WOMAN. The night my husband was done away with.

LAWYER FOR PROSECUTION. Before that night your husband was murdered – you never saw them? Never before then?

YOUNG WOMAN. No sir.

LAWYER FOR PROSECUTION. You are quite sure of that!

YOUNG WOMAN. Yes.

LAWYER FOR PROSECUTION. Mrs. Jones, do you remember about a year ago, a year ago this spring, bringing home to your house – a lily, a Chinese water lily?

YOUNG WOMAN. No – I don't think I do.

LAWYER FOR PROSECUTION. You don't think you remember bringing home a water lily growing in a bowl filled with small stones?

YOUNG WOMAN. No – No I don't.

LAWYER FOR PROSECUTION. I'll show you this bowl, Mrs. Jones. Does that refresh your memory?

YOUNG WOMAN. I remember the bowl – but I don't remember – the lily.

LAWYER FOR PROSECUTION. You recognize the bowl then?

YOUNG WOMAN. Yes.

LAWYER FOR PROSECUTION. It is yours, isn't it?

YOUNG WOMAN. It was in my house – yes.

LAWYER FOR PROSECUTION. How did it come there?

YOUNG WOMAN. How did it come there?

LAWYER FOR PROSECUTION. Yes – where did you get it?

YOUNG WOMAN. I don't remember.

LAWYER FOR PROSECUTION. You don't remember?

YOUNG WOMAN. No.

LAWYER FOR PROSECUTION. You don't remember about a year ago bringing this bowl into your bedroom filled with small stones and some water and a lily? You don't remember tending very carefully that lily till it died? And when it died you don't remember hiding the bowl full of little stones away on the top shelf of your closet – and keeping it there until – you don't remember?

YOUNG WOMAN. No, I don't remember.

LAWYER FOR PROSECUTION. You may have done so?

YOUNG WOMAN. No – no – I didn't! I didn't! I don't know anything about all that.

LAWYER FOR PROSECUTION. But you do remember the bowl?

YOUNG WOMAN. Yes. It was in my house – you found it in my house.

LAWYER FOR PROSECUTION. But you don't remember the lily or the stones?

YOUNG WOMAN. No – No I don't!

LAWYER FOR PROSECUTION *turns to look among his papers in a brief case.*

FIRST REPORTER (*writing*). Under the heavy artillery fire of the State's attorney's brilliant cross-questioning, the accused woman's defense was badly riddled. Pale and trembling she –

SECOND REPORTER (*writing*). Undaunted by the Prosecution's machine-gun attack, the defendant was able to maintain her position of innocence in the face of rapid-fire questioning that threatened, but never seriously menaced her defense. Flushed but calm she –

LAWYER FOR PROSECUTION (*producing paper*). Your Honor, I'd like to introduce this paper in evidence at this time.

JUDGE. What is it?

LAWYER FOR PROSECUTION. It is an affidavit taken in the State of Guanajato, Mexico.

LAWYER FOR DEFENSE. Mexico? Your Honor, I protest. A Mexican affidavit! Is this the United States of America or isn't it?

LAWYER FOR PROSECUTION. It's properly executed – sworn to before a notary – and certified to by an American Consul.

LAWYER FOR DEFENSE. Your Honor! I protest! In the name of this great United States of America – I protest – are we to permit our sacred institutions to be thus –

JUDGE. What is the purpose of this document – who signed it?

LAWYER FOR PROSECUTION. It is signed by one Richard Roe, and its purpose is to refresh the memory of the witness on the point at issue – and incidentally supply a motive for this murder – this brutal and cold-blooded murder of a sleeping man by –

LAWYER FOR DEFENSE. I protest, your Honor! I object!

JUDGE. Objection sustained. Let me see the document. (*Takes paper which is handed to him – looks at it.*) Perfectly regular. Do you offer this affidavit as evidence at this time for the purpose of refreshing the memory of the witness at this time?

LAWYER FOR PROSECUTION. Yes, your Honor.

JUDGE. You may introduce the evidence.

LAWYER FOR DEFENSE. I object! I object to the introduction of this evidence at this time as irrelevant, immaterial, illegal, biased, prejudicial, and –

JUDGE. Objection overruled.

LAWYER FOR DEFENSE. Exception.

JUDGE. Exception noted. Proceed.

LAWYER FOR PROSECUTION. I wish to read the evidence to the jury at this time.

JUDGE. Proceed.

LAWYER FOR DEFENSE. I object.

JUDGE. Objection overruled.

LAWYER FOR DEFENSE. Exception.

JUDGE. Noted.

LAWYER FOR DEFENSE. Why is this witness himself not brought into court – so he can be cross-questioned?

LAWYER FOR PROSECUTION. The witness is a resident of the Republic of Mexico and as such not subject to subpoena as a witness to this court.

LAWYER FOR DEFENSE. If he was out of the jurisdiction of this court how did you get this affidavit out of him?

LAWYER FOR PROSECUTION. This affidavit was made voluntarily by the deponent in the furtherance of justice.

LAWYER FOR DEFENCE. I suppose you didn't threaten him with extradition on some other trumped-up charge so that –

JUDGE. Order!

BAILIFF. Order!

JUDGE. Proceed with the evidence.

LAWYER FOR PROSECUTION (*reading*). In the matter of the State of ——— vs. Helen Jones, I Richard Roe, being of sound mind, do herein depose and state that I know the accused, Helen Jones, and have known her for a period of over one year immediately preceding the date of the signature on this affidavit. That I first met the said Helen Jones in a so-called speak-easy somewhere in the West 40s in New York City. That on the day I met her, she went with me to my room, also somewhere in the West 40s in New York City, where we had intimate relations –

YOUNG WOMAN (*moans*). Oh!

LAWYER FOR PROSECUTION (*continues reading*). – and where I gave her a blue bowl filled with pebbles, also containing a flowering lily. That from the first day we met until I departed for Mexico in the Fall, the said Helen Jones was an almost daily visitor to my room where we continued to –

YOUNG WOMAN. No! No! (*Moans.*)

LAWYER FOR PROSECUTION. What is it, Mrs. Jones – what is it?

YOUNG WOMAN. Don't read any more! No more!

LAWYER FOR PROSECUTION. Why not!

YOUNG WOMAN. I did it! I did it! I did it!

LAWYER FOR PROSECUTION. You confess?

YOUNG WOMAN. Yes – I did it!

LAWYER FOR DEFENSE. I object, your Honor.

JUDGE. You confess you killed your husband?

YOUNG WOMAN. I put him out of the way – yes.

JUDGE. Why?

YOUNG WOMAN. To be free.

JUDGE. To be free? Is that the only reason?

YOUNG WOMAN. Yes.

JUDGE. If you just wanted to be free – why didn't you divorce him?

YOUNG WOMAN. Oh I couldn't do that!! I couldn't hurt him like that!

Burst of laughter from all in the court. The YOUNG WOMAN *stares out at them, and then seems to go rigid.*

JUDGE. Silence!

BAILIFF. Silence!

There is a gradual silence.

JUDGE. Mrs. Jones, why –

YOUNG WOMAN *begins to moan – suddenly – as though the realization of the enormity of her isolation had just come upon her. It is a sound of desolation, of agony, of human woe. It continues until the end of the scene.*

Why – ?

YOUNG WOMAN *cannot speak.*

LAWYER FOR DEFENSE. Your Honor, I ask a recess to –

JUDGE. Court's adjourned.

SPECTATORS *begin to file out. The* YOUNG WOMAN *continues in the witness box, unseeing, unheeding.*

FIRST REPORTER. Murderess confesses.

SECOND REPORTER. Paramour brings confession.

THIRD REPORTER. I did it! Woman cries!

There is a great burst of speed from the telegraphic instruments. They keep up a constant accompaniment to the WOMAN'*s moans. The scene blacks out as the courtroom empties, and two policemen go to stand by the woman. The sound of the telegraph instruments continues until the scene lights into Episode Nine – and the prayers of the* PRIEST.

EPISODE NINE

A Machine

Scene: a prison room. The front bars face the audience. They are set back far enough to permit a clear passageway across the stage.

Sounds; the voice of a NEGRO *singing; the whir of an aeroplane flying.*

Characters
    YOUNG WOMAN
    A PRIEST
    A JAILER
    TWO BARBERS
    A MATRON
    MOTHER
    TWO GUARDS

At rise: in front of the bars, at one side, sits a MAN; *at the opposite side, a* WOMAN – *the* JAILER *and the* MATRON.

Inside the bars, a MAN *and a* WOMAN – *the* YOUNG WOMAN *and a* PRIEST. *The* YOUNG WOMAN *sits still with folded hands. The* PRIEST *is praying.*

PRIEST. Hear, oh Lord, my prayer; and let my cry come to Thee. Turn not away Thy face from me; in the day when I am in trouble, incline Thy ear to me. In what day soever I shall call upon Thee, hear me speedily. For my days are vanished like smoke; and my bones are grown dry, like fuel for the fire. I am smitten as grass, and my heart is withered; because I forgot to eat my bread. Through the voice of my groaning, my bone hath cleaved to my flesh. I am become like to a pelican of the wilderness. I am like a night raven in the house. I have watched and become as a sparrow all alone on the housetop. All the day long my enemies reproach me; and they that praised me did swear against me. My days have declined like a shadow, and I am withered like grass. But Thou, oh Lord, end rest forever. Thou shalt arise and have mercy, for it is time to have mercy. The time is come.

Voice of NEGRO *offstage – begins to sing a Negro spiritual.*

PRIEST. The Lord hath looked upon the earth, that He might hear the groans of them that are in fetters, that He might release the children of –

Voice of NEGRO *grown louder.*

JAILER. Stop that nigger yelling.

YOUNG WOMAN. No, let him sing. He helps me.

MATRON. You can't hear the Father.

YOUNG WOMAN. He helps me.

PRIEST. Don't I help you, daughter?

YOUNG WOMAN. I understand him. He is condemned. I understand him.

The voice of the NEGRO *goes on louder, drowning out the voice of the* PRIEST.

PRIEST (*chanting in Latin*). Gratiam tuum, quaesumus, Domine, metibus nostris infunde, ut qui, angelo nuntiante, Christifilii tui incarnationem cognovimus, per passionem eius et crucem ad ressurectionis gloriam perducamus. Per eudem Christum Dominum nostrum.

Enter TWO BARBERS. *There is a rattling of keys.*

FIRST BARBER. How is she?

MATRON. Calm.

JAILER. Quiet.

YOUNG WOMAN (*rising*). I am ready.

FIRST BARBER. Then sit down.

YOUNG WOMAN (*in a steady voice*). Aren't you the death guard come to take me?

FIRST BARBER. No, we ain't the death guard. We're the barbers.

YOUNG WOMAN. The barbers.

MATRON. You hair must be cut.

JAILER. Must be shaved.

BARBER. Just a patch.

The BARBERS *draw near her.*

YOUNG WOMAN. No!

PRIEST. Daughter, you're ready. You know you are ready.

YOUNG WOMAN (*crying out*). Not for this! Not for this!

MATRON. The rule.

JAILER. Regulations.

BARBER. Routine.

The BARBERS *take her by the arms.*

YOUNG WOMAN. No! No! Don't touch me – touch me!

They take her and put her down in the chair, cut a patch from her hair.

I will not be submitted – this indignity! No! I will not be submitted! – Leave me alone! Oh my God am I never to be let alone! Always to have to submit – to submit! No more – not now – I'm going to die – I won't submit! Not now!

BARBER (*finishing cutting a patch from her hair*). You'll submit, my lady. Right to the end, you'll submit! There, and a neat job too.

JAILER. Very neat.

MATRON. Very neat.

Exit BARBERS.

YOUNG WOMAN (*her calm shattered*). Father, Father! Why was I born?

PRIEST. I came forth from the Father and have come into the world – I leave the world and go into the Father.

YOUNG WOMAN (*weeping*). Submit! Submit! Is nothing mine? The hair on my head! The very hair on my head –

PRIEST. Praise God.

YOUNG WOMAN. Am I never to be let alone! Never to have peace! When I'm dead, won't I have peace?

PRIEST. Ye shall indeed drink of my cup.

YOUNG WOMAN. Won't I have peace tomorrow?

PRIEST. I shall raise Him up at the last day.

YOUNG WOMAN. Tomorrow! Father! Where shall I be tomorrow?

PRIEST. Behold the hour cometh. Yea, is now come. Ye shall be scattered every man to his own.

YOUNG WOMAN. In Hell! Father! Will I be in Hell!

PRIEST. I am the Resurrection and the Life.

YOUNG WOMAN. Life has been hell to me, Father!

PRIEST. Life has been hell to you, daughter, because you never knew God! Gloria in excelsis Deo.

YOUNG WOMAN. How could I know Him, Father? He never was around me.

PRIEST. You didn't seek Him, daughter. Seek and ye shall find.

YOUNG WOMAN. I sought something – I was always seeking something.

PRIEST. What? What were you seeking?

YOUNG WOMAN. Peace. Rest and peace. Will I find it tonight, Father? Will I find it?

PRIEST. Trust in God.

A shadow falls across the passage in the front of the stage – and there is a whirring sound.

YOUNG WOMAN. What is that? Father! Jailer! What is that?

JAILER. An aeroplane.

MATRON. Aeroplane.

PRIEST. God in his Heaven.

YOUNG WOMAN. Look, Father! A man flying! He has wings! But he is not an angel!

JAILER. Hear his engine.

MATRON. Hear the engine.

YOUNG WOMAN. He has wings – but he isn't free! I've been free, Father! For one moment – down here on earth – I have been free! When I did what I did I was free! Free and not afraid! How is that, Father? How can that be? A great sin – a mortal sin – for which I must die and go to hell – but it made me free! One moment I was free! How is that, Father? Tell me that?

PRIEST. Your sins are forgiven.

YOUNG WOMAN. And that other sin – that other sin – that sin of love – That's all I ever knew of Heaven – heaven on earth! How is that, Father? How can that be – a sin – a mortal sin – all I know of heaven?

PRIEST. Confess to Almighty God.

YOUNG WOMAN. Oh, Father, pray for me – a prayer – that I can understand!

PRIEST. I will pray for you, daughter, the prayer of desire. Behind

the King of Heaven, behold Thy Redeemer and God, Who is
even now coming; prepare thyself to receive Him with love,
invite him with the ardor of thy desire; come, oh my Jesus,
come to thy soul which desires Thee! Before Thou givest
Thyself to me, I desire to give Thee my miserable heart. Do
Thou accept it, and come quickly to take possession of it! Come
my God, hasten! Delay no longer! My only and Infinite Good,
my Treasure, my Life, my Paradise, my Love, my all, my wish
is to receive Thee with the love with which –

Enter the MOTHER. *She comes along the passageway and
stops before the bars.*

YOUNG WOMAN (*recoiling*). Who's that woman?

JAILER. Your mother.

MATRON. Your mother.

YOUNG WOMAN. She's a stranger – take her away – she's a
stranger.

JAILER. She's come to say goodbye to you –

MATRON. To say goodbye.

YOUNG WOMAN. But she's never known me – never known
me – ever – (*To the* MOTHER.) Go away! You're a stranger!
Stranger! Stranger! (MOTHER *turns and starts away.
Reaching out her hands to her.*) Oh Mother! Mother! (*They
embrace through the bars.*)

Enter TWO GUARDS.

PRIEST. Come, daughter.

FIRST GUARD. It's time.

SECOND GUARD. Time.

YOUNG WOMAN. Wait! Mother, my child; my little strange
child! I never knew her! She'll never know me! Let her live,
Mother. Let her live! Live! Tell her –

PRIEST. Come, daughter.

YOUNG WOMAN. Wait! Wait! Tell her –

The JAILER *takes the* MOTHER *away.*

GUARD. It's time.

YOUNG WOMAN. Wait! Wait! Tell her! Wait! Just a minute
more! There's so much I want to tell her – Wait –

The JAILER *takes the* MOTHER *off. The* TWO GUARDS *take
the* YOUNG WOMAN *by the arms, and start through the door
in the bars and down the passage, across stage and off:*

the PRIEST *follows; the* MATRON *follows the* PRIEST; *the*
PRIEST *is praying. The scene blacks out. The voice of the*
PRIEST *gets dimmer and dimmer.*

PRIEST. Lord have mercy – Christ have mercy – Lord have mercy
– Christ hear us! God the Father of Heaven! God the Son,
Redeemer of the World, God the Holy Ghost – Holy Trinity
one God – Holy Mary – Holy Mother of God – Holy Virgin of
Virgins – St. Michael – St. Gabriel – St. Raphael –

His voice dies out. Out of the darkness come the voices of
REPORTERS.

FIRST REPORTER. What time is it now?

SECOND REPORTER. Time now.

THIRD REPORTER. Hush.

FIRST REPORTER. Here they come.

THIRD REPORTER. Hush.

PRIEST (*his voice sounds dimly – gets louder – continues until the
end*). St. Peter pray for us – St. Paul pray for us – St. James
pray for us – St. John pray for us – all ye holy Angels and
Archangels – all ye blessed orders of holy spirits – St. Joseph –
St. John the Baptist – St. Thomas –

FIRST REPORTER. Here they are!

SECOND REPORTER. How little she looks! She's gotten smaller.

THIRD REPORTER. Hush.

PRIEST. St. Phillip pray for us. All you Holy Patriarchs and
prophets – St. Phillip – St. Matthew – St. Simon – St. Thaddeus
– All ye holy apostles – all ye holy disciples – all ye holy
innocents – Pray for us – Pray for us – Pray for us –

FIRST REPORTER. Suppose the machine shouldn't work!

SECOND REPORTER. It'll work! – It always works!

THIRD REPORTER. Hush!

PRIEST. Saints of God make intercession for us – Be merciful –
Spare us, oh Lord – be merciful –

FIRST REPORTER. Her lips are moving – what is she saying?

SECOND REPORTER. Nothing.

THIRD REPORTER. Hush!

PRIEST. Oh Lord deliver us from all evil – from all sin – from
Thy wrath – from the snares of the devil – from anger and
hatred and every evil will –.from –

FIRST REPORTER. Did you see that? She fixed her hair under the cap – pulled her hair out under the cap.

THIRD REPORTER. Hush!

PRIEST. – Beseech Thee – hear us – that Thou would'st spare us – that Thou would'st pardon us – Holy Mary – pray for us –

SECOND REPORTER. There –

YOUNG WOMAN (*calling out*). Somebody! Somebod –

Her voice is cut off.

PRIEST. Christ have mercy – Lord have mercy – Christ have mercy –

Curtain

Praise for
The Mrs. Murphy Series

THE TAIL OF THE TIP-OFF

"You don't have to be a cat lover to enjoy Brown's eleventh Mrs. Murphy novel. . . . Brown writes so compellingly . . . [she] breathes believability into every aspect of this smart and sassy novel." —*Publishers Weekly* (starred review)

"Rita Mae Brown's series remains one of the best cat mysteries. . . . Brown keeps the series fresh."
—*The Post & Courier* (Charleston, SC)

"The animals' droll commentary provides comic relief and clues helpful in solving the crime."
—*The Washington Post*

"A tightly woven mystery, peopled with the delightful characters of small-town Virginia . . . a real three-point play: an intriguing mystery, great characters, and an engaging sense of humor." —*I Love a Mystery*

"A fast-paced plot and enough animated feline personalities to keep readers entertained."
—*Daily News* (New York)

"A not-to-be-missed exciting cozy."
—*The Midwest Book Review*

"Nobody can put words in the mouths of animals better than Rita Mae Brown . . . fast-paced action . . . Harry and her menagerie are simply great."
—*Abilene Reporter-News*

CATCH AS CAT CAN

"This latest is as good as its predecessors ... thoroughly enjoyable." —*Winston-Salem Journal*

"Brown's proven brand of murder and mayhem played out against a background of Virginia gentility and idealized animals is once again up to scratch." —*Publishers Weekly*

"Any new Mrs. Murphy is a joyful reading experience, and *Catch as Cat Can* is no exception. . . . An adult mystery that appeals to the child in all of us."
—*The Midwest Book Review*

"The[se] mysteries continue to be a true treat."
—*The Post & Courier* (Charleston, SC)

"An entertaining read in a fun series." —*Mystery News*

CLAWS AND EFFECT

"Reading a Mrs. Murphy mystery is like eating a potato chip. You always go back for more. . . . Whimsical and enchanting . . . the latest expert tale from a deserving bestselling series."
—*The Midwest Book Review*

"Mrs. Murphy, the incomparable feline sleuth with attitude, returns to captivate readers. . . . An intriguing and well-executed mystery . . . Grateful fans will relish this charming addition by a master of the cozy cat genre."
—*Publishers Weekly*

"As charming as ever." —*The Tennessean*

"With intricate plot twists that will keep readers guessing right up until the end, *Claws and Effect* once again blends murder and mayhem with animal antics." —*Pet Life*

PAWING THROUGH THE PAST

involved with plots, plans, and emotional entanglements. *Pawing Through the Past* is no exception."
—*I Love a Mystery*

CAT ON THE SCENT

"Rita and Sneaky Pie know how to grab a reader. This fun-loving and delightful mystery is a must even if you're not a cat lover." —*The Pilot* (Southern Pines, NC)

"These provocative mysteries just glow."
—*Mystery Lovers Bookshop News*

"Features all the traits of purebred fun.... The antics of the animals, Brown's witty observations, the history-revering Virginians, and the Blue Ridge setting make this a pleasurable read for lovers of this popular genre."
—*BookPage*

"Animal antics and criminal capers combine captivatingly in *Cat on the Scent*."
—*The San Diego Union-Tribune*

"A charming and keen-eyed take on human misdeeds and animal shenanigans... Told with spunk and plenty of whimsy, this is another delightful entry in a very popular series." —*Publishers Weekly*

"A fine murder mystery... For fans of Mrs. Murphy and her pals, both two- and four-legged, *Cat on the Scent* smells like a winner." —*The Virginian-Pilot*

"Charming." —*People*

Murder on the Prowl

RITA MAE BROWN
& SNEAKY PIE BROWN

ILLUSTRATIONS BY WENDY WRAY

BANTAM BOOKS   NEW YORK · TORONTO · LONDON · SYDNEY · AUCKLAND

MURDER ON THE PROWL
A Bantam Book

PUBLISHING HISTORY
Bantam hardcover edition published April 1998
Bantam mass market edition / February 1999
Bantam mass market reissue / April 2004

Published by
Bantam Dell
A Division of Random House, Inc.
New York, New York

This is a work of fiction. Names, characters, places, and incidents either are
the product of the author's imagination or are used fictitiously. Any
resemblance to actual persons, living or dead, events, or locales
is entirely coincidental.

Bantam Books and the rooster colophon are registered trademarks of
Random House, Inc.

ISBN 0-553-57540-6

Manufactured in the United States of America
Published simultaneously in Canada

OPM   19 18 17 16 15 14 13 12

To Mr. Wonderful—sometimes
David Wheeler

Cast of Characters

Mary Minor Haristeen (Harry), the young postmistress of Crozet

Mrs. Murphy, Harry's gray tiger cat

Tee Tucker, Harry's Welsh corgi, Mrs. Murphy's friend and confidante

Pharamond Haristeen (Fair), veterinarian, formerly married to Harry

Mrs. George Hogendobber (Miranda), a widow who works with Harry in the post office

Market Shiflett, owner of Shiflett's Market, next to the post office

Pewter, Market's shamelessly fat gray cat, who now lives with Harry and family

Susan Tucker, Harry's best friend

Big Marilyn Sanburne (Mim), Queen of Crozet society

Rick Shaw, sheriff

Cynthia Cooper, police officer

Herbert C. Jones, pastor of Crozet Lutheran Church

Roscoe Fletcher, headmaster of the exclusive St. Elizabeth's private school

Naomi Fletcher, principal of the lower school at St. Elizabeth's. She supports her husband's vision 100%

Alexander Brashiers (Sandy), an English teacher at St. Elizabeth's who believes he should be headmaster

April Shively, secretary to the headmaster, whom she loves

Maury McKinchie, a film director who's lost his way, lost his fire, and seems to be losing his wife

Brooks Tucker, Susan Tucker's daughter. She has transferred to St. Elizabeth's

Karen Jensen, irreverent, a star of the field hockey team, and lusted after by most of the boys

Jody Miller, another good field hockey player, seems to be suffering the ill effects of an evaporating romance with Sean Hallahan

Sean Hallahan, the star of the football team

Roger Davis, calm, quiet, and watchful, he is overshadowed by Sean

Kendrick Miller, driven, insular, and hot-tempered, he's built a thriving nursery business as he's lost his family ... he barely notices them

Irene Miller, a fading beauty who deals with her husband's absorption in his work and her daughter's mood swings by ignoring them

Father Michael, priest at the Catholic church, a friend of the Reverend Herbert Jones

Jimbo Anson, owner of the technologically advanced car wash on Route 29

Coach Renee Hallvard, a favorite with the St. Elizabeth's students, she coaches the girls' field hockey team

Murder on the Prowl

$$\boxed{1}$$

Towns, like people, have souls. The little town of Crozet, Virginia, latitude 38°, longitude 78° 60′, had the soul of an Irish tenor.

On this beautiful equinox day, September 21, every soul was lifted, if not every voice—for it was perfect: creamy clouds lazed across a turquoise sky. The Blue Ridge Mountains, startling in their color, hovered protectively at the edge of emerald meadows. The temperature held at 72° F with low humidity.

This Thursday, Mary Minor Haristeen worked unenthusiastically in the post office. As she was the postmistress, she could hardly skip out, however tempted she was. Her tiger cat, Mrs. Murphy, and her corgi, Tee Tucker, blasted in and out of the animal door, the little flap echoing with each arrival or departure. It was the animals' version of teenagers slamming the door, and each whap reminded Harry that while they could escape, she was stuck.

Harry, as she was known, was industrious if a bit undirected. Her cohort at the P.O., Mrs. Miranda Hogendobber, felt that if Harry remarried, this questioning of her life's purpose would evaporate. Being quite a bit older than Harry, Miranda viewed marriage as purpose enough for a woman.

"What are you humming?"

" 'A Mighty Fortress Is Our God.' Martin Luther wrote it in 1529," Mrs. H. informed her.

"I should know that."

"If you'd come to choir practice you would."

"There is the small matter that I am not a member of your church." Harry folded an empty canvas mail sack.

"I can fix that in a jiffy."

"And what would the Reverend Jones do? He baptized me in Crozet Lutheran Church."

"Piffle."

Mrs. Murphy barreled through the door, a large cricket in her mouth.

Close in pursuit was Pewter, the fat gray cat who worked days next door at the grocery store: nights she traveled home with Harry. Market Shiflett, the grocer, declared Pewter had never caught a mouse and never would, so she might as well go play with her friends.

In Pewter's defense, she was built round; her skull was round, her ears, small and delicate, were round. Her tail was a bit short. She thought of herself as stout. Her gray paunch swung when she walked. She swore this was the result of her having "the operation," not because she was fat. In truth it was both. The cat lived to eat.

Mrs. Murphy, a handsome tiger, stayed fit being a ferocious mouser.

The two cats were followed by the dog, Tee Tucker.

Mrs. Murphy bounded onto the counter, the cricket wriggling in her mouth.

"That cat has brought in a winged irritant. She lives to kill," Miranda harrumphed.

"A cricket doesn't have wings."

Miranda moved closer to the brown shiny prey clamped in the cat's jaws. "It certainly is a major cricket—it ought to have wings. Why, I believe this cricket is as big as a praying mantis." She cupped her chin in her hand, giving her a wise appearance.

Harry strolled over to inspect just as Mrs. Murphy dispatched the insect with a swift bite through the innards, then laid the remains on the counter.

The dog asked, *"You're not going to eat that cricket, are you?"*

"No, they taste awful."

"I'll eat it," Pewter volunteered. *"Well, someone has to keep up appearances! After all, we are predators."*

"Pewter, that's disgusting." Harry grimaced as the rotund animal gobbled down the cricket.

"Maybe they're like nachos." Miranda Hogendobber heard the loud crunch.

"I'll never eat a nacho again." Harry glared at her coworker and friend.

"It's the crunchiness. I bet you any money," Miranda teased.

"It is." Pewter licked her lips in answer to the older

woman. She was glad cats didn't wear lipstick like Mrs. Hogendobber. Imagine getting lipstick on a cricket or mouse. Spoil the taste.

"Hey, girls." The Reverend Herbert Jones strolled through the front door. He called all women girls, and they had long since given up hope of sensitizing him. Ninety-two-year-old Catherine I. Earnhart was called a girl. She rather liked it.

"Hey, Rev." Harry smiled at him. "You're late today."

He fished in his pocket for his key and inserted it in his brass mailbox, pulling out a fistful of mail, most of it useless advertisements.

"If I'm late, it's because I lent my car to Roscoe Fletcher. He was supposed to bring it back to me by one o'clock, and here it is three. I finally decided to walk."

"His car break down?" Miranda opened the backdoor for a little breeze and sunshine.

"That new car of his is the biggest lemon."

Harry glanced up from counting out second-day air packets to see Roscoe pulling into the post office parking lot out front. "Speak of the devil."

Herb turned around. "Is that my car?"

"Looks different with the mud washed off, doesn't it?" Harry laughed.

"Oh, I know I should clean it up, and I ought to fix my truck, too, but I don't have the time. Not enough hours in the day."

"Amen," Miranda said.

"Why, Miranda, how nice of you to join the service." His eyes twinkled.

"Herb, I'm sorry," Roscoe said before he closed the door behind him. "Mim Sanburne stopped me in the hall, and I thought I'd never get away. You know how the Queen of Crozet talks."

"Indeed," they said.

"Why do they call Mim the Queen of Crozet?" Mrs. Murphy licked her front paw. *"Queen of the Universe is more like it."*

"No, just the Solar System," Tucker barked.

"Doesn't have the same ring to it," Mrs. Murphy replied.

"Humans think they are the center of everything. Bunch of dumb Doras." Pewter burped.

The unpleasant prospect of cricket parts being regurgitated on the counter made Mrs. Murphy take a step back.

"How do you like your car?" Roscoe pointed to the Subaru station wagon, newly washed and waxed.

"Looks brand-new. Thank you."

"You were good to lend me wheels. Gary at the dealership will bring my car to the house. If you'll drop me home, I'll be fine."

"Where's Naomi today?" Miranda inquired about his wife.

"In Staunton. She took the third grade to see the Pioneer Museum." He chuckled. "Better her than me. Those lower-school kids drive me bananas."

"That's why she's principal of the lower school, and you're headmaster. We call you 'the Big Cheese.' " Harry smiled.

"No, it's because I'm a good fund-raiser. Anyone want to cough up some cash?" He laughed, showing broad, straight teeth, darkened by smoking. He reached into his pocket and pulled out a pack of Tootsie Rolls, then offered them around.

"You're not getting blood from this stone. Besides, I graduated from Crozet High." Harry waved off the candy.

"Me, too, a bit earlier than she did," Miranda said coyly.

"I graduated in 1945," Herb said boldly.

"I can't get arrested with you guys, can I? You don't even

want my Tootsie Rolls." Roscoe smiled. He had a jovial face as well as manner. "Tell you what, if you win the lottery, give St. Elizabeth's a little bit. Education is important."

"For what?" Pewter stared at him. *"You-all don't do a damn thing except fuss at each other."*

"Some humans farm," Tucker responded.

Pewter glared down at the pretty corgi. *"So?"*

"It's productive," Mrs. Murphy added.

"It's only productive so they can feed each other. Doesn't have anything to do with us."

"They can fish," Tucker said.

"Big deal."

"It's a big deal when you want your tuna." Murphy laughed.

"They're a worthless species."

"Pewter, that cricket made you out of sorts. Gives you gas. You don't see me eating those things," Mrs. Murphy said.

"You know, my car does look new, really." Herb again cast his blue eyes over the station wagon.

"Went to the car wash on Twenty-ninth and Greenbrier Drive," Roscoe told him. "I love that car wash."

"You love a car wash?" Miranda was incredulous.

"You've got to go there. I'll take you." He held out his meaty arms in an expansive gesture. "You drive up—Karen Jensen and some of our other kids work there, and they guide your left tire onto the track. The kids work late afternoons and weekends—good kids. Anyway, you have a smorgasbord of choices. I chose what they call 'the works.' So they beep you in, car in neutral, radio off, and you lurch into the fray. First, a yellow neon light flashes, a wall of water hits you, and then a blue neon light tells you your undercarriage is being cleaned, then there's a white light and a pink light and a green light—why it's almost like a Broadway show. And"—he pointed outside—"there's the result. A hit."

"Roscoe, if the car wash excites you that much, your life needs a pickup." Herb laughed good-naturedly.

"You go to the car wash and see for yourself."

The two men left, Herb slipping into the driver's seat as Harry and Miranda gazed out the window.

"You been to that car wash?"

"No, I feel like I should wear my Sunday pearls and rush right out." Miranda folded her arms across her ample chest.

"I'm not going through any car wash. I hate it," Tucker grumbled.

"You hear thunder and you hide under the bed."

The dog snapped at Murphy, *"I do not, that's a fib."*

"Slobber, too." Since Murphy was on the counter, she could be as hateful as she pleased; the dog couldn't reach her.

"You peed in the truck," Tucker fired back.

Mrs. Murphy's pupils widened. *"I was sick."*

"Were not."

"Was, too."

"You were on your way to the vet and you were scared!"

"I was on my way to the vet because I was sick." The tiger vehemently defended herself.

"Going for your annual shots," Tucker sang in three-quarter time.

"Liar."

"Chicken."

"That was two years ago."

"Truck smelled for months." Tucker rubbed it in.

Mrs. Murphy, using her hind foot, with one savage kick pushed a stack of mail on the dog's head. *"Creep."*

"Hey!" Harry hollered. "Settle down."

"Vamoose!" Mrs. Murphy shot off the counter, soaring over the corgi, who was mired in a mudslide of mail, as she zoomed out the opened backdoor.

Tucker hurried after her, shedding envelopes as she ran.

Pewter relaxed on the counter, declining to run.

Harry walked to the backdoor to watch her pets chase one another through Miranda's yard, narrowly missing her mums, a riot of color. "I wish I could play like that just once."

"They are beguiling." Miranda watched, too, then noticed the sparkling light. "The equinox, it's such a special time, you know. Light and darkness are in perfect balance."

What she didn't say was that after today, darkness would slowly win out.

2

On her back, legs in the air, Mrs. Murphy displayed her slender beige tummy, the stripes muted, unlike the tiger stripes on her back, which were shiny jet-black. She heard the Audi Quattro a quarter of a mile down the driveway, long before Harry realized anyone had turned onto the farm drive.

Tucker, usually on guard, had trotted over to the creek that divided Harry's farm from Blair Bainbridge's farm on the southern boundary. A groundhog lived near the huge hickory there. Tucker, being a herding animal, possessed no burning desire to kill. Still, she enjoyed watching quarry, occasionally engaging a wild animal in conversation. She was too far away to sound a warning about the car.

Not that she needed to, for the visitor was Susan Tucker, Harry's best friend since toddler days. As Susan had traded in her old Volvo for an Audi Quattro, the tire sound was different and Tucker wasn't used to it yet. Mrs. Murphy possessed a better memory for such sounds than Tucker.

Pewter, flopped under the kitchen table, could not have cared less about the visitor. She was dreaming of a giant marlin garnished with mackerel. What made the dream especially sweet was that she didn't have to share the fish with anyone else.

Harry, on an organizing jag, was dumping the contents of her bureau drawers onto her bed.

Mrs. Murphy opened one eye. She heard the slam of the car door. A second slam lifted her head. Usually Susan cruised out to Harry's alone. Escaping her offspring saved her mental health. The back screen door opened. Susan walked in, her beautiful fifteen-year-old daughter, Brooks, following behind. No escape today.

"Toodle-oo," Susan called out.

Pewter, irritated at being awakened, snarled, *"I have never heard anything so insipid in my life."*

Mrs. Murphy rested her head back down on her paw. *"Crab."*

"Well, that's just it, Murphy, I was having the best dream of my life and now—vanished." Pewter mourned the loss.

"Hi, Murphy." Susan scratched behind the cat's delicate ears.

"Oh, look, Pewts is underneath the kitchen table." Brooks, who loved cats, bent down to pet Pewter. Her auburn hair fell in a curtain across her face.

"What I endure," the gray cat complained; however, she made no effort to leave, so the complaint was pro forma.

"I'm organizing," Harry called from the bedroom.

"God help us all." Susan laughed as she walked into the chaos. "Harry, you'll be up all night."

"I couldn't stand it anymore. It takes me five minutes to find a pair of socks that match and"—she pointed to a few pathetic silken remnants—"my underwear is shot."

"You haven't bought new lingerie since your mother died."

Harry plopped on the bed. "As long as Mom bought the stuff, I didn't have to—anyway, I can't stand traipsing into Victoria's Secret. There's something faintly pornographic about it."

"Oh, bull, you just can't stand seeing bra sizes bigger than your own."

"I'm not so bad."

Susan smiled. "I didn't say you were, I only hinted that you are a touch competitive."

"I am not. I most certainly am not. If I were competitive, I'd be applying my art history degree somewhere instead of being the postmistress of Crozet."

"I seem to remember one vicious field hockey game our senior year."

"That doesn't count."

"You didn't like BoomBoom Craycroft even then," Susan recalled.

"Speaking of jugs...I hear she seduced my ex-husband wearing a large selection of lingerie."

"Who told you that?"

"She did, the idiot."

Susan sat down on the opposite side of the bed because she was laughing too hard to stand up.

"She did! Can you believe it? Told me all about the black

lace teddy she wore when he came out to the farm on a call," Harry added.

Pharamond Haristeen, "Fair," happened to be one of the best equine vets in the state.

"Mom, Pewter's hungry," Brooks called from the kitchen.

Tucker, having raced back, pushed open the screen door and hurried over to Susan only to sit on her foot. As it was Susan who bred her and gave her to Harry, she felt quite close to the auburn-haired woman.

"Pewter's always hungry, Brooks; don't fall for her starving kitty routine."

"*Shut up,*" Pewter called back, then purred and rubbed against Brooks's leg.

"Mom, she's really hungry."

"Con artist." Walking back to the kitchen, Harry sternly addressed the cat, who was frantically purring. "If they gave Academy Awards to cats, you would surely win 'best actress.' "

"*I am so-o-o-o hungry,*" the cat warbled.

"*If I could use the electric can opener, I'd feed you just to shut you up.*" Mrs. Murphy sat up and swept her whiskers forward, then back.

Harry, arriving at the same conclusion, grabbed a can of Mariner's Delight. "What's up?"

"We're having a family crisis." Brooks giggled.

"No, we're not."

"Mom." Brooks contradicted her mother by the tone of her voice.

"I'm all ears." Harry ladled out the fishy-smelling food. Pewter, blissfully happy, stuck her face in it. Mrs. Murphy approached her food with more finesse. She liked to pat the edge of her dish with her paw, sniff, then take a morsel in her teeth, carefully chewing it. She believed this was an aid to digestion, also keeping her weight down. Pewter gobbled everything. Calorie Kitty.

"I hate my teachers this year, especially Home Room." Brooks dropped onto a brightly painted kitchen chair.

"Miss Tucker, you were not invited to sit down." Susan put her hands on her hips.

"Mom, it's Harry. I mean, it's not like I'm at Big Mim's or anything." She referred to Mim Sanburne, a fierce enforcer of etiquette.

"Practice makes perfect."

"Please have a seat." Harry invited her to the seat she already occupied.

"Thank you," Brooks replied.

"Just see that you don't forget your manners."

"Fat chance." Brooks laughed at her mother.

They strongly resembled each other, and despite their spats, a deep love existed between mother and daughter.

Danny, Susan's older child, was also the recipient of oceans of maternal affection.

Brooks abruptly got up and dashed outside.

"Where are you going?"

"Back in a flash."

Susan sat down. "I ask myself daily, sometimes hourly, whatever made me think I could be a mother."

"Oh, Susan." Harry waved her hand. "Stop trolling for compliments."

"I'm not."

"You know you're a good mother."

Brooks reappeared, Saturday newspaper in hand, and placed it on the table. "Sorry."

"Oh, thanks. I didn't get out to the mailbox this morning." She took the rubber band off the folded newspaper. The small white envelope underneath the rubber band contained the monthly bill. "I don't know why I pay for this damned paper. Half the time it isn't delivered."

"Well, they delivered it today."

"Hallelujah. Well—?" Harry shrugged. "What's the family crisis?"

"We're not having a family crisis," Susan replied calmly. "Brooks doesn't like her teachers, so we're discussing—"

"I hate my teachers, and Mom is getting bent out of shape. Because she graduated from Crozet High, she wants me to graduate from Crozet High. Danny graduates this year. That ought to be enough. Batting five hundred, Mom," Brooks interrupted.

Harry's eyes widened. "You can't drop out, Brooks."

"I don't want to drop out. I want to go back to St. Elizabeth's."

"That damned snob school costs an arm and a leg." Susan looked up at Pewter, who was eating very loudly. "That cat sounds like an old man smacking his gums."

Pewter, insulted, whirled around to face Susan, but she only proved the statement as little food bits dangled from her whiskers.

Susan smiled. "Like an old man who can't clean his mustache."

"Ha!" Mrs. Murphy laughed loudly.

"She really does look like that," Tucker agreed as she sat on the floor under the counter where Pewter chowed down. In case the cat dropped any food, Tucker would vacuum it up.

"Hey, I've got some cookies," Harry said.

"Thank you, no. We ate a big breakfast."

"What about coffee, tea?"

"No." Susan smiled.

"You don't think you can get along with your teachers or overlook them?" Harry switched back to the subject at hand.

"I hate Mrs. Berryhill."

"She's not so bad." Harry defended a middle-aged lady widowed a few years back.

"Gives me heaves." Brooks pretended to gag.

"If it's that bad, you aren't going to learn anything."

"See, Mom, see—I told you."

"I think it's important not to bail out before you've given it a month or two."

"By that time I'll have *failed French*!" She knew her mother especially wanted her to learn French.

"Don't be so dramatic."

"Go on, be dramatic." Harry poked at Susan's arm while encouraging Brooks.

"We need a little drama around here." Tucker agreed with Harry.

"I won't learn a thing. I'll be learning-deprived. I'll shrink into oblivion—"

Harry interrupted, "Say, that's good, Brooks. You must be reading good novels or studying vocabulary boosters."

Brooks smiled shyly, then continued. "I will be disadvantaged for life, and then I'll never get into Smith."

"That's a low blow," said Susan, who had graduated from Smith with Harry.

"Then you'll marry a gas station attendant and—"

"Harry, don't egg her on. She doesn't have to pay the bills."

"What does Ned say?" Harry inquired of Susan's husband, a lawyer and a likable man.

"He's worried about the money, too, but he's determined that she get a good foundation."

"St. Elizabeth's is a fine school even if I do think they're a bunch of snobs," Harry said forthrightly. "Roscoe Fletcher is doing a good job. At least everyone says he is. I can't say that I know a lot about education, but remember last year's graduating class put two kids in Yale, one in Princeton, one in Harvard." She paused. "I think everyone got into great schools. Can't argue with that."

"If I'm going to spend that much money, then I should send her to St. Catherine's in Richmond," Susan replied to Harry.

"Mom, I don't want to go away from home. I just want to get out of Crozet High. I'll be away soon enough when I go to college. Smith, Mom, Smith," she reminded her mother.

"Well—" Susan considered this.

"Call Roscoe Fletcher," Harry suggested. "Brooks has only been in school for two weeks. See if he'll let her transfer now or if she'll have to wait for the second semester."

Susan stood up to make herself a cup of tea.

"I asked you if you wanted tea," Harry said.

"I changed my mind. You want some?"

"Yeah, sure." Harry sat back down.

"I already called Roscoe. That officious bombshell of a secretary of his, April Shively, took forever to put me through. It's a contradiction in terms, bombshell and secretary." She thought a moment, then continued. "Of course, he said wondrous things about St. Elizabeth's, which one would expect. What headmaster won't take your money?"

"He has raised a lot of money, at least, that's what Mim says." Harry paused, "Mim graduated from Madeira, you know. You'd think she would have gone to St. Elizabeth's. Little Mim didn't graduate from St. Elizabeth's either."

"Mim is a law unto herself," Susan replied.

"Miranda will know why Big Mim didn't go there."

"If she chooses to tell. What a secret keeper that one is." Susan loved Miranda Hogendobber, being fully acquainted with her quirks. Miranda's secrets usually involved age or the petty politics of her various civic and church organizations.

"The big question: Can Brooks get in?"

"Of course she can get in," Susan replied in a loud voice. "She's carrying a three point eight average. And her record was great when she was there before, in the lower school."

"What about Danny? Will he be jealous?"

"No," Brooks answered. "I asked him."

Harry took her cup of tea as Susan sat back down.

"I just bought that Audi Quattro," Susan moaned. "How can I pay for all of this?"

"I can work after school," Brooks volunteered.

"I want those grades to stay up, up, up. By the time you get into college, you might have to win a scholarship. Two kids in college at the same time—when I got pregnant, why didn't I space them four years apart instead of two?" She wailed in mock horror.

"Because this way they're friends, and this way Danny can drive Brooks everywhere."

"And that's another thing." Susan smacked her hand on the table. "They'll be going to different after-school activities. He won't be driving her anywhere."

"Mom, half my friends go to St. Elizabeth's. I'll cop rides."

"Brooks, I am not enamored of the St. Elizabeth's crowd. They're too—superficial, and I hear there's a lot of drugs at the school."

"Get real. There's a lot of drugs at Crozet High. If I wanted to take drugs, I could get them no matter where I went to school." She frowned.

"That's hell of a note," Harry exclaimed.

"It's true, I'm afraid." Susan sighed. "Harry, the world looks very different when you have children."

"I can see that," Harry agreed. "Brooks, just who are your friends at St. Elizabeth's?"

"Karen Jensen. There's other kids I know, but Karen's my best friend there."

"She seems like a nice kid," Harry said.

"She is. Though she's also older than Brooks." Susan was frustrated. "But the rest of them are balls-to-the-wall consumers. I'm telling you, Harry, the values there are so superficial and—"

Harry interrupted her. "But Brooks is not superficial, and St. E isn't going to make her that way. It didn't before and it won't this time. She's her own person, Susan."

Susan dipped a teaspoon in her tea, slowly stirring in clover honey. She hated refined sugar. "Darling, go visit Harry's horses. I need a private word with my best bud."

"Sure, Mom." Brooks reluctantly left the kitchen, Tucker at her heels.

Putting the teaspoon on the saucer, Susan leaned forward. "It's so competitive at that school, some kids can't make it. Remember last year when Courtney Frere broke down?"

Trying to recall the incident, Harry dredged up vague details. "Bad college-board scores—was that it?"

"She was so afraid she'd disappoint her parents and not get

into a good school that she took an overdose of sleeping pills."

"Now I remember." Harry pressed her lips together. "That can happen anywhere. She's a high-strung girl. She got into, uh, Tulane, wasn't it?"

"Yes." Susan nodded her head. "But it isn't just competitive between the students, it's competitive between the faculty and the administration. Sandy Brashiers is still fuming that he wasn't made upper-school principal."

"Politics exists in every profession. Even mine," Harry calmly stated. "You worry too much, Susan."

"You don't know what it's like being a mother!" Susan flared up.

"Then why ask my opinion?" Harry shot back.

"Because—" Susan snapped her teaspoon on the table.

"Hey!" Tucker barked.

"Hush, Tucker," Harry told her.

"What's the worst that can happen?" Harry grabbed the spoon out of Susan's hand. "If she hates it, you take her out of there. If she falls in with the wrong crowd, yank her out."

"This little detour could destroy her grade-point average."

"Well, she'll either go to a lesser college than our alma mater or she can go to a junior college for a year or two to pull her grades back up. Susan, it isn't the end of the world if Brooks doesn't do as well as you wish—but it's a hard lesson."

"I don't think Mrs. Berryhill is that bad."

"We aren't fifteen. Berryhill's not exactly a barrel of laughs even for us."

Susan breathed deeply. "The contacts she makes at St. Elizabeth's could prove valuable later, I suppose."

"She's a good girl. She'll bloom where planted."

"You're right." Susan exhaled, then reached over for the

folded paper. "Speaking of the paper, let's see what fresh hell the world is in today."

She unfolded the first section of the paper, the sound of which inflamed Mrs. Murphy, who jumped over from the counter to sit on the sports section, the living section, and the classifieds.

"Murphy, move a minute." Harry tried to pull the living section out from under the cat.

"I enjoy sitting on the newspaper. Best of all, I love the tissue paper in present boxes, but this will do."

Harry gently lifted up Mrs. Murphy's rear end and pulled out a section of paper as the tail swished displeasure. "Thank you."

"I beg your pardon," Mrs. Murphy grumbled as Harry let her rear end down.

"Another fight in Congress over the federal budget," Susan read out loud.

"What a rook." Harry shrugged. "Nobody's going to do anything anyway."

"Isn't that the truth? What's in your section?"

"Car wreck on Twenty-ninth and Hydralic. Officer Crystal Limerick was on the scene."

"Anything in there about Coop?" She mentioned their mutual friend who was now a deputy for the Albemarle County Sheriff's Department.

"No." Harry flipped pages, disappointed that she didn't find what she was looking for.

"You've got the obit section, let's see who went to their reward."

"You're getting as bad as Mom."

"Your mother was a wonderful woman, and it's one's civic

duty to read the obituary column. After all, we must be ready to assist in case—"

She didn't finish her sentence because Harry flipped open the section of the paper to the obituary page suddenly shouting, "Holy shit!"

3

"I just spoke to him yesterday." Susan gasped in shock as she read over Harry's shoulder the name Roscoe Harvey Fletcher, forty-five, who died unexpectedly September 22. She'd jumped up to see for herself.

"The paper certainly got it in the obit section quickly." Harry couldn't believe it either.

"Obit section has the latest closing." Susan again read the information to be sure she wasn't hallucinating. "Doesn't say how he died. Oh, that's not good. When they don't say it means suicide or—"

"AIDS."

"They never tell you in this paper how people die. I think it's important." Susan snapped the back of the paper.

" 'The family requests donations be made to the Roscoe Harvey Fletcher Memorial Fund for scholarships to St. Elizabeth's. . . .' What the hell happened?" Harry shot up and grabbed the phone.

She dialed Miranda's number. Busy. She then dialed Dr. Larry Johnson. He knew everything about everybody. Busy. She dialed the Reverend Herbert Jones.

"Rev," she said as he picked up the phone, "it's Mary Minor."

"I know your voice."

"How did Roscoe die?"

"I don't know." His voice lowered. "I was on my way over there to see what I could do. Nobody knows anything. I've spoken to Mim and Miranda. I even called Sheriff Shaw to see if there had been a late-night accident. Everyone is in the dark, and there's no funeral information. Naomi hasn't had time to select a funeral home. She's probably in shock."

"She'll use Hill and Wood."

"Yes, I would think so, but, well—" His voice trailed off a moment, then he turned up the volume. "He wasn't sick. I reached Larry. Clean bill of health, so this has to be an accident of some kind. Let me get over there to help. I'll talk to you later."

"Sorry," Harry apologized for slowing him down.

"No, no, I'm glad you called."

"Nobody called me."

"Miranda did. If you had an answering machine you'd have known early on. She called at seven A.M., the minute she saw the paper."

"I was in the barn."

"Called there, too."

"Maybe I was out on the manure spreader. Well, it doesn't

matter. There's work to be done. I'll meet you over at the Fletchers'. I've got Susan and Brooks with me. We can help do whatever needs to be done."

"That would be greatly appreciated. See you there." He breathed in sharply. "I don't know what we're going to find."

As Harry hung up the phone, Susan stood up expectantly. "Well?"

"Let's shoot over to the Fletchers'. Herbie's on his way."

"Know anything?" They'd been friends for so long they could speak in shorthand to each other, and many times they didn't need to speak at all.

"No."

"Let's move 'em out." Susan made the roundup sign.

Tucker, assisted by Brooks, sneaked into the roundup. She lay on the floor of the Audi until halfway to Crozet. Mrs. Murphy and Pewter, both livid at being left behind, stared crossly as the car pulled out of the driveway.

Once at the Fletchers' the friends endured another shock. Fifty to sixty cars lined the street in the Ednam subdivision. Deputy Cynthia Cooper directed traffic. This wasn't her job, but the department was shorthanded over the weekend.

"Coop?" Harry waved at her.

"Craziest thing I've ever heard of," the nice-looking officer said.

"What do you mean?" Susan asked.

"He's not dead."

"WHAT?" all three humans said in unison.

Tucker, meanwhile, wasted no time. She walked in the front door, left open because of the incredible number of friends, acquaintances, and St. Elizabeth's students who were paying condolence calls. Tucker, low to the ground, threaded her way through the humans to the kitchen.

Brooks quickly found her friends, Karen Jensen and Jody Miller. They didn't know anything either.

As Harry and Susan entered the living room, Roscoe held up a glass of champagne, calling to the assembled, "The reports of my death are greatly exaggerated!" He sipped. "Bierce."

"Twain," Sandy Brashiers corrected. He was head of the English department and a rival for Roscoe's power.

"Ambrose Bierce." Roscoe smiled but his teeth were clenched.

"It doesn't matter, Roscoe, you're alive." Naomi, a handsome woman in her late thirties, toasted her husband.

April Shively, adoringly staring at her florid boss, clinked her glass with that of Ed Sugarman, the chemistry teacher.

"Hear, hear," said the group, which contained most of Harry's best friends, as well as a few enemies.

Blair Bainbridge, not an enemy but a potential suitor, stood next to Marilyn, or Little Mim, the well-groomed daughter of Big Mim Sanburne.

"When did you get home?" Harry managed to ask Blair after expressing to Roscoe her thanks for his deliverance.

"Last night."

"Hi, Marilyn." She greeted Little Mim by her real name.

"Good to see you." It wasn't. Marilyn was afraid Blair liked Harry more than herself.

Fair Haristeen, towering above the other men, strode over to his ex-wife, with whom he was still in love. "Isn't this the damnedest thing you've ever seen?" He reached into the big bowl of hard candies sitting on an end table. Roscoe always had candy around.

"Pretty weird." She kissed him on the cheek and made note that Morris "Maury" McKinchie, Roscoe Fletcher's best friend, was absent.

Meanwhile Tucker sat in the kitchen with Winston, the family English bulldog, a wise and kind animal. They had been exchanging pleasantries before Tucker got to the point.

"What's going on, Winston?"

"I don't know," came the grave reply.

"Has he gone to doctors in Richmond or New York? Because Harry heard from Herb Jones that he was healthy."

"Nothing wrong with Roscoe except too many women in his life."

The corgi cocked her head. *"Ah, well,"* she said, *"a prank, I guess, this obit thing."*

"Roscoe now knows how many people care about him. If people could attend their funerals, they'd be gratified, I should think," Winston said.

"Never thought of that."

"Umm." Winston waddled over to the backdoor, overlooking the sunken garden upon which Naomi lavished much attention.

"Winston, what's worrying you?"

The massive head turned to reveal those fearsome teeth. *"What if this is a warning?"*

"Who'd do a thing like that?"

"Tucker, Roscoe can't keep it in his pants. I've lost count of his affairs, and Naomi has reached the boiling point. She always catches him. After many lies, he does finally confess. He promises never to do it again. Three months, six months later—he's off and running."

"Who?"

"The woman?" The wrinkled brow furrowed more deeply. *"April, maybe, except she's so obvious even the humans get it. Let's see, a young woman from New York, I forget her name. Oh, he's made a pass at BoomBoom, but I think she's otherwise engaged. You know, I lose count."*

"Bet Naomi doesn't," the little corgi sagely replied.

4

That evening a heavy fog crept down Yellow Mountain. Harry, in the stable, walked outside to watch a lone wisp float over the creek. The wisp was followed by fingers spreading over the meadow until the farm was enveloped in gray.

She shivered; the temperature was dropping.

"Put on your down vest, you'll catch your death," Mrs. Murphy advised.

"What are you talking about, Miss Puss?" Harry smiled at her chatty cat.

"You, I'm talking about you. You need a keeper." The tiger sighed, knowing that the last person Harry would take care of would be herself.

Tucker lifted her head. Moisture carried good scent. *"That bobcat's near."*

"Let's get into the barn then." The cat feared her larger cousin.

As the little family plodded into the barn, the horses nickered. Darkness came as swiftly as the fog. Harry pulled her red down vest off a tack hook. She flipped on the light switch. Having stayed overlong at Roscoe Fletcher's to celebrate, she was now behind on her farm chores.

Tomahawk, the oldest horse in the barn, loved the advent of fall. A true foxhunting fellow, he couldn't wait for the season to begin. Gin Fizz and Poptart, the younger equines, perked their ears.

"That old bobcat is prowling around." Mrs. Murphy leapt onto the Dutch door, the top held open by a nickel-plated hook.

Tomahawk gazed at her with his huge brown eyes. *"Mean, that one."*

Two bright beady black eyes appeared at the edge of the hayloft. *"What's this I hear about a bobcat?"*

"Simon, I thought you'd still be asleep," Tucker barked.

The opossum moved closer to the edge, revealing his entire light gray face. *"You-all make enough noise to wake the dead. Any minute now and Flatface up there will swoop down and bitterly chastise us."*

Simon referred to the large owl who nested in the cupola. The owl disliked the domesticated animals, especially Mrs. Murphy. There was also a black snake who hibernated in the hayloft, but she was antisocial, even in summertime. A cornucopia of mice kept the predators fat and happy.

The hayloft covered one-third of the barn, which gave the space a lighter, airier feeling than if it had run the full length of the structure. Harry, using salvaged lumber, had built a hay shed thirty yards from the barn. She had painted it dark green with white trim; that was her summer project. Each summer she tried to improve the farm. She loved building, but after nailing on shingles in the scorching sun, she had decided she'd think long and hard before doing that again.

Mrs. Murphy climbed the ladder to the hayloft. *"Fog is thick as pea soup."*

"Doesn't matter. I can smell her well enough." Simon referred to the dreaded bobcat.

"Maybe so, but she can run faster than anyone here except for the horses."

"I'm hungry."

"I'll get Mom to put crunchies in my bowl. You can have that."

Simon brightened. *"Goody."*

Mrs. Murphy walked the top beam of the stalls, greeting each horse as she passed over its head. Then she jumped down on the tall wooden medicine chest standing next to the tackroom door. From there it was an easy drop to the floor.

Harry, having fed the horses, knelt on her hands and knees in the feed room. Little holes in the wooden walls testified to the industry of the mice. She lined her feed bins in tin, which baffled them, but they gobbled every crumb left on the floor. They also ate holes in her barn jacket, which enraged her.

"Mother, you aren't going to catch one."

"Murphy, do something!"

The cat sat next to Harry and patted the hole in the wall. *"They've got a system like the New York subway."*

"You're certainly talkative," Harry commented.

"And you don't understand a word I'm saying." The cat smiled. *"I'm hungry."*

"Jeez, Murphy, lower the volume."

"*Food, glorious food*— " She sang the song from *Oliver.*

Tucker, reposing in the tack room, hollered, "*You sing about as well as I do.*"

"*Thanks. I could have lived my whole life without knowing that.*"

Her entreaties worked. Harry shook triangular crunchies out of the bag, putting the bowl on top of the medicine cabinet so Tucker wouldn't steal the food.

"*Thanks,* " Simon called down, showing his appreciation.

"*Anytime.*" Murphy nibbled a few mouthfuls to satisfy Harry.

"I suppose Pewter will be hungry." Harry checked her watch. "She's not an outdoor girl." She laughed.

"*If she gets any fatter, you'll need to buy a red wagon so you can haul her gut around,*" Mrs. Murphy commented.

Harry sat on her old tack trunk. She glanced around. While there were always chores to be done, the regular maintenance ones were finished: feed, water, muck stalls, clean tack, sweep out the barn.

As soon as the horses finished eating, she would turn them out. With the first frost, usually around mid-October, she would flip their schedule. They'd be outside during the day and in their stalls at night. In the heat of summer they stayed inside the barn during the day; it was well ventilated by the breeze always blowing down the mountain. Kept the flies down, too.

She got up, her knees cracking, and walked to the open barn door. "You know, we could have an early frost." She returned to Fizz's stall. "I wonder if we should get on the new schedule now."

"Go ahead. If there are a couple of hot days, we'll come inside during the day. We're flexible."

"Let's stay inside." Poptart ground his sweet feed.

"Who wants to argue with the bobcat? I don't," Tomahawk said sensibly.

Harry cupped her chin with her hand. "You know, let's go to our fall schedule."

"Hooray!" the horses called out.

"Nighty night," she called back, turning off the lights.

Although the distance between the stable and the house couldn't have been more than one hundred yards, the heavy fog and mist soaked the three friends by the time they reached the backdoor.

The cat and dog shook themselves in the porch area. Harry would pitch a fit if they did it in the kitchen. Even Harry shook herself. Once inside she raced to put on the kettle for tea. She was chilled.

Pewter, lounging on the sofa, head on a colorful pillow, purred, *"I'm glad I stayed inside."*

"You're always glad you stayed inside," Tucker answered.

Harry puttered around. She drank some tea, then walked back into her bedroom. "Oh, no." In the turmoil of the day, she'd rushed out with Susan and Brooks, forgetting the mess she had left behind. The contents of her bureau drawers lay all over her bed. "I will not be conquered by underpants."

She gulped her tea, ruthlessly tossing out anything with holes in it or where the fabric was worn thin. That meant she had only enough socks left for half a drawer, one satin bra, and three pairs of underpants.

"Mom, you need to shop," said Mrs. Murphy, who adored shopping although she rarely got the opportunity for it.

Harry beheld the pile of old clothes. "Use it up, wear it out, make it do, or do without."

"You can't wear these things. They're tired," Pewter, now in the middle of the pile, told her. *"I'm tired, too."*

"You didn't do anything." Murphy laughed.

Harry stomped out to the pantry, returning armed with a big scissors.

"What's she going to do?" Pewter wondered aloud.

"Make rags. Mother can't stand to throw anything out if it can be used for something. She'll cut everything into squares or rectangles and then divide the pile between the house and the barn."

"The bras, too?"

"No, I think those are truly dead," Mrs. Murphy replied.

"Harry is a frugal soul," Pewter commented. She herself was profligate.

"She has to be." Tucker cleaned her hind paws, not easy for a corgi. *"That post office job pays for food and gas and that's all. Luckily, she inherited the farm when her parents died. It's paid for, but she doesn't have much else. A little savings and a few stocks her father left her, but he wasn't a financial wizard either. Her one extravagance, if you can call it that, is the horses. 'Course, they help in 'mowing' the fields."*

"Humans are funny, aren't they?" Pewter said thoughtfully. *"Big Mim wallows in possessions, and Harry has so little. Why doesn't Mim give things to Harry?"*

"You forget, she gave her Poptart. She and Fair went halfsies on it."

"I did forget. Still, you know what I mean."

Tucker shrugged. *"They're funny about things. Things mean a lot to them. Like bones to us, I guess."*

"*I couldn't care less about bones. Catnip is another matter,*" the tiger said gleefully, wishing for a catnip treat.

"*Ever see that T-shirt? You know, the one that says 'He who dies with the most toys wins'?*" Pewter, snuggling in the new rag pile, asked.

"*Yeah. Samson Coles used to wear it—before he was disgraced by dipping into escrow funds.*" Tucker giggled.

"*Stupid T-shirt,*" Mrs. Murphy said briskly. "*When you're dead, you're dead. You can't win anything.*"

"*That reminds me. The bobcat's out there tonight,*" Tucker told Pewter.

"*I'm not going outside.*"

"*We know that.*" Mrs. Murphy swished her tail. "*Wonder if the Fletchers will find out who put that phony obituary in the paper? If they don't, Mother will. You know how nosy she gets.*"

The phone rang. Harry put down her scissors to pick it up. "Hi."

Blair Bainbridge's deep voice had a soothing quality. "Sorry I didn't call on you the minute I got home, but I was dog tired. I happened to be down at the café when Marilyn ran in to tell me about Roscoe dying. We drove over to his house, and I—"

"Blair, it's okay. She's crazy about you, as I'm sure you know."

"Oh, well, she's lonesome." Since he was one of the highest paid male models in the country, he knew perfectly well that women needed smelling salts in his presence. All but Harry. Therefore she fascinated him.

"Susan and I are riding tomorrow after church if you want to come along."

"Thanks. What time?"

"Eleven."

He cheerfully said, "I'll see you at eleven, and, Harry, I can tack my own horse. Who do you want me to ride?"

"Tomahawk."

"Great. See you then. 'Bye."

" 'Bye."

The animals said nothing. They knew she was talking to Blair, and they were divided in their opinions. Tucker wanted Harry to get back with Fair. She knew it wasn't unusual for humans to remarry after divorcing. Pewter thought Blair was the better deal because he was rich and Harry needed help in that department. Mrs. Murphy, while having affection for both men, always said that Mr. Right hadn't appeared. Be patient.

The phone rang again.

"Coop. How are you?"

"Tired. Hey, don't want to bug you, but did you have any idea who might have put that false obit in the papers?"

"No."

"Roscoe says he hasn't a clue. Naomi doesn't think it's quite as funny as he does. Herb doesn't have any ideas. April Shively thinks it was Karen Jensen since she's such a cutup. BoomBoom says Maury McKinchie did it, and he'll use our reactions as the basis for a movie. I even called the school chaplain, Father Michael. He was noncommittal."

"What do you mean?"

Father Michael, the priest of the Church of the Good Shepherd between Crozet and Charlottesville, had close ties to the private school. Although nondenominational for a number of years, St. Elizabeth's each year invited a local clergyman to be the chaplain of the school. This exposed the students to different religious approaches. This year it was the

Catholics' turn. Apart from a few gripes from extremists, the rotating system worked well.

"He shut up fast," Coop replied.

"That's weird."

"I think so, too."

"What does Rick think?" Harry referred to Sheriff Shaw by his first name.

"He sees the humor in this, but he wants to find out who did it. If kids were behind this, they need to learn that you can't jerk people around like that."

"If I hear of anything, I'll buzz."

"Thanks."

"Don't work too hard, Coop."

"Look who's talking. See you soon. 'Bye."

Harry hung up the phone and picked up the small throw-out pile. Then she carefully divided the newly cut rags, placing half by the kitchen door. That way she would remember to take them to the barn in the morning. She noticed it was ten at night.

"Where does the time go?"

She hopped in the shower and then crawled into bed.

Mrs. Murphy, Pewter, and Tucker were already on the bed.

"What do you guys think about Roscoe's fake obituary?" she asked her animal friends.

Like many people who love animals, she talked to them, doing her best to understand. They understood her, of course.

"*Joke.*" Pewter stuck out one claw, which she hooked into the quilt.

"*Ditto.*" Tucker agreed. "*Although Winston said Naomi is furious with him. Mad enough to kill.*"

"Humans are boring—" Pewter rested her head on an out-stretched arm.

"See, you think like I do." Harry wiggled under the blankets. "Just some dumb thing. For all I know, Roscoe did it himself. He's not above it."

"Winston said Roscoe's running the women. Can't leave them alone." Tucker was back on her conversation with the bull-dog.

"Maybe this isn't a joke." Mrs. Murphy, who had strong opinions about monogamy, curled on Harry's pillow next to her head.

"Oh, Murphy, it will all blow over." Tucker wanted to go to sleep.

5

The woody aroma of expensive tobacco curled up from Sandy Brashiers's pipe. The leather patches on his tweed jacket were worn to a perfect degree. His silk rep tie, stripes running in the English direction, left to right, was from Oxford University Motor Car Club. He had studied at Oxford after graduating from Harvard. A cashmere V neck, the navy underscoring the navy stripe in the tie, completed his English-professor look.

However, the Fates or Sandy himself had not been kind. Not only was he not attached to a university, he was teaching high-school English, even if it *was* at a good prep school. This was not the future his own professors or he himself had envisioned when he was a star student.

He never fell from grace because he never reached high enough to tumble. Cowardice and alcohol already marred his good looks at forty-two. As for the cowardice, no one but Sandy seemed to know why he hung back when he was capable of much more. Then again, perhaps even he didn't know.

He did know he was being publicly humiliated by headmaster Roscoe Fletcher. When the ancient Peter Abbott retired as principal of the upper school at the end of last year's term, Sandy should have automatically been selected to succeed Abbott. Roscoe dithered, then dallied, finally naming Sandy principal pro tem. He declared a genuine search should take place, much as he wished to promote from within.

This split the board of directors and enraged the faculty, most of whom believed the post should go to Sandy. If Roscoe was going to form a search committee each time a position opened, could any faculty member march assuredly into administration?

Fortunately for Brooks Tucker, she knew nothing of the prep school's politics. She was entranced as Mr. Brashiers discussed the moral turpitude of Lady Macbeth in the highly popular Shakespeare elective class.

"What would have happened if Lady Macbeth could have acted directly, if she didn't have to channel her ambition through her husband?"

Roger Davis raised his hand. "She would have challenged the king right in his face."

"No way," pretty Jody Miller blurted before she raised her hand.

"Would you like to expand on that theme after I call on you?" Sandy wryly nodded to the model-tall girl.

"Sorry, Mr. Brashiers." She twirled her pencil, a nervous

habit. "Lady Macbeth was devious. It would be out of character to challenge the king openly. I don't think her position i society would change that part of her character. She'd b sneaky even if she were a man."

Brooks, eyebrows knit together, wondered if that was true She wanted to participate, but she was shy in her new sur roundings even though she knew many of her classmate from social activities outside of school.

Sean Hallahan, the star halfback on the football team, wa called on and said in his deep voice, "She's devious, Jody, be cause she has to hide her ambition."

This pleased Sandy Brashiers, although it did not pleas Jody Miller, who was angry at Sean. Ten years ago the boy rarely understood the pressures on women's lives, but enoug progress had been made that his male students could read text bearing those pressures in mind.

Karen Jensen, blond and green-eyed, the most popular gir in the junior class, chirped, "Maybe she was having a ba hair day."

Everyone laughed.

After class Brooks, Karen, and Jody walked to the cafete ria—or the Ptomaine Pit, as it was known. Roger Davis, tal and not yet filled out, trailed behind. He wanted to talk t Brooks. Still awkward, he racked his brain about how to ope a conversation.

He who hesitates is lost. Sean scooted by him, skiddin next to the girls, secure in his welcome.

"Think the president's wife is Lady Macbeth?"

The three girls kept walking while Jody sarcastically said "Sean, how long did it take you to think of that?"

"You inspire me, Jody." He cocked his head, full of him self.

Roger watched this from behind them. He swallowed hard, took two big strides and caught up.

"Hey, bean," Sean offhandedly greeted him, not at all happy that he might have to share the attention of three pretty girls.

If Roger had been a smart-ass kid, he would have called Sean a bonehead or something. Sean was bright enough, but his attitude infuriated the other boys. Roger was too nice a guy to put someone else down, though. Instead he smiled and forgot what he was going to say to Brooks.

Luckily, she initiated the conversation. "Are you still working at the car wash?"

"Yes."

"Do they need help? I mean, I'd like to get a job and—" Her voice faced away.

"Jimbo always needs help. I'll ask him," Roger said firmly, now filled with a mission: to help Brooks.

Jimbo C. Anson, as wide as he was tall, owned the car wash, the local heating-fuel company, and a small asphalt plant that he had bought when the owner, Kelly Craycroft, died unexpectedly. Living proof of the capitalist vision of life, Jimbo was also a soft touch. Brooks would be certain to get that after-school job.

Brooks was surprised when she walked through the backdoor of her house that afternoon to find her mother on the phone with Roger. He'd already gotten her the job. She needed to decide whether to work after school, weekends, or both.

After Brooks profusely thanked Roger, she said she'd call him back since she needed to talk to her mother.

"I guess you do." Susan stared at her after Brooks hung up the phone.

"Mom, St. Elizabeth's is expensive. I want to make money."

"Honey, we aren't on food stamps. At least, not yet." Susan sighed, loath to admit that the few fights she ever had with Ned were over money.

"If I can pay for my clothes and stuff, that will help some."

Susan stared into those soft hazel eyes, just like Ned's. Happy as she was to hear of Brooks's willingness to be responsible, she was oddly saddened or perhaps nostalgic: her babies were growing up fast. Somehow life went by in a blur. Wasn't it just yesterday she was holding this beautiful young woman in her arms, wondering at her tiny fingers and toes?

Susan cleared her throat. "I'm proud of you." She paused. "Let's go take a look at the car wash before you make a decision."

"Great." Brooks smiled, revealing the wonders of orthodontic work.

"Yeehaw!" came a holler from outside the backdoor.

"I'm here, too," Tucker barked.

Neither Mrs. Murphy nor Pewter was going to brazenly advertise her presence.

The Tucker's own corgi, Tee Tucker's brother, Owen Tudor, raced to the backdoor as it swung open. Their mother had died of old age that spring. It was now a one-corgi household.

"Tucker." Owen kissed his sister. He would have kissed the two cats except they deftly sidestepped his advances.

"I didn't hear your truck," Susan said.

"Dead. This time it's the carburetor." Harry sighed. "One of these years I will buy a new truck."

"And the cows will fly," Pewter added sardonically.

"Mom might win the lottery." Tucker, ever the optimist, pricked up her ears.

"Need a ride home?" Susan offered.

"I'll walk. Good for me and good for the critters."

"It's not good for me," Pewter objected instantly. *"My paws are too delicate."*

"You're too fat," Mrs. Murphy said bluntly.

"I have big bones."

"Pewter—" Tucker started to say something but was interrupted by Susan, who reached down to pet her.

"Why don't you all hop in the car, and we'll go to the car wash? Brooks took a job there, but I want to check it out. If you go with me, I'll feel better."

"Sure."

Everyone piled into the Audi. Mrs. Murphy enjoyed riding in cars. Pewter endured it. The two dogs loved every minute of it, but they were so low to the ground the only way they could see out the window was to sit on human laps, which were never in short supply.

They waved to Big Mim in her Bentley Turbo R, heading back toward Crozet.

Mrs. Murphy, lying down in the back window, watched the opulent and powerful machine glide by. *"She's still in her Bavarian phase."*

"Huh?" Tucker asked.

"Caps with pheasant feathers, boiled wool jackets. For all I know she's wearing lederhosen, or one of those long skirts that weigh a sweet ton."

"You know, if I were German, I'd be embarrassed when Americans dress like that," Pewter noted sagely.

"If I were German, I'd be embarrassed if Germans dressed like that," Owen Tudor piped up, which made the animals laugh.

"You-all are being awfully noisy," Harry chided them.

"They're just talking," Brooks protested.

"If animals could talk, do you know what they'd say?" Susan then told them: "What's to eat? Where's the food? Can I sleep with it? Okay, can I sleep on it?"

"I resent that," Mrs. Murphy growled.

"Who cares?" Pewter airily dismissed the human's gibe.

"What else can they do but joke about their betters? Low self-esteem." Owen chuckled.

"Yeah, and whoever invented that term ought to be hung at sundown." Mrs. Murphy, not one given to psychologizing, put one paw on Harry's shoulder. "In fact, the idea that a person is fully formed in childhood is absurd. Only a human could come up with that one."

"They can't help it," Tucker said.

"Well, they could certainly shut up about it," Mrs. Murphy suggested strongly.

"BoomBoom Craycroft can sure sling that crap around." Tucker didn't really dislike the woman, but then again, she didn't really like her either.

"You haven't heard the latest!" Pewter eagerly sat up by Brooks in the backseat.

"What?" The other animals leaned toward the cat.

"Heard it at Market's."

"Well!" Mrs. Murphy imperiously prodded.

"As I was saying before I was so rudely interrupted—"

"I did not interrupt you." Tucker was testy.

Owen stepped in. *"Shut up, Tucker, let her tell her story."*

"Well, BoomBoom was buying little glass bottles and a mess of Q-Tips, I mean enough Q-Tips to clean all the ears in Albemarle County. So Market asks, naturally enough, what is she going to do with all this stuff. Poor guy, next thing you know she launches

into an explanation about fragrance therapy. No kidding. How certain essences will create emotional states or certain smells will soothe human ailments. She must have blabbed on for forty-five minutes. I thought I would fall off the counter laughing at her."

"She's off her nut," Owen said.

"Market asked for an example." Pewter relished her tale. *"She allowed as how she didn't have any essence with her but, for instance, if he felt a headache coming on, he should turn off the lights, sit in a silent room, and put a pot of water on the stove with a few drops of sage essence. It would be even better if he had a wood-burning stove. Then he could put the essence of sage in the little humidifier on top."*

"Essence of bullshit," Mrs. Murphy replied sardonically.

"Will you-all be quiet? This is embarrassing. Susan will never let you in her car again," Harry complained.

"All right by me," Pewter replied saucily, which made the animals laugh again.

Brooks petted Pewter's round head. "They have their own language."

"You know, that's a frightening thought." Susan glanced at her daughter in the rearview mirror, surrounded as she was by animals. "My Owen and poor dear departed Champion Beatitude of Grace—"

"Just call her Shortstop. I hate it when Susan uses Mom's full title." Owen's eyes saddened.

"She was a champion. She won more corgi firsts than Pewter and Murphy have fleas," Tucker said.

Murphy swatted at Tucker's stump. *"If you had a tail, I would chew it to bits."*

"I saw you scratching."

"Tucker, that was not fleas."

"What was it then, your highness? Eczema? Psoriasis? Hives?"

"Shut up." Mrs. Murphy bopped her hard.

"That is enough!" Harry twisted around in the front passenger seat and missed them because the car reached the entrance to the brand-new car wash, and the stop threw her forward.

Roger dashed out of the small glass booth by the entrance to the car-wash corridor.

"Hi, Mrs. Tucker." He smiled broadly. "Hi, Brooks. Hi, Mrs. Haristeen . . . and everybody."

"Is Jimbo here?"

"Yes, ma'am."

A car pulled up behind them, and one behind that. Roscoe Fletcher squirmed impatiently in the second car.

"Roger, I want to zip through this extravaganza." Susan reached in her purse for the $5.25 for exterior wash only.

"Mom, let's shoot the works."

"That's eleven ninety-five."

"I'll contribute!" Harry fished a five out of her hip pocket and handed it to Roger.

"Harry, don't do that."

"Shut up, Suz, we're holding up traffic."

"Here's the one." Brooks forked over a one-dollar bill.

"Okay then, a little to the right, Mrs. Tucker. There, you've got it. Now put your car in neutral and turn off the radio, if you have it on. Oh, and roll up the windows."

She rolled up the driver's-side window as Roger picked up a long scrub brush to scrub her headlights and front grille while Karen Jensen worked the rear bumper. She waved.

"Hey, I didn't know Karen worked here. Jody, too." She saw Jody putting on mascara as she sat behind the cash register.

"Brooks, don't you dare open that window," Susan commanded as she felt the belt hook under the left car wheel. They lurched forward.

"Hey, hey, I can't see!" Pewter screeched.

"Early blindness," Mrs. Murphy said maliciously as the yellow neon light flashed on, a bell rang, and a wall of water hit them with force.

Each cleansing function—waxing, underbody scrub and coat, rinsing—was preceded by a neon light accompanied by a bell and buzzer noise. By the time they hit the blowers, Pewter frothed at the mouth.

"Poor kitty." Brooks petted her.

"Pewter, it really is okay. We're not in any danger." Mrs. Murphy felt bad that she had tormented her.

The gray kitty shook.

"Last time I take her through a car wash." Harry, too, felt sorry for the cat's plight.

They finally emerged with a bump from the tunnel of cleanliness. Susan popped the car in gear and parked it in a lot on the other side of the car wash.

As she and Brooks got out to meet with Jimbo Anson, Harry consoled Pewter, who crawled into her lap. The other animals kept quiet.

A light rap on the window startled Harry, she was so intent on soothing the cat.

"Hi, Roscoe. You're right, it is like a Broadway show with all those lights."

"Funny, huh?" He offered her a tiny sweet, a miniature strawberry in a LaVossienne tin, French in origin. "Just discovered these. Les Fraises Bonbon Fruits pack a punch. Go on and try one."

"Okay." She reached in and plucked out a miniature strawberry. "Whooo."

"That'll pucker those lips. Naomi is trying to get me to stop eating so much sugar but I love sweetness." He noticed Brooks and Susan in the small office with Jimbo Anson. "Has she said anything about school?"

"She likes it."

"Good, good. You been to the vet?"

"No, we're out for a family drive."

"I can't remember the times I've seen you without Mrs. Murphy and Tucker. Now you've got Pewter, too. Market said she was eating him out of house and home."

"No-o-o," the cat wailed, shaken but insulted.

"Hey, Pewter, we'll get even. We can pee on his mail before Mom stuffs it in his box," Murphy sang out gaily. *"Or we could shred it to bits, except the bills. Keep them intact."*

St. Elizabeth's mail was delivered directly to the school. Personal mail was delivered to the Crozet post office.

"Yeah." Pewter perked up.

"Good to see you, the animals too." He waved and Harry hit the button to close the window.

Then she called after him, "Where'd you get the strawberry drops?"

"Foods of All Nations," he replied.

She noticed Karen Jensen making a face after he passed by. Roger laughed. "Kids," Harry thought to herself. Then she remembered the time she stuck Elmer's Glue in the locks of her most unfavorite teacher's desk drawer.

After ten minutes Susan and Brooks returned to the car.

Books was excited. "I'll work after school on Monday 'cause there's no field hockey practice, and I'll work Saturdays. Cool!"

"Sounds good to me." Harry held up her hand for a high five as Brooks bounced into the backseat.

Susan turned on the ignition. "This way she won't miss practice. After all, part of school is sports."

"Can we go home now?" Pewter cried.

"Roscoe must live at this place," Susan said lightly as they pulled out of the parking lot.

6

Little squeaks behind the tack-room walls distracted Harry from dialing. She pressed the disconnect button to redial.

Mrs. Murphy sauntered into the tack room, then paused, her ears swept forward. *"What balls!"*

"Beg pardon?" Pewter opened one chartreuse eye.

"Mouse balls. Can you hear them?"

Pewter closed her eye. *"Yes, but it's not worth fretting over."*

Harry, finger still on the disconnect button, rested the telephone receiver on her shoulder. "What in the hell are they doing, Murphy?"

"Having a party," the tiger replied, frustrated that she couldn't get at her quarry.

Harry lifted the receiver off her shoulder, pointing at the

cat with it. "I can't put down poison. If you catch a sick mouse, then *you'll* die. I can't put the hose into their holes because I'll flood the tack room. I really thought you could solve this problem."

"If one would pop out of there, I would." The cat, angry, stomped out.

"Temper, temper," Harry called out after her, which only made things worse.

She redialed the number as Murphy sat in the barn aisle, her back to Harry and her ears swept back.

"Hi, Janice. Harry Haristeen."

"How are you?" the bright voice on the other end of the line responded.

"Pretty good. And you?"

"Great."

"I hope you'll indulge me. I have a question. You're still editing the obituary page, aren't you?"

"Yep. Ninety-five cents a line. Five dollars for a photo." Her voice softened. "Has, uh—"

"No. I'm curious about how Roscoe Fletcher's obituary appeared in the paper."

"Oh, that." Janice's voice dropped. "Boy, did I get in trouble."

"Sorry."

"All I can tell you is, two days ago I received a call from Hallahan Funeral Home saying they had Roscoe's body as well as the particulars."

"So I couldn't call in and report a death?"

"No. If you're a family member or best friend you might call or fax the life details, but we verify death with the funeral home or the hospital. Usually they call us. The hospital won't give me cause of death either. Sometimes family members will put it in, but we can't demand any information other than verification that the person is dead." She took a deep breath. "And I had that!"

"Do you generally deal with the same people at each of the funeral homes?"

"Yes, I do, and I recognize their voices, too. Skip Hallahan called in Roscoe's death."

"I guess you told that to the sheriff."

"Told it to Roscoe, too. I'm sick of this."

"I'm sorry, Janice. I made you go over it one more time."

"That's different—you're a friend. Skip is being a bung-hole, I can tell you that. He swears he never made the call."

"I think I know who did."

"Tell me."

"I will as soon as I make sure I'm right."

7

The high shine on Roscoe Fletcher's car surrendered to dust, red from the clay, as he drove down Mim Sanburne's two-mile driveway to the mansion Mim had inherited from her mother's family, the Urquharts.

He passed the mansion, coasting to a stop before a lovely cottage a quarter mile behind the imposing pile. Cars parked neatly along the farm road bore testimony to the gathering within.

Raising money for St. Elizabeth's was one of Little Mim's key jobs. She wanted to show she could be as powerful as her mother.

Breezing through Little Mim's front door, Roscoe heard

Maury McKinchie shout, "The phoenix rises from the ashes!"

The members of the fund-raising committee, many of them alumnae, laughed at the film director's quip.

"You missed the resurrection party, my man." Roscoe clapped McKinchie on the back. "Lasted until dawn."

"Every day is a party for Roscoe," April Shively, stenographer's notebook flipped open at the ready, said admiringly.

April, not a member of the committee, attended all meetings as the headmaster's secretary, which saved the committee from appointing one of its own. It also meant that only information deemed important by Roscoe made it to the typed minutes. Lastly, it gave the two a legitimate excuse to be together.

"Where were you this time?" Irene Miller, Jody's mother, asked, an edge of disapproval in her voice since Maury McKinchie missed too many meetings, in her estimation.

"New York." He waited until Roscoe took a seat then continued. "I have good news." The group leaned toward him. "I met with Walter Harnett at Columbia. He loves our idea of a film department. He has promised us two video cameras. These are old models, but they work fine. New, this camera sells for fifty-four thousand dollars. We're on our way." He beamed.

After the applause, Little Mim, chair of the fund-raising committee, spoke. "That is the most exciting news! With preparation on our part, I think we can get approval from the board of directors to develop a curriculum."

"Only if we can finance the department." Roscoe folded his hands together. "You know how conservative the board is. Reading, writing, and arithmetic. That's it. But if we can finance one year—and I have the base figures here—then I hope and believe the positive response of students and parents will see us through the ensuing year. The board will be forced into the twentieth century"—he paused for effect—"just as we cross into the twenty-first."

They laughed.

"Is the faculty for us?" Irene Miller asked, eager to hitch on to whatever new bandwagon promised to deliver the social cachet she so desired.

"With a few notable exceptions, yes," Roscoe replied.

"Sandy Brashiers," April blurted out, then quickly clamped her mouth shut. Her porcelain cheeks flushed. "You know what a purist he is," she mumbled.

"Give him an enema," Maury said, and noted the group's shocked expression. "Sorry. We say that a lot on a film shoot. If someone is really a pain in the ass, he's called the D.B. for douche bag."

"Maury." Irene cast her eyes down in fake embarrassment.

"Sorry. The fact remains, he is an impediment."

"I'll take care of Sandy," Roscoe Fletcher smoothly asserted.

"I wish someone would." Doak Mincer, a local bank president, sighed. "Sandy has been actively lobbying against this. Even when told the film department would be a one-year experimental program, totally self-sufficient, funded separately, the whole nine yards, he's opposed—adamantly."

"Has no place in academia, he says." Irene, too, had been lobbied.

"What about that cinematographer you had here mid-September? I thought that engendered enthusiasm." Marilyn pointed her pencil at Roscoe.

"She was a big hit. Shot film of some of the more popular kids, Jody being one, Irene."

"She loved it." Irene smiled. "You aren't going to encounter resistance from parents. What parent would be opposed to their child learning new skills? Or working with a pro like Maury? Why, it's a thrill."

"Thank you." Maury smiled his big smile, the one usually reserved for paid photographers.

He had enjoyed a wonderful directing career in the 1980s, which faded in the '90s as his wife's acting career catapulted into the stratosphere. She was on location so much that Maury often forgot he had a wife. Then again, he might have done so regardless of circumstances.

He had also promised Darla would lecture once a year at St. Elizabeth's. He had neglected to inform Darla, stage name Darla Keene. Real name Michelle Gumbacher. He'd cajole her into it on one of her respites home.

"Irene, did you bring your list of potential donors?" Little Mim asked. Irene nodded, launching into an intensely boring recitation of each potential candidate.

After the meeting Maury and Irene walked out to his country car, a Range Rover. His Porsche 911 was saved for warm days.

"How's Kendrick?" he inquired about her husband.

"Same old, same old."

This meant that all Kendrick did was work at the gardening center he had built from scratch and which at long last was generating profit.

She spied a carton full of tiny bottles in the passenger seat of the Rover. "What's all that?"

"Uh"—long pause—"essences."

"What?"

"Essences. Some cure headaches. Others are for success. Not that I believe it, but they can be soothing, I suppose."

"Did you bring this stuff back from New York?" Irene lifted an eyebrow.

"Uh—no. I bought them from BoomBoom Craycroft."

"Good God." Irene turned on her heel, leaving him next to his wildly expensive vehicle much favored by the British royals.

Later that evening when Little Mim reluctantly briefed her mother on the meeting—reluctant because her mother had to know everything—she said, "I think I can make the film department happen."

"That would be a victory, dear."

"Don't be so enthusiastic, Mother."

"I am enthusiastic. Quietly so, that's all. And I do think Roscoe enjoys chumming with the stars, such as they are, entirely too much. Greta Garbo. *That* was a star."

"Yes, Mother."

"And Maury—well, West Coast ways, my dear. Not Virginia."

"Not Virginia," a description, usually whispered by whites

and blacks alike to set apart those who didn't measure up. This included multitudes.

Little Mim bristled. "The West Coast, well, they're more open-minded."

"Open-minded? They're porous."

8

"What have you got to say for yourself?" A florid Skip Hallahan glared at his handsome son.

"I'm sorry, Dad," Sean muttered.

"Don't talk to me. Talk to him!"

"I'm sorry, Mr. Fletcher."

Roscoe, hands folded across his chest, unfolded them. "I accept your apology, but did you really think phoning in my obituary was funny?"

"Uh—at the time. Guess not," he replied weakly.

"Your voice does sound a lot like your father's." Roscoe leaned forward. "No detentions. But—I think you can volunteer at the hospital for four hours each week. That would satisfy me."

"Dad, I already have a paper route. How can I work at the hospital?"

"I'll see that he does his job," Skip snapped, still mortified.

"If he falters, no more football."

"What?" Sean, horrified, nearly leapt out of his chair.

"You heard me," Roscoe calmly stated.

"Without me St. Elizabeth's doesn't have a prayer," Sean arrogantly predicted.

"Sean, the football season isn't as important as you learning: actions have consequences. I'd be a sorry headmaster if I let you off the hook because you're our best halfback...because someday you'd run smack into trouble. Actions have consequences. You're going to learn that right now. Four hours a week until New Year's Day. Am I clearly understood?" Roscoe stood up.

"Yes, sir."

"I asked you this before. I'll ask it one last time. Were you alone in this prank?"

"Yes, sir," Sean lied.

9

A ruddy sun climbed over the horizon. Father Michael, an early riser, enjoyed his sunrises as much as most people enjoyed sunsets. Armed with hot Jamaican coffee, his little luxury, he sat reading the paper at the small pine breakfast table overlooking the church's beautifully tended graveyard.

The Church of the Good Shepherd, blessed with a reasonably affluent congregation, afforded him a pleasant albeit small home on the church grounds. A competent secretary, Lucinda Payne Coles, provided much-needed assistance Mondays through Fridays. He liked Lucinda, who, despite moments of bitterness, bore her hardships well.

After her husband, Samson, lost all his money and got caught with his pants down in the bargain in an extramarital affair, Lucinda sank into a slough of despond. She applied when the job at the church became available and was happily hired even though she'd never worked a day in her life. She typed adequately, but, more important, she knew everyone and everyone knew her.

As for Samson, Father Michael remembered him daily in his prayers. Samson had been reduced to physical labor at Kendrick Miller's gardening business. At least he was in the best shape of his life and was learning to speak fluent Spanish, as some of his coworkers were Mexican immigrants.

Father Michael, starting on a second cup of coffee—two lumps of brown sugar and a dollop of Devonshire cream— blinked in surprise. He thought he saw a figure sliding through the early-morning mist.

That needed jolt of caffeine blasted him out of his seat. He grabbed a Barbour jacket to hurry outside. Quietly he moved closer to a figure lurking in the graveyard.

Samson Coles placed a bouquet of flowers on Ansley Randolph's grave.

Father Michael, a slightly built man, turned to tiptoe back to the cottage, but Samson heard him.

"Father?"

"Sorry to disturb you, Samson. I couldn't see clearly in the mist. Sometimes the kids drink in here, you know. I thought I could catch one in the act. I am sorry."

Samson cleared his throat. "No one visits her."

"She ruined herself, poor woman." Father Michael sighed.

"I know. I loved her anyway. I still loved Lucinda but . . . I couldn't stay away from Ansley." He sighed. "I don't know why Lucinda doesn't leave me."

"She loves you, and she's working on forgiveness. God sends us the lessons we need."

"Well, if mine is humility, I'm learning." He paused. "You won't tell her you saw me here, will you?"

"No."

"It's just that...sometimes I feel so bad. Warren doesn't visit her grave, and neither do the boys. You'd think at least once they'd visit their mother's grave."

"They're young. They think if they ignore pain and loss, it will fade away. Doesn't."

"I know." He turned, and both men left the graveyard, carefully shutting the wrought-iron gate behind them.

At the northwest corner of the graveyard a massive statue of the Avenging Angel seemed to follow them with his eyes.

"I just so happen to have some of the best Jamaican coffee you would ever want to drink. How about joining me for a cup?"

"I hate to trouble you, Father."

"No trouble at all."

They imbibed the marvelous coffee and talked of love, responsibility, the chances for the Virginia football team this fall, and the curiousness of human nature as evidenced by the false obituary.

A light knock on the backdoor got Father Michael out of his chair. He opened the door. Jody Miller, one of his parishioners, wearing her sweats as she was on her way to early-morning field hockey practice, stood in the doorway, a bruise prominent on her cheek and a red mark near her eye that would soon blacken.

"Father Michael, I have to talk to you." She saw Samson at the table. "Uh—"

"Come on in."

"I'll be late for practice." She ran down the back brick

walkway as Father Michael watched her with his deep brown eyes. He finally closed the door.

"Speaking of curious." Samson half smiled. "Everything is so important at that age."

It was.

Five minutes after Samon left, Skip Hallahan pulled into Father Michael's driveway with Sean in the passenger seat. Reluctantly, Sean got out.

"Father!" Skip bellowed.

Father Michael stuck his head out the backdoor. "Come in, Skip and Sean, I'm not deaf, you know."

"Sorry," Skip mumbled, then launched into Sean's misdeed before he'd taken a seat.

After Skip ranted for a half hour, Father Michael asked him to leave the room for a few minutes.

"Sean, I can see the humor in calling in the obituary. I really can. But can you see how you've upset people? Think of Mrs. Fletcher."

"I'm getting the idea," Sean replied ruefully.

"I suggest you call on Mrs. Fletcher and apologize. I also suggest you call Janice Walker, editor of the obituary page at the paper, and apologize, and lastly, write a letter of apology and send it to 'Letters to the Editor.' After that, I expect the paper will take your route away from you." The good priest tried to prepare him for retaliation.

Sean sat immobile for a long time. "All right, Father, I will."

"What possessed you to do this? Especially to your headmaster."

"Well, that was kind of the point." Sean suppressed a smile. "It wouldn't have been nearly as funny if I'd called in, uh, your obituary."

Father Michael rapped the table with his fingertips. "I see. Well, make your apologies. I'll calm down your father." He stood up to summon Skip Hallahan.

Sean stood also. "Thanks, Father."

"Go on. Get out of here." The priest clapped the young man on the back.

10

Every hamlet and town has its nerve centers, those places where people congregate to enjoy the delights of gossip. Not that men admit to gossiping: for them it's "exchanging information."

A small group of men stood outside the post office on the first Monday in October in buttery Indian-summer sunshine. The Reverend Herbert Jones, Fair Haristeen, Ned Tucker, Jim Sanburne—the mayor of Crozet—and Sandy Brashiers spoke forcefully about the football teams of Virginia, Tech, William and Mary, and, with a shudder, Maryland.

"Maryland's the one to beat, and it hurts me to say that," the Reverend Jones intoned. "And I never will say it in front of John Klossner."

John, a friend of Herb's, graduated from Maryland and never let his buddies forget it.

Another one of the "in" group, Art Bushey—absent this morning—had graduated from Virginia Military Institute, so there was no reason for argument there. Poor VMI's team couldn't do squat, a wretched reality for those who loved the institution and a sheer joy for those who did not.

"This is the year for Virginia, Herb. I don't care how hot Maryland has been up to now." Sandy Brashiers crossed his arms over his chest.

"Say, why aren't you in school today?" Herb asked.

"I've worked out a schedule with King Fletcher, so I don't go in until noon on Mondays." Sandy breathed in. "You know, I love young people, but they'll suck you dry."

"Too young to know what they're asking of us." Fair toed the gravel. "Now before we get totally off the subject, I want to put in a good word for William and Mary."

"Ha!" Jim Sanburne, a huge man in his middle sixties, almost as tall as Fair but twice as broad, guffawed.

"Give it up, Fair." Ned laughed.

"One of these days the Tribe will prevail." Fair, an undergraduate alumnus, held up the Victory V.

"How come you don't root for Auburn? That's where you went to veterinary school," Sandy said.

"Oh, I like Auburn well enough."

Harry, from the inside, opened the door to the post office and stood, framed in the light. "What are you guys jawing about? This is government property. No riffraff."

"Guess you'll have to go, Fair," Ned said slyly.

The other men laughed.

"We're picking our teams for this year." Jim explained the reasoning behind each man's choice.

"I pick Smith!"

"Since when does Smith have a football team?" Sandy Brashiers asked innocently.

"They don't, but if they did they'd beat VMI," Harry replied. "Think I'll call Art Bushey and torment him about it."

This provoked more laughter. Mrs. Murphy, roused from a mid-morning catnap, walked to the open doorway and sat down. She exhaled, picked up a paw, and licked the side of it, which she rubbed on her face. She liked football, occasionally trying to catch the tiny ball as it streaked across the television screen. In her mind she'd caught many a bomb. Today football interested her not a jot. She ruffled her fur, smoothed it down, then strolled alongside the path between the post office and the market. She could hear Harry and the men teasing one another with outbursts of laughter. Then Miranda joined them to even more laughter.

Mrs. Murphy had lived all her life on this plot of Virginia soil. She watched the news at six and sometimes at eleven, although usually she was asleep by then. She read the newspapers by sitting right in front of Harry when she read. As near as she could tell, humans lived miserable lives in big cities. It was either that or newspapers worked on the Puritan principle of underlining misery so the reader would feel better about his or her own life. Whatever the reason, the cat found human news dull. It was one murder, car wreck, and natural disaster after another.

People liked one another here. They knew one another all their lives, with the occasional newcomer adding spice and speculation to the mix. And it wasn't as though Crozet never had bad things happen. People being what they are, jealousy, greed, and lust existed. Those caught paid the price. But in the main, the people were good. If nothing else they took care of their pets.

She heard a small, muffled sob behind Market Shiflett's store. She trotted to the back. Jody Miller, head in hands, was crying her heart out. Pewter sat at her sneakers, putting her paw on the girl's leg from time to time, offering comfort.

"*I wondered where you were.*" Murphy touched noses with Pewter, then stared at the girl.

Jody's blackening eye caught her attention when the girl removed her hands from her face. She wiped her nose with the back of her hand, blinking through her tears. "Hello, Mrs. Murphy."

"*Hello, Jody. What's the matter?*" Murphy rubbed against her leg.

Jody stared out at the alleyway, absentmindedly stroking both cats.

"*Did she say anything to you?*"

"*No,*" Pewter replied.

"*Poor kid. She took a pounding.*" Mrs. Murphy stood on her hind legs, putting her paws on Jody's left knee for a closer look at the young woman's injury. "*This just happened.*"

"*Maybe she got in a fight on the way to school.*"

"*She has field hockey practice early in the morning—Brooks does, too.*"

"*Oh, yeah.*" Pewter cocked her head, trying to capture Jody's attention. "*Maybe her father hit her.*"

Kendrick Miller possessed a vicious temper. Not that anyone outside of the family ever saw him hit his wife or only child, but people looked at him sideways sometimes.

The light crunch of a footfall alerted the cats. Jody, still crying, heard nothing. Sandy Brashiers, whose car was parked behind the market, stopped in his tracks.

"Jody!" he exclaimed, quickly bending down to help her.

She swung her body away from him. The cats moved out of the way. "I'm all right."

He peered at her shiner. "You've been better. Come on, I'll run you over to Larry Johnson. Can't hurt to have the doctor take a look. You can't take a chance with your eyes, honey."

"Don't call me honey." Her vehemence astonished even her.

"I'm sorry." He blushed. "Come on."

"No."

"Jody, if you won't let me take you to Dr. Johnson, then I'll have to take you home. I can't just leave you here."

The backdoor of the post office swung open, and Harry stepped out; she had heard Jody's voice. Miranda was right behind her.

"Oh, dear," Miranda whispered.

Harry came over. "Jody, that's got to hurt."

"I'm all right!" She stood up.

"That's debatable." Sandy was losing patience.

Miranda put a motherly arm around the girl's shoulders. "What happened?"

"Nothing."

"She got pasted away," Pewter offered.

"I suggested that I take her to Larry Johnson—to be on the safe side." Sandy shoved his hands into his corduroy pockets.

Jody balefully implored Miranda with her one good eye. "I don't want anyone to see me."

"You can't hide for two weeks. That's about how long it will take for your raccoon eye to disappear." Harry didn't like the look of that eye.

"Now, Jody, you just listen to me," Miranda persisted. "I

am taking you to Larry Johnson's. You can't play Russian roulette with your health. Mr. Brashiers will tell Mr. Fletcher that you're at the doctor's office so you won't get in trouble at school."

"Nobody cares about me. And don't call Mr. Fletcher. Just leave him out of it."

"People care." Miranda patted her and hugged her. "But for right now you come with me."

Encouraged and soothed by Miranda, Jody climbed into the older woman's ancient Ford Falcon.

Harry knitted her eyebrows in concern. Sandy, too. Without knowing it they were mirror images of one another.

Sandy finally spoke. "Coach Hallvard can be rough, but not that rough."

"Maybe she got into a fight with another kid at school," Harry said, thinking out loud.

"Over what?" Pewter asked.

"Boys. Drugs. PMS." Mrs. Murphy flicked her tail in irritation.

"You can be cynical." Pewter noticed a praying mantis in the crepe myrtle.

"Not cynical. Realistic."

Tucker waddled out of the post office. Fast asleep, she had awakened to find no one in the P.O. *"What's going on?"*

"High-school drama." The cats rubbed it in. *"And you missed it."*

Larry Johnson phoned Irene Miller, who immediately drove to his office. But Jody kept her mouth shut...especially in front of her mother.

Later that afternoon, Janice Walker dropped by the post office. "Harry, you ought to be a detective! How did you know it was Sean Hallahan? When you called me back yesterday to tell me, I wasn't sure, but he came by this morning to apologize. He even took time off from school to do it."

"Two and two." Harry flipped up the divider between the mail room and the public area. "He sounds like his dad. He can be a smart-ass, and hey, wouldn't it be wild to do something like that? He'll be a hero to all the kids at St. Elizabeth's."

"Never thought of it that way," Janice replied.

"You know, I was thinking of calling in BoomBoom Craycroft's demise." Harry's eyes twinkled.

Janice burst out laughing. "You're awful!"

11

Roscoe glanced out his window across the pretty quad that was the heart of St. Elizabeth's. Redbrick buildings, simple Federal style, surrounded the green. Two enormous oaks anchored either end, their foliage an electrifying orange-yellow.

Behind the "home" buildings, as they were known, stood later additions, and beyond those the gym and playing fields beckoned, a huge parking lot between them.

The warm oak paneling gave Roscoe's office an inviting air. A burl partner's desk rested in the middle of the room. A leather sofa, two leather chairs, and a coffee table blanketed with books filled up one side of the big office.

Not an academic, Roscoe made a surprisingly good headmaster. His lack of credentials bothered the teaching staff, who had originally wanted one of their own, namely Sandy Brashiers or even Ed Sugarman. But Roscoe over the last seven years had won over most of them. For one thing, he knew how to raise money as he had a "selling" personality and a wealth of good business contacts. For another, he was a good administrator. His MBA from the Wharton School at University of Pennsylvania stood him in good stead.

"Come in." He responded to the firm knock at the door, then heard a loud "Don't you dare!"

He quickly opened the door to find his secretary, April, and Sandy Brashiers yelling at each other.

April apologized. "He didn't ask for an appointment. He walked right by me."

"April, stop being so officious." Sandy brushed her off.

"You have no right to barge in here." She planted her hands on her slim hips.

Roscoe, voice soothing, patted her on her padded shoulder. "That's all right. I'm accustomed to Mr. Brashiers's impetuosity."

He motioned for Sandy to come in while winking at April, who blushed with pleasure.

"What can I do for you, Sandy?"

"Drop dead" was what Sandy wanted to say. Instead he cleared his throat. "I'm worried about Jody Miller. She's become withdrawn, and this morning I found her behind the post office. She had a bruised cheek and a black eye and refused to talk about it."

"There is instability in the home. It was bound to surface in Jody eventually." Roscoe did not motion for Sandy to sit down. He leaned against his desk, folding his arms across his chest.

"A black eye counts for more than instability. That girl needs help."

"Sandy," Roscoe enunciated carefully, "I can't accuse her parents of abuse without her collaboration. And who's to say Kendrick hit her? It could have been anybody."

"How can you turn away?" Sandy impulsively accused the florid, larger man.

"I am not turning away. I will investigate the situation, but I advise you to be prudent. Until we know what's amiss or until Jody herself comes forward, any accusation would be extremely irresponsible."

"Don't lecture *me*."

"Don't lecture me."

"You don't give a damn about that girl's well-being. You sure as hell give a damn about her father's contributions to your film project—money we could use elsewhere."

"I've got work to do. I told you I'll look into it." Roscoe dropped his folded arms to his sides, then pointed a finger in Sandy's reddening face. "Butt out. If you stir up a hornet's nest, you'll get stung worse than the rest of us."

"What's that shopworn metaphor supposed to mean?" Sandy clenched his teeth.

"That I know your secret."

Sandy blanched. "I don't have any secrets."

Roscoe pointed again. "Try me. Just try me. You'll never teach anywhere again."

Livid, Sandy slammed the door on his way out. April stuck her blond-streaked head back in the office.

Roscoe smiled. "Ignore him. The man thrives on emotional scenes. The first week of school he decried the fostering of competition instead of cooperation. Last week he thought Sean Hallahan should be censured for a sexist remark that I think was addressed to Karen Jensen—'Hey, baby!'" Roscoe imitated Sean. "Today he's frothing at the mouth because Jody Miller has a black eye. My God."

"I don't know how you put up with him," April replied sympathetically.

"It's my job." Roscoe smiled expansively.

"Maury McKinchie's on line two."

"Who's on line one?"

"Your wife."

"Okay." He punched line one. "Honey, let me call you back. Are you in the office?"

Naomi said she was, her office being in the building opposite his on the other side of the quad. He then punched line two. "Hello."

"Roscoe, I'd like to shoot some football and maybe field hockey practice . . . just a few minutes. I'm trying to pull together dynamic images for the alumni dinner in December."

"Got a date in mind?"

"Why don't I just shoot the next few games?" The director paused. "I've got footage for you to check. You'll like it."

"Fine." Roscoe smiled.

"How about a foursome this Saturday? Keswick at nine?"

"Great."

Roscoe hung up. He buzzed April. "You handled Sandy Brashiers very well," he told her.

"He gives me a pain. He just pushed right by me!"

"You did a good job. Your job description doesn't include tackling temporary principals and full-time busybodies."

"Thank you."

"Remind me to tell the coaches that Maury will be filming some football and hockey games."

"Will do."

He took his figner off the intercom button and sat in his swivel chair, feeling satisfied with himself.

12

Harry sorted her own mail, tossing most of it into the wastebasket. She spent each morning stuffing mailboxes. By the time she got to her own mail, she hadn't the patience to wade through appeals for money, catalogs, and flyers. Each evening she threw a canvas totebag jammed with her mail onto the bench seat of the old Ford truck. On those beautiful days when she walked home from work, she slung it over her shoulder.

She'd be walking for the next week regardless of weather because not only was the carburetor fritzed out on the truck, but a mouse had nibbled through the starter wires. Mrs. Murphy needed to step up her rodent control.

Harry dreaded the bill. No matter how hard she tried, she

couldn't keep up with expenses. She lived frugally, keeping within a budget, but no matter how careful her plans, telephone companies changed rates, the electric company edged up its prices, and the county commissioners lived to raise Albemarle taxes.

She often wondered how people with children made it. They'd make it better if they didn't work for the postal service, she thought to herself.

Gray clouds, sodden, dropped lower and lower. The first big raindrop splattered as she was about two miles from home. Tee Tucker and Mrs. Murphy moved faster. Pewter, with a horror of getting wet, ran ahead.

"I've never seen that cat move that fast," Harry said out loud.

A dark green Chevy half-ton slowly headed toward her. She waved as Fair braked.

"Come on, kids," she called as the three animals raced toward Fair.

As if on cue the clouds opened the minute Harry closed the passenger door of the truck.

"Hope you put your fertilizer down."

"Back forty," she replied laconically.

He slowed for another curve as they drove in silence.

"You're Mary Sunshine."

"Preoccupied. Sorry."

They drove straight into the barn. Harry hopped out and threw on her raincoat. Fair put on his yellow slicker, then backed the truck out, parking at the house so Pewter could run inside. He returned to help Harry bring in the horses, who were only too happy to get fed.

Mrs. Murphy and Tucker stayed in the barn.

"These guys look good." Fair smiled at Gin Fizz, Tomahawk, and Poptart.

"Thanks. Sometimes I forget how old Tomahawk's getting to be, but then I forget how old I'm getting to be."

"We're only in our thirties. It's a good time."

She scooped out the sweet feed. "Some days I think it is. Some days I think it isn't." She tossed the scoop back into the feed bin. "Fair, you don't have to help. Lucky for me you came along the road when you did."

"Many hands make light work. You won't be riding tonight."

The rain, like gray sheets of iron, obscured the house from view.

"The weatherman didn't call for this, nor did Miranda."

"Her knee failed." He laughed. Miranda predicted rain according to whether her knee throbbed or not.

She clapped on an ancient cowboy hat, her rain hat. "Better make a run for it."

"Why don't you put me under your raincoat?" Mrs. Murphy asked politely.

Hearing the plaintive meow, Harry paused, then picked up the kitty, cradling her under her coat.

"Ready, steady, GO!" Fair sang out as he cut the lights in the barn.

He reached the backdoor first, opening it for Harry and a wet Tucker.

Once inside the porch they shook off the rain, hung up their coats, stamped their feet, and hurried into the kitchen. A chill had descended with the rain. The temperature plunged ten degrees and was dropping still.

She made fresh coffee while he fed the dog and cats.

Harry had doughnuts left over from the morning.

They sat down and enjoyed this zero-star meal. It was better than going hungry.

"Well—?"

"Well, what?" She swallowed, not wishing to speak with her mouth full.

"What's the matter?"

She put the rest of her glazed doughnut on the plate. "Jody Miller had a black eye and wouldn't tell anyone how she got it. The kid was crying so hard it hurt to see her."

"How'd you find out?"

"She cut classes and was sitting on the stoop behind Market's store."

"I found her first." Pewter lifted her head out of the food bowl.

"Pewter, you're such an egotist."

"Look who's talking," the gray cat answered Mrs. Murphy sarcastically. *"You think the sun rises and sets on your fur."*

"Miranda drove her over to Larry Johnson's. She stayed until Irene arrived. Irene wasn't too helpful, according to Miranda, a reliable source if ever there was one."

"Jody's a mercurial kid."

"Aren't they all?"

"I suppose." He got up to pour himself another coffee. "I'm finally warming up. Of course, it could be your presence."

"I'm going to throw up." Pewter gagged.

"You don't have a romantic bone in your body," Tucker complained.

"In fact, Pewter, no one can see the bones in your body."

"Ha, ha," the gray cat said dryly.

"Do you think it would be nosy if I called Irene? I'm worried."

"Harry, everyone in Crozet is nosy, so that's not an issue." He smiled. "Besides which, you and Miranda found her."

"I found her," Pewter interjected furiously.

"You are not getting another morsel to eat." Harry shook her finger at the gray cat, who turned her back on her, refusing to have anything to do with this irritating human.

Harry picked up the old wall phone and dialed. "Hi, Irene, it's Mary Minor." She paused. "No trouble at all. I know Miranda was glad to help. I was just calling to see if Jody's all right."

On the other end of the line Irene explained, "She got into a fight with one of the girls at practice—she won't say which one—and then she walked into chemistry class and pulled a D on a pop quiz. Jody has never gotten a D in her life. She'll be fine, and thank you so much for calling. 'Bye."

" 'Bye." Harry hung up the receiver slowly. "She doesn't know any more than I do. She said the girls got into a fight at field hockey practice, and Jody got a D on a pop quiz in chemistry."

"Now you can relax. You've got your answer."

"Fair"—Harry gestured, both hands open—"there's no way that vain kid is going to walk into chemistry class with a fresh shiner. Jody Miller fusses with her makeup more than most movie stars. Besides, Ed Sugarman would have sent her to the infirmary. Irene Miller is either dumb as a stick or not telling the truth."

"I vote for dumb as a stick." He smiled. "You're making a mountain out of a molehill. If Jody Miller lied to her mother, it's not a federal case. I recall you fibbing to your mother on the odd occasion."

"Not very often."

"Your nose is growing." He laughed.

Harry dialed Ed Sugarman, the chemistry teacher. "Hi, Ed, it's Mary Minor Haristeen." She paused a moment. "Do I need chemistry lessons? Well, I guess it depends on the kind of chemistry you're talking about." She paused. "First off, excuse me for butting in, but I want to know if Jody Miller came to your class today."

"Jody never came to class today," Ed replied.

"Well—that answers my question."

"In fact, I was about to call her parents. I know she was at field hockey practice because I drove by the field on my way in this morning. Is something wrong?"

"Uh—I don't know. She was behind Market's store this morning sporting a black eye and tears."

"I'm sorry to hear that. She's a bright girl, but her grades are sliding..." He hesitated. "One sees this often if there's tension in the home."

"Thanks, Ed. I hope I haven't disturbed you."

"You haven't disturbed me." He paused for a moment and then said as an aside, "Okay, honcy." He then returned to Harry. "Doris says hello."

"Tell Doris I said hello also," Harry said.

Harry bid Ed good-bye, pressed the disconnect button, and thought for a minute.

"Want to go to a movie?"

"I'm not going out in that."

The rain pounded even harder on the tin roof. "Like bullets."

"I rented *The Madness of King George*. We could watch that."

"Popcorn?"

"Yep."

"If you'd buy a microwave, you could pop the corn a lot

faster." He read the directions on the back of the popcorn packet.

"I'm not buying a microwave. The truck needs new starter wires—the mice chewed them—needs new tires, too, and I'm even putting that off until I'm driving on threads." She slapped a pot on the stove. "And it needs a new carburetor."

After the movie, Fair hoped she'd ask him to stay. He made comment after comment about how slick the roads were.

Finally Harry said, "Sleep in the guest room."

"I was hoping I could sleep with you."

"Not tonight." She smiled, evading hurting his feelings. Since she was also evading her own feelings, it worked out nicely for her, temporarily, anyway.

The next morning, Fair cruised out to get the paper. The rain continued steady. He dashed back into the kitchen. As he removed the plastic wrapping and opened the paper, an eight-by-ten-inch black-bordered sheet of paper, an insert, fell on the floor. Fair picked it up. "What in the hell is this?"

13

"Maury McKinchie, forty-seven, died suddenly in his home October third," Fair mumbled as he read aloud Maury's cinematic accomplishments and the fact that he lettered in football at USC. He peered over Mrs. Murphy, who jumped on the paper to read it herself.

Both humans and the cat stood reading the insert. Pewter reposed on the counter. She was interested, but Murphy jumped up first. Why start the day with a fight? Tucker raced around the table, finally sitting on her mother's foot.

"What's going on?" Tucker asked.

"Tucker, Maury McKinchie is dead," Mrs. Murphy answered her.

"Miranda," Harry said when she picked up the phone, "I've just seen it."

"Well, I just saw Maury McKinchie jog down the lane between my house and the post office not ten minutes ago!"

"This is too weird." Harry's voice was even. "As weird as that rattail hair of his." She referred to the short little ponytail Maury wore at the nape of his neck. Definitely not Virginia.

"He wore a color-coordinated jogging suit. Really, the clothes that man wears." Miranda exhaled through her nostrils. "Roscoe was jogging with him."

"Guess he hasn't read the paper." Harry laughed.

"No." She paused. "Isn't this the most peculiar thing. If Sean's behind this again, he realized he can't phone in an obituary anymore. It can't be Sean, though—his father would kill him." She thought out loud.

"And he lost his paper route. Fired. At least, that's what I heard," Harry added.

"Bombs away!" Pewter launched herself from the counter onto the table and hit the paper, tearing it. Both cats and paper skidded off the table.

"Pewter!" Fair exclaimed.

"Aha!" Mrs. Hogendobber exclaimed when she heard Fair's voice in the background. "I knew you two would get back together," she gloated to Harry.

"Don't jump the gun, Miranda." Harry gritted her teeth, knowing a grilling would occur at the post office.

"See you at work," Miranda trilled.

14

"Not another prank!" the Reverend Herbert Jones said when he picked up his mail, commenting on the obituary insert in his paper that morning.

"A vicious person with unresolved authority-figure conflicts," BoomBoom Craycroft intoned. "A potent mixture of chamomile and parsley would help purify this tortured soul."

"Disgusting and not at all funny," Big Mim Sanburne declaimed.

"A sick joke," Lucinda Payne Coles said, picking up her mail and that of the Church of the Good Shepherd.

"Hasn't Maury been working with you on the big alumni fund-raising dinner?" Harry inquired.

"Yes," Little Mim replied.

"What's going on at St. Elizabeth's?" Harry walked out front.

"Nothing. Just because Roscoe and Maury are associated with the school doesn't make the school responsible for these—what should I call them—?" Little Mim flared.

Her mother, awash in navy blue cashmere, tapped Little Mim's hand with a rolled-up magazine.

"Premature death notices." Mim laughed. "Sooner or later they will be accurate. Sean Hallahan has apologized to everyone involved. At least, that's what his father told me. Who has the paper route? That's the logical question."

Marilyn sniffed. Her mother could get her goat faster than anyone on earth. "Roger Davis has the paper route."

"Call his mother," Mim snapped. "And . . . are you listening to me?"

"Yes, Mother."

"Whoever is writing these upsetting things knows a lot about both men."

"Or is a good researcher," Herb's grave voice chimed in.

"Don't look at me," Harry joked. "I never learned how to correctly write in footnotes. You have to do that to be a good researcher."

"Don't be silly. You couldn't have graduated from Smith with honors without learning how to do footnotes." Big Mim unrolled the magazine, grimaced at the photo of an exploded bus, and rolled it back up again. "I'll tell you what's worse than incorrect footnotes . . . lack of manners. Our social skills are so eroded that people don't write thank-you notes anymore . . . and if they did, they couldn't spell."

"Mother, what does that have to do with Roscoe's and Maury's fake obits?"

"Rude. Bad manners." She tapped the magazine sharply on the edge of the counter.

"Hey!" Little Mim blurted, her head swiveling in the direction of the door.

Maury McKinchie pushed through, beheld the silence and joked, "Who died?"

"You," Harry replied sardonically.

"Ah, come on, my last movie wasn't that bad."

"Haven't you opened your paper?" Little Mim edged toward him.

"No."

Herb handed the insert to Maury. "Take a look."

"Well, I'll be damned." Maury whistled.

"Who do you think did this?" Miranda zoomed to the point.

He laughed heartily. "I can think of two ex-wives who would do it, only they'd shoot me first. The obit would be for real."

"You really don't have any idea?" Herb narrowed his eyes.

"Not a one." Maury raised his bushy eyebrows as well as his voice.

Big Mim checked her expensive Schaffhausen watch. "I'm due up at the Garden Club. We vote on which areas to beautify today. A big tussle, as usual. Good-bye, all. Hope you get to the bottom of this."

" 'Bye," they called after her.

Maury, though handsome, had developed a paunch. Running would remove it, he hoped. Being a director, he had a habit of taking charge, giving orders. He'd discovered that didn't work in Crozet. An even bigger shock had befallen him when Darla became the breadwinner. He was searching for the right picture to get his career back on track. He flew to

L.A. once a month and burned up the phone and fax lines the rest of the time.

"Mother wants to create a garden around the old railroad station. What do you bet she gets her way?" Little Mim jumped to a new topic. There wasn't anything she could do about the fake obituary anyway.

"The odds are on her side." Harry picked up the tall metal wastebasket overflowing with paper.

"I can do that for you." Maury seized the wastebasket. "Where does it go?"

"Market's new dumpster," Miranda said.

"Take me one minute."

As he left, Little Mim said, "He's a terrible flirt, isn't he?"

"Don't pay any attention to him," Harry advised.

"I didn't say he bothered me."

Maury returned, placing the wastebasket next to the table where people sorted their mail.

"Thank you," Harry said.

He winked at her. "My pleasure. You can say you've encountered an angel today."

"Beg pardon?" Harry said.

"If I'm dead, I'm living uptown, Harry, not downtown." He laughed and walked out with a wave.

Susan Tucker arrived just as Miranda had begun her third degree on the subject of Fair staying over.

"Miranda, why do you do this to me?" Harry despaired.

"Because I want to see you happy."

"Telling everyone that my ex-husband spent the night isn't going to make me happy, and I told you, Miranda, nothing happened. I am so tired of this."

"Methinks the lady doth protest too much." Mrs. Hogendobber coyly quoted Shakespeare.

"Oh, pul-lease." Harry threw up her hands.

Susan, one eyebrow arched, said, "Something did happen. Okay, maybe it wasn't sex, but he got his foot in the door."

"And his ass in the guest room. It was raining cats and dogs."

"*I beg your pardon,*" Mrs. Murphy, lounging in the mail cart, called out.

"All right." Harry thought the cat wanted a push so she gave her a ride in the mail cart.

"*I love this....*" Murphy put her paws on the side of the cart.

"Harry, I'm waiting."

"For what?"

"For what's going on with you and Fair."

"NOTHING!"

Her shout made Tucker bark.

Pewter, hearing the noise, hurried in through the back animal door. "*What's the matter?*"

"*Mrs. H. and Susan think Mom's in love with Fair because he stayed at the house last night.*"

"*Oh.*" Pewter checked the wastebasket for crumbs. "*They need to stop for tea.*"

Susan held up her hands. "You are so sensitive."

"Wouldn't you be?" Harry fired back.

"I guess I would."

"Harry, I didn't mean to upset you." Miranda, genuinely contrite, walked over to the small refrigerator, removing the pie she'd baked the night before.

Pewter was ecstatic.

Harry sighed audibly. "I want his attention, but I don't think I want him. I'm being perverse."

"Maybe vengeful is closer to the mark." Miranda pulled no punches.

"Well—I'd like to think I was a better person than that, but maybe I'm not." She glanced out the big front window. "Going to be a nice day."

"Well, my cherub is playing in the field hockey game, rain or shine," Susan said. "Danny's got football practice, so I'll watch the first half of Brooks's game and the last half of Danny's practice. I wish I could figure out how to be in two places at the same time."

"If I get my chores done, I'll drop by," Harry said. "I'd love to see Brooks on the attack. Which reminds me, got to call and see if my truck is ready."

"I thought you didn't have the money to fix it," Susan said.

"He'll let me pay over time." As she was making the call, Miranda and Susan buzzed about events.

"Miranda, do you think these false obituaries have anything to do with Halloween?" Harry asked as she hung up the phone.

"I don't know."

"*It's only the first week of October.*" Tucker thought out loud. "*Halloween is a long way away.*"

"*What about all those Christmas catalogs clogging the mail?*" Pewter hovered over the pie.

"*Humans like to feel anxious,*" Tucker declared.

"*Imagine worrying about Christmas now. They might not live to Christmas,*" Mrs. Murphy cracked.

The other two animals laughed.

"*You know what I would do if I were one of them?*" Pewter flicked off the dishcloth covering the pie. "*I'd go to an Arab country. That would take care of Christmas.*"

"Take care of a lot else, too," Mrs. Murphy commented wryly.

Miranda noticed in the nick of time. "Shoo!"

Harry grabbed the phone. "Hello, may I have the obituary department?"

Miranda, Susan, the two cats, and the dog froze to listen.

"Obituary."

"Janice, have you heard about the insert?"

"Yes, but it's only in the papers of one route, Roger Davis's route. I can't be blamed for this one."

"I wouldn't want to be in Roger Davis's shoes right now," Harry said.

15

"I didn't do it." Roger, hands in his pants pockets, stared stubbornly at the headmaster and the temporary principal.

"You picked up the newspapers from the building at Rio Road?" Sandy questioned.

"Yes."

"Did you go through the papers?" Roscoe asked.

"No, I just deliver them. I had no idea that death notice on Mr. McKinchie was in there."

"Did anyone else go with you this morning? Like Sean Hallahan?"

"No, sir," Roger answered Roscoe Fletcher. "I don't like Sean."

Sandy took another tack. "Would you say that you and Sean Hallahan are rivals?"

Roger stared at the ceiling, then leveled his gaze at Sandy. "No. I don't like him, that's all."

"He's a bit of a star, isn't he?" Sandy continued his line of reasoning.

"Good football players usually are."

"No, I mean he's really a star now for putting the false obituary in the paper, Mr. Fletcher's obituary."

Roger looked from Sandy to Roscoe, then back to Sandy. "Some kids think it was very cool."

"Did you?" Roscoe inquired.

"No, sir," Roger replied.

"Could anyone have tampered with your papers without you knowing about it?" Roscoe swiveled in his chair to glance out the window. Children were walking briskly between classes.

"I suppose they could. Each of us who has a route goes to pick up our papers . . . they're on the landing. We've each got a spot because each route has a different number of customers. We're supposed to have the same number, but we don't. People cancel. Some areas grow faster than others. So you go to your place on the loading dock and pick up your papers. All I do is fold them to stick them in the tube. And on rainy days, put them in plastic bags."

"So someone could have tampered with your pile?" Roscoe persisted.

"Yes, but I don't know how they could do it without being seen. There are always people at the paper. Not many at that hour." He thought. "I guess it could be done."

"Could someone have followed after you on your route, pulled the paper out of the tube and put in the insert?" Sandy liked Roger but he didn't believe him. "One of your friends, perhaps?"

"Yes. It would be a lot of work."

"Who knows your paper route?" Roscoe glanced at the Queen Anne clock.

"Everyone. I mean, all my friends."

"Okay, Roger. You can go." Roscoe waved him away.

Sandy opened the door for the tall young man. "I really hope you didn't do this, Roger."

"Mr. Brashiers, I didn't."

Sandy closed the door, turning to Roscoe. "Well?"

"I don't know." Roscoe held up his hands. "He's an unlikely candidate, although circumstances certainly point to him."

"Damn kids," Sandy muttered, then spoke louder. "Have you investigated the Jody Miller incident further?"

"I spoke to Coach Hallvard. She said no fight occurred at practice. I'm going to see Kendrick Miller later today. I wish I knew what I was going to say."

16

Rumbling along toward St. Elizabeth's, Harry felt her heart sink lower and lower. The truck repairs cost $289.16, which demolished her budget. Paying over time helped, but $289 was $289. She wanted to cry but felt that it wasn't right to cry over money. She sniffled instead.

"*There's got to be a way to make more money,*" Mrs. Murphy whispered.

"*Catnip,*" Pewter replied authoritatively. "*She could grow acres of catnip, dry it, and sell it.*"

"*Not such a bad idea—could you keep out of the crop?*"

"*Could you?*" Pewter challenged.

They pulled into the school parking lot peppered with

Mercedes Benzes, BMWs, Volvos, a few Porsches, and one Ford Falcon.

The game was just starting with the captains in the center of the field, Karen Jensen for St. Elizabeth's and Darcy Kelly for St. Anne's Belfield from Charlottesville.

Roscoe had pride of place on the sidelines. Naomi squeezed next to him. April Shively sat on Roscoe's left side. She took notes as he spoke, which drove Naomi wild. She struggled to contain her irritation. Susan and Miranda waved to Harry as she climbed up to them. Little Mim sat directly behind Roscoe. Maury, flirtatious, amused her with Hollywood stories about star antics. He told her she was naturally prettier than those women who had the help of plastic surgery, two-hundred-dollar haircuts, and fabulous lighting. Little Mim began to brighten.

Pretty Coach Renee Hallvard, her shiny blond pageboy swinging with each stride, paced the sidelines. St. Anne's won the toss. While Karen Jensen trotted to midfield, the other midfielder, Jody Miller, twirled her stick in anticipation.

Irene and Kendrick Miller sat high in the stands for a better view. Kendrick had requested that he and Roscoe get together after the game. His attendance was noted since he rarely turned up at school functions, claiming work kept him pinned down.

People commented on the fact that Sean Hallahan and Roger Davis weren't at the game. Everyone had an opinion on that.

St. Anne's, a powerhouse in field hockey and lacrosse, worked the ball downfield, but Karen Jensen, strong and fast, stole the ball from the attacker in a display of finesse that brought the Redhawk supporters to their feet.

Brooks, an attacker, sped along the side, then cut in, a basic pattern, but Brooks, slight and swift, dusted her defender to pick up Karen's pinpoint pass. She fired a shot at the goalie, one of the best in the state, who gave St. Anne's enormous confidence.

The first quarter, speedy, resulted in no score.

"Brooks has a lot of poise under pressure." Harry was proud of the young woman.

"She's going to need it," Susan predicted.

"Quite a game." Miranda, face flushed, was remembering her days of field hockey for Crozet High in 1950.

The second quarter the girls played even faster and harder. Darcy Kelly drew first blood for St. Anne's. Karen Jensen, jogging back to the center, breathed a few words to her team. They struck back immediately with three razorsharp passes resulting in a goal off the stick of Elizabeth Davis, Roger's older sister.

At halftime both coaches huddled with their girls. The trainers exhausted themselves putting the teams back together. The body checks, brutal, were taking their toll.

Sandy Brashiers, arriving late, sat on the corner of the bleachers.

"Jody's playing a good game." Roscoe leaned down to talk low to Sandy. "Maybe this will be easier than I thought."

"Hope so," Sandy said.

"Roscoe," Maury McKinchie teased him, "what kind of headmaster are you when a kid puts your obituary in the paper?"

"Looks who's talking. Maury, the walking dead," Roscoe bellowed.

"Only in Hollywood," Maury said, making fun of himself. "Oh, well, I've made a lot of mistakes on all fronts."

Father Michael, sitting next to Maury, said, "To err is human, to forgive divine."

"To err is human, to forgive is extraordinary." Roscoe chuckled.

They both shut up when Mrs. Florence Rubicon, the aptly, or perhaps prophetically, named Latin teacher, waved a red-and-gold Redhawks pennant and shouted, *"Carpe diem—"*

Sandy shouted back, finishing the sentence, *"Quam minimum credula postero."* Meaning "Don't trust in tomorrow."

Those who remembered their Latin laughed.

A chill made Harry shiver.

"Cold?" Miranda asked.

"No—just"—she shrugged—"a notion."

The game was turning into a great one. Both sides cheered themselves hoarse, and at the very end Teresa Pietro scored a blazing goal for St. Anne's. The Redhawks, crestfallen, dragged off the field, hurt so badly by the defeat that they couldn't rejoice in how spectacularly they had played. It would take time for them to realize they'd participated in one of the legendary field hockey games.

Jody Miller, utterly wretched because Teresa Pierro had streaked by her, was stomping off the field, her head down. Her mother ran out to console her; her father stayed in the stands to talk to people and to wait for Roscoe, besieged, as always.

When Maury McKinchie walked over to soothe her, she hit him in the gut with her stick. He keeled over.

Irene, horrified, grabbed the stick from her daughter's hand. She looked toward Kendrick, who had missed the incident.

Coach Hallvard quickly ran over. Brooks, Karen, Elizabeth, and Jody's other teammates stared in disbelief.

"Jody, go to the lockers—NOW," the coach ordered.

"I think she'd better come home with me," Irene said tightly.

"Mrs. Miller, I'll send her straight home. In fact, I'll drive her home, but I need to talk to her first. Her behavior affects the entire team."

Jody, white-lipped, glared at everyone, then suddenly laughed. "I'm sorry, Mr. McKinchie. If only I'd done that to Teresa Pietro."

Maury, gasping for breath, smiled gamely. "I don't look anything like Teresa Pietro."

"Are you all right?" Coach Hallvard asked him.

"Yes, it's the only time I've been grateful for my spare tire."

Coach Hallvard put her hand under Jody's elbow, propelling her toward the lockers.

Roscoe turned around to look up to Kendrick, who was being filled in on the incident. He whispered to his wife, "Go see what you can do for Maury." Then he said to April, hovering nearby, "I think you'd better go to the locker room with Coach Hallvard and the team, right?"

"Right." April trotted across the field, catching up with Naomi, who pretended she was happy for the company.

Father Michael felt a pang for not pursuing Jody the morning she came to see him. He was realizing how much she had needed him then.

Brooks, confused like the rest of her teammates, obediently walked back to the locker room while the St. Anne's team piled on the bus.

Mrs. Murphy, prowling the bleachers now that everyone

was down on the sidelines, jerked her head up when she caught a whiff, a remnant of strong perfume.

"*Ugh.*" Pewter seconded her opinion.

They watched Harry chat with her friends about the incident as Roscoe glided over to Kendrick Miller. Sandy Brashiers also watched him, his eyes narrow as slits.

The two men strolled back to the bleachers, not thinking twice about the cats sitting there.

Kendrick glanced across the field at a now upright Maury attended by Irene and Naomi. "He's got both our wives buzzing around him. I guess he'll live."

Roscoe, surprised at Kendrick's cool response, said, "Doesn't sound as if you want him to—"

Kendrick, standing, propped one foot on the bleacher higher than the one he was standing on. "Don't like him. One of those dudes who comes here with money and thinks he's superior to us. That posture of detached amusement wears thin."

"Perhaps, but he's been very good to St. Elizabeth's."

Quickly Kendrick said, "I understand your position, Roscoe, you'd take money from the devil if you had to. You're a good businessman."

"I'd rather be a good headmaster," Roscoe replied coolly. "I was hoping you could illuminate me concerning Jody."

"Because she hit Maury?" His voice rose. "Wish I'd seen it."

"No, although that's an issue now. She skipped school the other day with a black eye. She said she got it in practice, but Coach Hallvard said, no, she didn't and as far as she knew there were no fights after practice. Does she roughhouse with neighborhood kids or—?"

"Do I beat her?" Kendrick's face darkened. "I know what

people say behind my back, Roscoe. I don't beat my daughter. I don't beat my wife. Hell, I'm not home enough to get mad at them. And yes—I have a bad temper."

Roscoe demurred. "Please, don't misunderstand me. My concern is the well-being of every student at St. Elizabeth's. Jody, a charming young girl, is, well, more up and down lately. And her grades aren't what they were last year."

"I'll worry about it when the first report card comes out." Kendrick leaned on his knee.

"That will be in another month. Let's try to pull together and get those grades up before then." Roscoe's smile was all mouth, no eyes.

"You're telling me I'm not a good father." Kendrick glowered. "You've been talking to my bride, I suppose." The word "bride" dripped with venom.

"No, no, I haven't." Roscoe's patience began to erode.

"You're a rotten liar." Kendrick laughed harshly.

"Kendrick, I'm sorry I'm wasting your time." He stepped down out of the bleachers and left a furious Kendrick to pound down and leave in the opposite direction.

Sandy Brashiers awaited Roscoe at the other end. "He doesn't look too happy."

"He's an ass." Roscoe, sensitive and tired, thought he heard implicit criticism in Sandy's voice.

"I waited for you because I think we need to have an assembly or small workshop about how to handle losing. Jody's behavior was outrageous."

Roscoe hunched his massive shoulders. "I don't think we have to make that big a deal out of it."

"You and I will never see eye to eye, will we?" Sandy said.

"I'll handle it," Roscoe said sternly.

A pause followed, broken by Sandy. "I don't want to make

you angry. I'm not trying to obstruct you, but this gives us a chance to address the subject of winning and losing. Sports are blown out of proportion anyway."

"They may be blown out of proportion, but they bring in alumni funds." Roscoe shifted his weight.

"We're an institution of learning, not an academy for sports."

"Sandy, not now. I'm fresh out of patience," Roscoe warned.

"If not now, when?"

"This isn't the time or place for a philosophical discussion of the direction of secondary education in general or St. Elizabeth's in particular." Roscoe popped a hard strawberry candy in his mouth and moved off in the direction of the girls' locker room. Perhaps April had some information for him. He noticed that Naomi had shepherded Maury toward the quad, so he assumed she would be serving him coffee, tea, or spirits in her office. She had a sure touch with people.

The cats scampered out from under the bleachers, catching up with Harry, who was in the parking lot calling for them.

17

Late that night the waxing moon flitted between inky boiling clouds. Mrs. Murphy, unable to sleep, was hunting in the paddock closest to the barn. A sudden gust of wind brought her nose up from the ground. She sniffed the air. A storm, a big one, was streaking in.

Simon, moving fast for him, ran in from the creek. Overhead Flatface swooped low, banked, then headed out to the far fields for one more pass before the storm broke.

"That's it for me." Simon headed to the open barn door. *"Besides, bobcat tracks in the creekbed."*

"Good enough reason."

"Are you coming in?"

"In a minute." She watched the gray animal with the long rat tail shuffle into the barn.

A light wind rustled the leaves. She saw the cornstalks sway, then wiggle in Harry's small garden by the corner of the barn. This proved a handy repository for her "cooked" manure. A red fox, half grown, sashayed out the end, glanced over her shoulder, beheld Mrs. Murphy, put her nose up, and walked away.

Mrs. Murphy loved no fox, for they competed for the same game.

"You stay out of my corn rows," she growled.

"You don't own the world," came the belligerent reply.

A lone screech froze both of them.

"She's a killer." The fox flattened for a minute, then got up.

"You're between a storm and a bobcat. Where's your den?"

"I'm not telling you."

"Don't tell me, but you'd better hike to it fast." A big splat landed on the cat. She thought about the fox's predicament. *"Go into the shavings shed until the storm blows over and the bobcat's gone. Just don't make a habit of it."*

Without a word the fox scooted into the shavings shed, burrowing down in the sweet-smelling chips as the storm broke overhead.

The tiger cat, eyes widened, listened for the bobcat. Another more distant cry, like a woman screaming, told her that the beast headed back to the forest, her natural home. Since the pickings were so good in the fall—lots of fat mice and rats gorged on fallen grain plus fruits left drying on the vine—the bobcat ventured closer to the human habitation.

The wind stiffened, the trees gracefully bent lower. The

field mouse Mrs. Murphy patiently tracked wanted to stay dry. She refused to poke her nose out of her nest.

More raindrops sent the cat into the barn. She climbed the ladder. Simon was arranging his sleeping quarters. His treasures, spread around him, included a worn towel, one leather riding glove, a few scraps of newspaper, and a candy bar that he was saving for a rainy day, which it was.

"Simon, don't you ever throw anything out?"

He smiled. "My mother said I was a pack rat, not a possum."

The force of the rain, unleashed, hit like a baseball bat against the north side of the barn. Flatface, claws down, landed in her cupola. She glanced down at the two friends, ruffled her feathers, then shut her eyes. She disdained earth-bound creatures.

"Flatface," Simon called up to her, "before you go to sleep, how big is the bobcat?"

"Big enough to eat you." She laughed with a whooing sound.

"Really, how big?" he pressed.

She turned her big head nearly upside down. "Thirty to forty pounds and still growing. She's quick, lightning-quick, and smart. Now, if you two peons don't mind, I'm going to sleep. It's turning into a filthy night."

Mrs. Murphy and Simon caught up on the location of the latest beaver dam, fox dens, and one bald-eagle nest. Then the cat told him about the false obituaries.

"Bizarre, isn't it?"

Simon pulled his towel into his hollowed-out nest in the straw. "People put out marshmallows to catch raccoons. Us, too. We love marshmallows. Sure enough, one of us will grab the marshmallow. If we're lucky, the human wants to watch us. If

we're unlucky, we're trapped or the marshmallow is poisoned. I think a human is putting out a marshmallow for another human."

Mrs. Murphy sat a long time, the tip of her tail slowly wafting to and fro. *"It's damned queer bait, Simon, telling someone he's dead."*

"Not just him—everyone."

18

The storm lashed central Virginia for two days, finally moving north to discomfort the Yankees.

Harry's father said storms did Nature's pruning. The farm, apart from some downed limbs, suffered little damage, but a tree was down on the way to Blair Bainbridge's house.

On Saturday, Harry borrowed his thousand-dollar power washer. Merrily she blasted the old green-and-yellow John Deere tractor, her truck, the manure spreader, and, in a fit of squeaky-clean mania, the entire interior of the barn. Not a cobweb remained.

The three horses observed this from the far paddock. By now they were accustomed to Harry's spring and fall fits.

Other humans feeling those same urges worked on Saturday. Miranda aired her linens as she planted her spring bulbs. She'd need the rest of Sunday to finish the bulbs.

The Reverend Jones stocked his woodpile and greeted the chimney sweep by touching his top hat. A little superstition never hurt a pastor.

Fair Haristeen decided to run an inventory on equine drugs at the clinic only to repent as the task devoured the day.

BoomBoom Craycroft, adding orange zest to her list of essences, peeled a dozen of them.

Susan Tucker attacked the attic while Ned edged every tree and flower bed until he thought his fillings would fall out of his teeth from the vibrations of the machine.

Big Mim supervised the overhaul of her once-sunk pontoon boat.

Little Marilyn transferred the old records of St. Elizabeth's benefactors to a computer. Like Fair, she was sorry she had started the job.

Sandy Brashiers made up the questions for a quiz on *Macbeth*.

Jody Miller worked at the car wash with Brooks, Karen, and Roger.

Because of the storm, the car wash was jam-packed. The kids hadn't had time for lunch, so Jody took everyone's order. It was her turn to cross Route 29 and get sandwiches at the gas station–deli on the southwest corner. The Texaco sat between the car wash and the intersection. If only that station had a deli, she wouldn't have to cross the busy highway.

Jimbo Anson slipped her twenty-five dollars for everyone's lunch, his included, as they were famished.

As the day wore on, the temperature climbed into the midsixties. The line of cars extended out to Route 29.

Roscoe Fletcher, his Mercedes station wagon caked in

mud, patiently waited in line. He had turned off Route 29 and moved forward enough to be right in front of the Texaco station. The car wash was behind the gas station itself, so the kids did not yet know their headmaster was in line and he didn't know how many cars were in front of him. The car stereo played *The Marriage of Figaro.* He sang aloud with gusto.

The line crept forward.

Jody headed down to the intersection. Five minutes later she dashed back into the office.

"Where's the food?" Roger, hungry, inquired as he reached in for another dry towel.

She announced, "Mr. Fletcher is in line! He hasn't seen me yet. I'll go as soon as he gets through the line."

"I'll starve by then," Roger said.

"He'll be cool." Karen stuck her head in the door as Roger threw her a bottle of mag washer for aluminum hubcaps.

"Maybe—but I don't want a lecture. I know I was wrong to hit Mr. McKinchie." Her voice rose. "I've had about all the help I can stand. I was wrong. Okay. I apologized. Guess you don't want to see him either." She pointed at Roger, who ignored her.

"Well, he's past the Texaco station. You'd better hide under the desk," Karen yelled. "Jeez, I think everyone in the world is here today." She heard horns beeping out on Route 29. Irene Miller had pulled in behind Roscoe, then Naomi Fletcher in her blue Miata. BoomBoom Craycroft, car wafting fragrances, was just ahead of him.

Roger waved up another car. He bent his tall frame in two as the driver rolled down the window. "What will it be?"

"How about a wash only?"

"Great. Put it in neutral and turn off your car radio."

The driver obeyed instructions while Karen and Brooks slopped the big brushes into the soapy water, working off the worst of the mud.

"Hey, there's Father Michael." Karen noticed the priest's black old-model Mercury. "You'd think the church would get him a better car." She yelled so Jody, scrunched under the desk, could hear her.

"It runs," Brooks commented on the car.

"How many are in the line now?" Roger wiped the sweat from his forehead with the back of his arm as Jimbo walked down to the intersection to direct drivers to form a double line. He needed to unclog the main north-south artery of Charlottesville.

"Number twenty-two just pulled in," Brooks replied.

"Unreal." Karen whistled.

Roscoe rolled down his window, flooding the car wash with Mozart. He was three cars away from his turn.

"You-all should learn your Mozart," he called to them. "Greatest composer who ever lived."

His wife shouted from her car, "It's the weekend, Roscoe. You can't tell them what to do."

"Right!" Karen laughed, waving at Naomi.

"I bet you listen to Melissa Etheridge and Sophie B. Hawkins," Roscoe said as he offered her strawberry hard candy, which she refused.

"Yeah." Karen turned her attention to the car in front of her. "They're great. I like Billy Ray Cyrus and Reba McEntire, too."

Irene rolled her window down. "Where's Jody?"

"She went to the deli to get our lunches, and I hope she hurries up!" Roger told a half-truth.

"What about Bach?" Roscoe sang out, still on his music topic.

"The Beatles," Karen answered. "I mean, that's like rock Bach."

"No, Bill Haley and the Comets are like rock Bach," Roscoe said as he sucked on the candy in his mouth. "Jerry Lee Lewis."

The kids took a deep breath and yelled and swung their hips in unison, "Elvis!"

By the time Roscoe put his left tire into the groove, everyone was singing "Hound Dog," which made him laugh. He noticed Jody peeking out of the office. The laughter, too much for her, had lured her from under the desk.

He pointed his finger at her. "You ain't nothin' but a hound dog."

She laughed, but her smile disappeared when her mother yelled at her. "I thought you were at the deli."

"I'm on my way. We're backed up," she said since she'd heard what Roger told her mother.

"Mr. Fletcher, shut your window," Karen advised as the station wagon lurched into the car wash.

"Oh, right." He hit the electric button, and the window slid shut with a hum.

As the tail end of the Mercedes disappeared in a sheet of water, the yellow neon light flashed on and Karen waved Irene on. "He's so full of shit," she said under her breath.

BoomBoom hollered out her window, "Stress. Irene, this is too much stress. Come meet me at Ruby Tuesday's after the car wash."

"Okay," Irene agreed. Her left tire was in the groove now. "I want the works." Irene handed over fifteen dollars. Karen made change.

Roger, at the button to engage the track, waited for Roscoe to finish. The light telling him to put through the next vehicle didn't come on. Minutes passed.

"I'm in a hurry." Irene tried to sound pleasant.

"It's been like this all day, Mrs. Miller." Karen smiled tightly.

Brooks looked down the line. "Maybe Mr. Fletcher's out but the light didn't come on. I'll go see."

Brooks loped alongside the car wash, arriving at the end where the brown station wagon, nose out, squatted. The tail of the vehicle remained on the track. The little metal cleats in the track kept pushing the car.

Brooks knocked on the window. Roscoe, sitting upright, eyes straight ahead, didn't reply.

"Mr. Fletcher, you need to move out."

No reply. She knocked harder. Still no reply.

"Mr. Fletcher, please drive out." She waited, then opened the door. The first thing she noticed was that Mr. Fletcher had wet his pants, which shocked her. Then she realized he was dead.

19

It wasn't funny, but Rick Shaw wanted to laugh. Mozart blared through the speakers, and the car's rear end shone like diamonds after endless washings.

Naomi Fletcher, in shock, had been taken home by an officer.

Diana Robb, a paramedic with the rescue squad, patiently waited while Sheriff Shaw and Deputy Cooper painstakingly examined the car.

Jimbo Anson turned off the water when Rick told him it was okay.

Roget Davis directed traffic around the waiting line. He was relieved when a young officer pulled up in a squad car.

"Don't go yet," Tom Kline told Roger. "I'll need your help."

Obediently, Roger continued to direct traffic onto the Greenbrier side street. He wanted to comfort Brooks for the shock she had suffered, but that would have to wait.

Rick said under his breath to Coop, "Ever tell you about the guy who died on the escalator over in Richmond? I was fresh out of school. This was my first call as a rookie. No one could get on or off until cleared, and the store didn't turn off the motor. People were running in place. Super aerobics. 'Course the stiff rolled right up to the step-off, where his hair caught in the steps. By the time I reached him, he was half scalped."

"Gross." She knew that Rick wasn't unfeeling, but a law enforcement officer sees so much that a protective shell develops over emotions.

"Let's have the boys take photos, bag the contents of the station wagon." He reached in and, with his gloves on, snapped off the stereo. "Okay, we're done," he called over his shoulder to Diana Robb and Cooper behind him.

"Sheriff, what do you think?" the paramedic asked him.

"Looks like a heart attack. He's the right age for it. I've learned over the years, though, to defer to the experts. Unless Mrs. Fletcher objects, we'll send the body to Bill Moscowitz—he's a good coroner."

"If you don't stop smoking those Chesterfields, I'll be picking you up one of these days."

"Ah, I've stopped smoking so many times." He should have taken his pack out of his pocket and left it in the unmarked car; then she wouldn't have noticed. "Drop him at the morgue. I'll stop by Naomi's, so tell Bill to hold off until he hears from me." He turned to Coop. "Anything else?"

"Yeah, Roscoe's obituary was in the paper, remember?"

He rubbed his chin, the light chestnut stubble already appearing even though he'd shaved at six this morning. "We thought it was a joke."

"Boss, let's question a few people, starting with Sean Hallahan."

He folded his arms and leaned against the green unmarked car. "Let's wait—well, let me think about it. I don't want to jump the gun."

"Maury McKinchie's obituary was stuffed in the paper as well."

"I know. I know." He swept his eyes over the distressed Irene Miller and BoomBoom. Father Michael had administered the last rites. In the corner of his eye the lumpish figure of Jimbo Anson loomed. "I'd better talk to him before he runs to Dunkin' Donuts and eats another dozen jelly rolls." Jimbo ate when distressed. He was distressed a lot.

He half whispered, "Coop, take the basics from these folks, then let them go. I think BoomBoom is going to code on us." He used the medic slang word for "die."

Rick straightened his shoulders and walked the thirty yards to Jimbo.

"Sheriff, I don't know what to do. Nothing like this has ever happened to me. I just feel awful. Poor Naomi."

"Jimbo, death always upsets the applecart. Breathe deeply." He clapped the man on the back. "That's better. Now you tell me what happened."

"He went through the car wash, well I mean, I didn't see him, the kids were up front, and when the car didn't roll off she, I mean Brooks, ran around to see if the pedal hadn't released on the belt and, well, Roscoe was gone."

"Did you see him at all?"

"No, I mean, not until I came back with Brookie. Kid had some sense, I can tell you. She didn't scream or cry. She ran to my office, told me Roscoe was dead, and I followed her to there." He pointed.

"That's fine. I may be talking to you again, but it looks like a heart attack or stroke. These things happen."

"Business was great today." A mournful note crept into his voice.

"You'll be able to reopen before long. I'm going to impound the car, just routine, Jimbo. You won't have to worry about the vehicle being parked here."

"Thanks, Sheriff."

Rick clapped him on the back again and walked into the air-conditioned office—the day had turned unusually hot—where Brooks, Jody, and Karen sat. Cooper was already there.

"Sheriff, we were establishing a time line." Coop smiled at the three young women.

"One thirty, about," Brooks said.

"Mr. Anson said you showed presence of mind," Rick complimented Brooks.

"I don't know. I feel so bad for Mr. Fletcher. He helped me get into St. Elizabeth's after the semester started."

"Well, I'm not the Reverend Jones but I do believe that Roscoe Fletcher is in a better place. Much as you'll miss him, try to think of that."

"Jody, did you notice anything?" Coop asked.

"No. He said 'hi' and that was it. Karen and Brooks scrubbed down his bumpers. I think Roger pressed the button to send him in."

"Where is Roger?" Rick said.

"Directing traffic," Karen replied.

"Good man to have around."

This startled the two girls, who had never thought of Roger as anything other than a tall boy who was quiet even in kindergarten. Brooks was beginning to appreciate Roger's special qualities.

"Was there anything unusual about Mr. Fletcher or anyone else today?"

"No." Karen twirled a golden hair around her forefinger.

"Girls, if anything comes to mind, call me." He handed around his card.

"Is something wrong, something other than the fact that Mr. Fletcher is dead?" Brooks inquired shrewdly.

"No. This is routine."

"It's weird to be questioned." Brooks was forthright.

"I'm sorry you all lost Mr. Fletcher. I know it was a shock. I have to ask questions, though. I don't mean to further upset you. My job is to collect details, facts, like little pieces of a mosaic."

"We understand," Karen said.

"We're okay," Brooks fibbed.

"Okay then." He rose and Coop also handed her card to the three girls.

As she trudged across the blacktop to motion Roger from Greenbrier Drive, she marveled at the self-possession of the three high school girls. Usually, something like this sent teenage girls into a crying jag. As far as she could tell, not one tear had fallen, but then BoomBoom, never one to pass up the opportunity to emote, was crying enough for all of them.

20

Johnny Pop, the 1958 John Deere tractor, rolled through the meadow thick with goldenrod. Tucker pouted by a fallen walnut at the creek. Mrs. Murphy sat in Harry's lap. Tucker, a trifle too big and heavy, envied the tiger her lap status.

As the tractor popped by, she turned and gazed into the creek. A pair of fishy eyes gazed right back. Startled, Tucker took a step back and barked, then sheepishly sat down again.

The baking sun and two days of light winds had dried out the wet earth. Harry, determined to get in one more hay cutting before winter, fired up Johnny Pop the minute she thought she wouldn't get stuck. She couldn't hear anything, so Mrs. Hogendobber startled her when she walked out into the meadow.

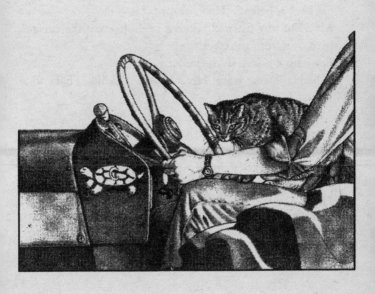

Tucker, intent on her bad mood, missed observing the black Falcon rumbling down the drive.

Miranda waved her arms over her head. "Harry, stop!"

Harry immediately flipped the lever to the left, cutting off the motor. "Miranda, what's the matter? What are you doing out here on gardening day?"

"Roscoe Fletcher's dead—for real, this time."

"What happened?" Harry gasped.

Mrs. Murphy listened. Tucker, upon hearing the subject, hurried over from the creek.

Pewter was asleep in the house.

"Died at the car wash. Heart attack or stroke. That's what Mim says."

"Was she there?"

"No. I forgot to ask her how she found out. Rick Shaw told Jim Sanburne, most likely, and Jim told Mim."

"It's ironic." Harry shuddered.

"The obit?"

Harry nodded. Mrs. Murphy disagreed. *"It's not ironic. It's murder. Wait and see. Cat intuition."*

21

Sean Hallahan pushed a laundry cart along a hallway so polished it reflected his image.

The double doors at the other end of the corridor swung open. Karen and Jody hurried toward him.

"How'd you get in here?" he asked.

Ignoring the question, Jody solemnly said, "Mr. Fletcher's dead. He died at the car wash."

"What?" Sean stopped the cart from rolling into them.

Karen tossed her ponytail. "He went in and never came out."

"Went in what?" Sean appeared stricken, his face white.

"The car wash," Jody said impatiently. "He went in the car

wash, but at the other end, he just sat. Looks like he died of a heart attack."

"Are you making this up?" He smiled feebly.

"No. We were there. It was awful. Brooks Tucker found him."

"For real," he whispered.

"For real." Jody put her arm around his waist. "No one's going to think anything. Really."

"If only I hadn't put that phony obituary in the paper." He gulped.

"Yeah," the girls chimed in unison.

"Wait until my dad hears about this. He's going to kill me." He paused. "Who knows?"

"Depends on who gets to the phone first, I guess." Karen hadn't expected Sean to be this upset. She felt sorry for him.

"We came here first before going home. We thought you should know before your dad picks you up."

"Thanks," he replied, tears welling in his eyes.

22

Father Michael led the assembled upper and lower schools of St. Elizabeth's in a memorial service. Naomi Fletcher, wearing a veil, was supported by Sandy Brashiers with Florence Rubicon, the Latin teacher, on her left side. Ed Sugarman, the chemistry teacher, escorted a devastated April Shively.

Many of the younger children cried because they were supposed to or because they saw older kids crying. In the upper school some of the girls carried on, whipping through boxes of tissues. A few of the boys were red-eyed as well, including, to everyone's surprise, Sean Hallahan, captain of the football team.

Brooks reported all this to Susan, who told Harry and Miranda when they joined her at home for lunch.

"Well, he ate too much, he drank too much, and who knows what else he did—too much." Susan summed up Roscoe's life.

"How's Brooks handling it?" Harry inquired.

"Okay. She knows people die; after all, she watched her grandma die by inches with cancer. In fact, she said, 'When it's my time I want to go fast like Mr. Fletcher.'"

"I don't remember thinking about dying at all at her age," Harry wondered out loud.

"You didn't think of anything much at her age," Susan replied.

"Thanks."

"Children think of death often; they are haunted by it because they can't understand it." Miranda rested her elbows on the table to lean forward. "That's why they go to horror movies—it's a safe way to approach death, scary but safe."

Harry stared at Miranda's elbows on the table. "I never thought of that."

"I know I'm not supposed to have my elbows on the table, Harry, but I can't always be perfect."

Harry blinked. "It's not that at all—it's just that you usually are—perfect."

"Aren't you sweet."

"Harry puts her feet on the table, she's so imperfect."

"Susan, I do not."

"You know what was rather odd, though?" Susan reached for the sugar bowl. "Brooks told me Jody said she was glad Roscoe was dead. That she didn't like him anyway. Now that's a bit extreme even for a teenager."

"Yeah, but Jody's been extreme lately." Harry got up when the phone rang. Force of habit.

"Sit down. I'll answer it." Susan walked over to the counter and lifted the receiver.

"Yes. Of course, I understand. Marilyn, it could have an impact on your fund-raising campaign. I do suggest that you appoint an interim headmaster immediately." Susan paused and held the phone away from her ear so the others could hear Little Mim's voice. Then she spoke again. "Sandy Brashiers. Who else? No, no, and no," she said after listening to three questions. "Do you want me to call anyone? Don't fret, doesn't solve a thing."

"She'll turn into her mother," Miranda predicted as Susan hung up the receiver.

"Little Mim doesn't have her mother's drive."

"Harry, not only do I think she has her mother's drive, I think she'll run for her father's seat once he steps down as mayor."

"No way." Harry couldn't believe the timid woman she had known since childhood could become that confident.

"Bet you five dollars," Miranda smugly said.

"According to Little Mim, the Millers are divorcing."

"Oh, dear." Miranda hated such events.

"About time." Harry didn't like hearing of divorce either, but there were exceptions. "Still, there is no such thing as a good divorce."

"You managed," Susan replied.

"How quickly you forget. During the enforced six months' separation every married couple and single woman in this town invited my ex-husband to dinner. Who had me to dinner, I ask you?"

"I did." Miranda and Susan spoke in chorus.

"And that was it. The fact that I filed for the divorce made me an ogre. He was the one having the damned affair."

"Sexism is alive and well." Susan apportioned out seven-layer salad, one of her specialties. She stopped, utensils in midair. "Did either of you like Roscoe Fletcher?"

"De mortuis nil nisi bonum," Miranda advised.

"Speak nothing but good about the dead," Harry translated although it was unnecessary. "Maybe people said that because they feared the departed spirit was nearby. If they gave you trouble while alive, think what they could do to you as a ghost."

"Did you like Roscoe Fletcher?" Susan repeated her question.

Harry paused. "Yes, he had a lot of energy and good humor."

"A little too hearty for my taste." Miranda found the salad delicious. "Did you like him?"

Susan shrugged. "I felt neutral. He seemed a bit phony sometimes. But maybe that was the fund-raiser in him. He had to be a backslapper and glad-hander, I suppose."

"Aren't we awful, sitting here picking the poor man apart?" Miranda dabbed her lipstick-coated lips with a napkin.

The phone rang again. Susan jumped up. "Speaking of letting someone rest in peace, I'd like to eat in peace."

"You don't have to answer it," Harry suggested.

"Mothers always answer telephones." She picked up the jangling device. "Hello." She paused a long time. "Thanks for telling me. You've done the right thing."

Little Mim had rung back to say St. Elizabeth's had held an emergency meeting by conference call.

Sandy Brashiers had been selected interim headmaster.

23

Late that afternoon, a tired Father Michael bent his lean frame, folding himself into the confessional.

He usually read until someone entered the other side of the booth. The residents of Crozet had been particularly virtuous this week because traffic was light.

The swish of the fabric woke him as he half dozed over the volume of Thomas Merton, a writer he usually found provocative.

"Father, forgive me for I have sinned," came the formalistic opening.

"Go on, my child."

"I have killed and I will kill again." The voice was muffled, disguised.

He snapped to attention, but before he could open his mouth, the penitent slipped out of the booth. Confused, Father Michael pondered what to do. He felt he must stay in the booth for the confessional hours were well-known—he had a responsibility to his flock—but he wanted to call Rick Shaw immediately. Paralyzed, he grasped the book so hard his knuckles were white. The curtain swished again.

A man's voice spoke, deep and low. "Father forgive me for I have sinned."

"Go on, my child," Father Michael said as his mind raced.

"I've cheated on my wife. I can't help myself. I have strong desires." He stopped.

Father Michael advised him by rote, gave him a slew of Hail Marys and novenas. He kept rubbing his wristwatch until eventually his wrist began to hurt. As the last second of his time in the booth expired, he bolted out, grabbed the phone, and dialed Rick Shaw.

When Coop picked up the phone, he insisted he speak to the sheriff himself.

"Sheriff Shaw."

"Yes."

"This is Father Michael. I don't know"—sweat beaded on his forehead; he couldn't violate what was said in the confessional booth—"I believe a murder may have taken place."

"One has, Father Michael."

The priest's hands were shaking. "Oh, no. Who?"

"Roscoe Fletcher." Rick breathed deeply. "The lab report came back. He was poisoned by malathion. Not hard to get around here, so many farmers use it. It works with the speed of light so he had to have eaten it at the car wash. We've tested the strawberry hard candy in his car. Nothing."

"There couldn't be any mistake?"

"No. We have to talk, Father."

After Father Michael hung up the phone, he needed to collect his thoughts. He paced outside, winding up in the graveyard. Ansley Randolph's mums bloomed beautifully.

A soul was in peril. But if the confession he had heard was true, then another immortal soul was in danger as well. He was a priest. He should do something, but he didn't know what. It then occurred to him that he himself might be in danger—his body, not his soul.

Like a rabbit who hears the beagle pack, he twitched and cast his eyes around the graveyard to the Avenging Angel. It looked so peaceful.

24

His shirtsleeves rolled up, Kendrick Miller sat in his favorite chair to read the paper.

Irene swept by. "Looking for your obituary?" She arched a delicate eyebrow.

"Ha ha." He rustled the paper.

Jody, reluctantly doing her math homework at the dining-room table so both parents could supervise, reacted. "Mom, that's not funny."

"I didn't say it was."

"Who knows, maybe *your* obituary will show up." She dropped her pencil inside her book, closing it.

"If it does, Jody, you'll have placed it there." Irene sank gracefully onto the sofa.

Jody grimaced. "Sick."

"I can read it now: 'Beloved mother driven to death by child—and husband.'"

"Irene..." Kendrick reproved, putting down the paper.

"Yeah, Mom."

"Well"—she propped her left leg over an embroidered pillow—"I thought Roscoe Fletcher could have sold ice to Eskimos and probably did. He was good for St. Elizabeth's, and I'm sorry he died. I was even sorrier that we were all there. I would have preferred to hear about it rather than see it."

"He didn't look bad." Jody opened her book again. "I hope he didn't suffer."

"Too quick to suffer." Irene stared absently at her nails, a discreet pale pink. "What's going to happen at St. Elizabeth's?"

Kendrick lifted his eyebrows. "The board will appoint Sandy Brashiers headmaster. Sandy will try to kill Roscoe's film-course idea, which will bring him into a firefight with Maury McKinchie, Marilyn Sanburne, and April Shively. Ought to be worth the price of admission."

"How do you know that?" Jody asked.

"I don't know it for certain, but the board is under duress. And the faculty likes Brashiers."

"Oh, I almost forgot. Father Michael can see us tomorrow at two thirty."

"Irene, I have landscaping plans to show the Doubletree people tomorrow." He was bidding for the hotel's business. "It's important."

"I'd like to think I'm important. That this marriage is important," Irene said sarcastically.

"Then you pay the bills."

"You turn my stomach." Irene swung her legs to the floor and left.

"Way to go, Dad."

"You keep out of this."

"I love when you spend the evening at home. Just gives me warm fuzzies." She hugged herself in a mock embrace.

"I ought to—" He shut up.

"Hit me. Go ahead. Everyone thinks you gave me the shiner."

He threw the newspaper on the floor. "I've never once hit you."

"I'll never tell," she goaded him.

"Who did hit you?"

"Field hockey practice. I told you."

"I don't believe you."

"Fine, Dad. I'm a liar."

"I don't know what you are, but you aren't happy."

"Neither are you," she taunted.

"No, I'm not." He stood up, put his hands in his pockets. "I'm going out."

"Take me with you."

"Why?"

"I don't want to stay home with her."

"You haven't finished your homework."

"How come you get to run away and I have to stay home?"

"I—" He stopped because a determined Irene reentered the living room.

"Father Michael says he can see us at nine in the morning," she announced.

His face reddening, Kendrick sat back down, defeated. "Fine."

"Why do you go for marriage counseling, Mom? You go to mass every day. You see Father Michael every day."

"Jody, this is none of your business."

"If you discuss it in front of me, it is," she replied flippantly.

"She's got a point there." Kendrick appreciated how intelligent his daughter was, and how frustrated. However, he didn't know how to talk to her or his manipulative—in his opinion—wife. Irene suffocated him and Jody irritated him. The only place he felt good was at work.

"Dad, are you going to give St. E.'s a lot of money?"

"I wouldn't tell you if I were."

"Why not?"

"You'd use it as an excuse to skip classes." He half laughed.

"Kendrick"—Irene sat back on the sofa—"where do you get these ideas?"

"Contrary to popular opinion, I was young once, and Jody likes to—" He put his hand out level to the floor and wobbled it.

"Learned it from you." Jody flared up.

"Can't we have one night of peace?" Irene wailed, unwilling to really examine why they couldn't.

"Hey, Mom, we're dysfunctional."

"That's a bullshit word." Kendrick picked his paper up. "All those words are ridiculous. Codependent. Enabler. Jesus Christ. People can't accept reality anymore. They've invented a vocabulary for their illusions."

Both his wife and daughter stared at him.

"Dad, are you going to give us the lecture on professional victims?"

"No." He buried his nose in the paper.

"Jody, finish your homework," Irene directed.

Jody stood up. She had no intention of doing homework. "I hated seeing Mr. Fletcher dead. You two don't care. It was a shock, you know." She swept her books onto the floor; they hit with thuds equal to their differing weights. She stomped out the front door, slamming it hard.

"Kendrick, you deal with it. I was at the car wash, remember?"

He glared at her, rolled his paper up, threw it on the chair, and stalked out.

Irene heard him call for Jody. No response.

25

"You cheated!" Jody, angry, squared off at Karen Jensen.

"I did not."

"You didn't even understand *Macbeth*. There's no way you could have gotten ninety-five on Mr. Brashiers's quiz."

"I read it and I understand it."

"Liar."

"I went over to Brooks Tucker's and she helped me."

Jody's face twisted in sarcasm. "She read aloud to you?"

"No. Brooks gets all that stuff. It's hard for me."

"She's your new best friend."

"So what if she is?" Karen tossed her blond hair.

"You'd better keep your mouth shut."

"You're the one talking, not me."

"No, I'm not."

"You're weirding out."

Jody's eyes narrowed. "I lost my temper. That doesn't mean I'm weirding out."

"Then why call me a cheater?"

"Because"—Jody sucked in the cool air—"you're on a scholarship. You have to make good grades. And English is not your subject. I don't know why you even took Shakespeare."

"Because Mr. Brashiers is a great teacher." Karen Jensen glanced down the alleyway. She saw only Mrs. Murphy and Pewter, strolling through Mrs. Hogendobber's fall garden, a riot of reds, rusts, oranges, and yellows.

Taking a step closer, Jody leaned toward her. "You and I vowed to—"

Karen held up her hands, palms outward. "Jody, chill out. I'd be crazy to open my mouth. I don't want anyone to know I went to bed with a guy this summer, and neither do you. Just chill out."

Jody relaxed. "Everything's getting on my nerves... especially Mom and Dad. I just want to move out."

Karen noticed the tiger cat coming closer. "Guess everyone feels that way sometimes."

"Yeah," Jody replied, "but your parents are better than mine."

Karen didn't know how to answer that, so she said, "Let's go in and get the mail."

"Yeah." Jody started walking.

Pewter and Murphy, now at the backdoor of the post office, sat on the steps. Pewter washed her face. Mrs. Murphy dropped her head so Pewter could wash her, too.

"*Didn't you think the newspaper's write-up of Roscoe's death was strange?*" Murphy's eyes were half closed.

"*You mean the bit about an autopsy and routine investigation?*"

"*If he died of a heart attack, why a routine investigation? Mom better pump Coop when she sees her—and hey, she hasn't been in to pick up her mail for the last two days.*"

"*Nothing in there but catalogs.*" Pewter took it upon herself to check out everyone's mailbox. She said she wasn't being nosy, only checking for mice.

Shouting in the post office sent them zipping through the animal door.

They crossed the back section of the post office and bounded onto the counter. Both Harry and Mrs. Hogendobber were in the front section as were Jody, an astonished Samson Coles, and Karen Jensen. Tucker was at Harry's feet, squared off against Jody. The animals had arrived in the middle of an angry scene.

"You're the one!"

"Jody, that's enough," Mrs. Hogendobber, aghast, admonished the girl.

Samson, his gravelly voice sad, said quietly, "It's all right, Miranda."

"You're the one sleeping with Mom!" Jody shrieked.

"I am not having an affair with your mother." He was gentle.

"Jody, come on. I'll ride you home." Karen tugged at the tall girl's sleeve, at a loss for what to do. Her friend exploded when Samson put his arm around her shoulders, telling her how sorry he was that the headmaster had died.

"You cheated on Lucinda—everyone knows you did—and

then Ansley killed herself. She drove her Porsche into that pond because of you...and now you're fucking my mother."

"JODY!" Mrs. Hogendobber raised her voice, which scared everyone.

Jody burst into tears and Karen pushed her out the front door. "I'm sorry, Mrs. Hogendobber and Mr. Coles. I'm sorry, Mrs. Haristeen. She's, uh..." Karen couldn't finish her thought. She closed the door behind her.

Samson curled his lips inward until they disappeared. "Well, I know I'm the town pariah, but this is the first time I've heard that I caused Ansley's death."

A shocked Miranda grasped the counter for support. "Samson, no one in this town blames you for that unstable woman's unfortunate end. She caused unhappiness to herself and others." She gulped in air. "That child needs help."

"Help? She needs a good slap in the face." Pewter paced the counter.

Tucker grumbled. *"Stinks of fear."*

"They can't smell it. They only trust their eyes. Why, I don't know—their eyes are terrible." Mrs. Murphy, concerned, sat at the counter's edge watching Karen force Jody into her car, an old dark green Volvo.

"We'd better call Irene," Harry, upset, suggested.

"No." Samson shook his head. "Then the kid will think we're ganging up on her. Obviously, she doesn't trust her mother if she thinks she's having an affair with me."

"Then I'll call her father."

"Harry, Kendrick's no help," Mrs. Hogendobber, rarely a criticizer, replied. "His love affair with himself is the problem in that family. It's a love that brooks no rivals."

This made Harry laugh; Miranda hadn't intended to be funny, but she had hit the nail on the head.

Samson folded his arms across his chest. "Some people shouldn't have children. Kendrick is one of them."

"We can't let the child behave this way. She's going to make a terrific mess." Miranda added sensibly, "Not everyone will be as tolerant as we are." She tapped her chin with her fore-finger, shifting her weight to her right foot. "I'll call Father Michael."

Samson hesitated, then spoke. "Miranda, what does a middle-aged priest know of teenage girls ... of women?"

"About the same as any other man," Harry fired off.

"Touché," Samson replied.

"Samson, I didn't mean to sound nasty. You're probably more upset than you're letting on. Jody may be a kid, but a low blow is a low blow," Harry said.

"I could leave this town where people occasionally forgive but never forget. I think about it, you know, but"—he rammed his hands in his pockets—"I'm not the only person living in Crozet who's made a mistake. I'm too stubborn to turn tail. I belong here as much as the next guy."

"I hope you don't think I'm sitting in judgment." Miranda's hand fluttered to her throat.

"Me neither." Harry smiled. "It's hard for me to be open-minded about that subject, thanks to my own history ... I mean, BoomBoom Craycroft of all people. Fair could have picked someone—well, you know."

"That was the excitement for Fair. That BoomBoom was so obvious." Samson realized he'd left his mail on the counter. "I'm going back to work." He scooped his mail up before Pewter, recovering from the drama, could squat on it. "What I really feel bad about is tampering with the escrow accounts. That was rotten. Falling in love with Ansley may have been imprudent, but it wasn't criminal. Betraying a responsibility to clients, that was wrong." He sighed. "I've paid for it. I've lost my license. Lost respect. Lost my house. Nearly los Lucinda." He paused again, then said, "Well, girls, we've had enough soap opera for one day." He pushed the door open and breathed in the crisp fall air.

Miranda ambled over to the phone, dialed, and go Lucinda Coles. "Lucinda, is Father Michael there?"

He was, and she buzzed the good woman through.

"Father Michael, have you a moment?" Miranda accu- rately repeated the events of the afternoon.

When she hung up, Harry asked, "Is he going to talk to her?"

"Yes. He seemed distracted, though."

"Maybe the news upset him."

"Of course." She nodded. "I'm going to clean out that re- frigerator. It needs a good scrub."

"Before you do that, there's a pile of mail for Roscoe Fletcher. Why don't we sort it out and run it over to Naomi after work?"

The two women dumped the mail out on the work table in the back. A flutter of bills made them both feel guilty The woman had lost her husband. Handing over bills seemed heartless. Catalogs, magazines, and handwritten personal letters filled up one of the plastic boxes they used in the back to carry mail after sorting it out of the big canvas duffel bags.

A Jiffy bag, the end torn, the gray stuffing spilling out, sen Harry to the counter for Scotch tape.

Tucker observed this. She wanted to play, but the cats were hashing over the scene they'd just witnessed. She barked.

"Tucker, if you need to go to the bathroom, there's the door."

"Can't we walk, just a little walk? You deserve a break."

"Butterfingers." Harry dropped the bag. The tiny tear in the cover opened wider.

Mrs. Murphy and Pewter stopped their gabbing and jumped down.

"Yahoo!" Mrs. Murphy pounced on the tear and the gray stuffing burst out.

"Aachoo." Pewter sneezed as the featherlight stuffing floated into the air.

"I've got it!" Mrs. Murphy crowed.

Pewter pounced, both paws on one end of the bag, claws out as the tiger cat ripped away at the other corner, enlarging the tear until she could reach into the bag with her paw.

If Mrs. Murphy had been a boxer, she would have been hailed for her lightning hands.

Lying flat on her side, she fished in the Jiffy bag with her right paw.

"Anything to eat?"

"No, it's paper, but it's crisp and crinkly."

The large gray cat blinked, somewhat disappointed. Food, the ultimate pleasure, was denied her. She'd have to make do with fresh paper, a lesser pleasure but a pleasure nonetheless.

"You girls are loony tunes." Tucker, bored, turned her back. Paper held no interest for her.

"Hooked it. I can get it out of the bag. I know I can." Murphy yanked hard at the contents of the package, pulling the paper partway through the tear.

"Look!" Pewter shouted.

Mrs. Murphy stopped for a second to focus on her booty. *"Wow!"* She yanked harder.

Tucker turned back around thanks to the feline excitement. *"Give it to Mom. She needs it."*

Mrs. Murphy ripped into the bag so fast the humans hadn't time to react, and the cat turned a somersault to land on her side, then put her paw into the bag. Her antics had them doubled over.

However funny she was, Mrs. Murphy was destroying government property.

"Mom, we're rich!" Mrs. Murphy let out a jubilant meow.

Harry and Miranda, dumbfounded, bent over the demolished bag.

"My word." Miranda's eyes about popped from her head. She reached out with her left hand, fingers to the floor, to steady herself.

The humans and animals stared at a stack of one-hundred-dollar bills, freshly minted.

"We'd better call Rick Shaw. No one sends that much money in the mail." Harry stood up, feeling a little dizzy.

"Harry, I don't know the law on this, but we can't open this packet."

"I know that," Harry, a trifle irritated, snapped.

"It's not our business." Miranda slowly thought out loud. "I'll call Ned."

"No. That's still interfering in the proper delivery of the mail."

"Miranda, there's something fishy about this."

"Fishy or not, we are employees of the United States Postal Service, and we can't blow the whistle just because there's money in a package."

"We sure could if it were a bomb."

"But it's not."

"You mean we deliver it?"

"Exactly."

"Oh." Mrs. Murphy's whiskers drooped. *"We need that money."*

26

Naomi Fletcher called Rick Shaw herself. She asked Miranda and Harry to stay until the sheriff arrived.

Mrs. Murphy, Pewter, and Tucker languished in the cab of the truck. When the sheriff pulled in with Cooper at his side, the animals set up such a racket that Cynthia opened the truck door.

"Bet you guys need to go to the bathroom."

"Sure," they yelled over their shoulders as they made a bee-line for the front door.

"You'd better stop for a minute," Tucker advised the cats.

"I'm not peeing in public. You do it," the tiger, insulted, replied.

"Fine." The corgi found a spot under a tree, did enough to

convince Cynthia that she had saved the interior of Harry's truck, then hurried to the front door.

Once inside they huddled under the coffee table while Cynthia dusted the bag and the bills for prints.

After an exhaustive discussion Rick told Roscoe Fletcher's widow to deposit the money in her account. He could not impound the cash. There was no evidence of wrongdoing.

"There are no assumptions in my job, only facts." He ran his right hand through his thinning hair.

Naomi, both worried and thrilled, for the sum had turned out to be seventy-five thousand dollars, thanked the sheriff and his deputy for responding to her call.

Rick, hat in hand, said, "Mrs. Fletcher, brace yourself. The story will be out in the papers tomorrow. A coroner's report is public knowledge. Bill Moscowitz has delayed writing up the autopsy report for as long as he can."

"I know you're doing your best." Naomi choked up.

Harry and Miranda, confused, looked at each other and then back at Rick.

Naomi nodded at him, so he spoke. "Roscoe was poisoned."

"*What!*" Tucker exclaimed.

"*I told you,*" Mrs. Murphy said.

"*Don't be so superior,*" Pewter complained.

"Naomi, I'm sorry, so very sorry." Mrs. Hogendobber reached over and grasped Naomi's hand.

"*Who'd want to kill him?*" Pewter's long white eyebrows rose.

"*Someone who failed algebra?*" Mrs. Murphy couldn't resist.

"*Hey, where's Tucker?*" Pewter asked.

Tucker had sneaked off alone to find Winston, the bull-dog.

Harry said, "I'm sorry, Naomi."

Naomi wiped her thin nose with a pink tissue. "Poisoned! One of those strawberry drops was poison."

Cooper filled in the details. "He ingested malathion, which usually takes just minutes to kill someone."

Harry blurted out, "I ate one of those!"

"When?" Rick asked.

"Oh, two days before his death. Maybe three. You know Roscoe... always offering everyone candy." She felt queasy.

"Unfortunately, we don't know how he came to be poisoned. The candy in his car was safe."

They squeezed back into Harry's truck, the cats on Miranda's lap. Tucker, between the two humans, told everyone what Winston had said. *"Naomi cries all the time. She didn't kill him. Winston's positive."*

"There goes the obvious suspect in every murder case." Pewter curled up on Miranda's lap, which left little room for Mrs. Murphy.

"You could move over."

"Go sit on Harry's lap."

"Thanks, I will, you selfish toad."

Tucker nudged Murphy. *"Winston said Sandy Brashiers is over all the time."*

"Why?" Pewter inquired.

"Trying to figure out Roscoe's plans for this school year. He left few documents or guidelines, and April Shively is being a real bitch—according to Winston."

"Secretaries always fall in love with their bosses," Pewter added nonchalantly.

"Oh, Pewter." Murphy wrinkled her nose.

"*They do!*" ·

"*Even if she was in love with him, it doesn't mean she'd be an obstructionist—good word, huh?*" Tucker smiled, her big fangs gleaming.

"*I'm impressed, Tucker.*" The tiger laughed. "*Of course she's an obstructionist. April doesn't like Sandy. Roscoe didn't either.*"

"*Guess Sandy's in for a rough ride.*" Pewter noticed one of Herb Jones's two cats sitting on the steps to his house. "*Look at Lucy Fur. She always shows off after her visit to the beauty parlor.*"

"*That long hair is pretty, but can you imagine taking care of it?*" Mrs. Murphy, a practical puss, replied.

"I don't know what this world is coming to." Miranda shook her head.

"Poison is the coward's way to kill someone." Harry, still shaken from realizing she had eaten Roscoe's candies, growled, "Whoever it was was chickenshit."

"That's one way to put it." Miranda frowned.

"The question is, where did he get the poison and is there a tin of lethal candies out there waiting for another innocent victim?" Harry stroked Murphy, keeping her left hand on the wheel.

"We know one thing," Miranda pronounced firmly. "Whoever killed him was close to him . . . if malathion kills as fast as Coop says it does."

"Close and weak. I mean it. Poison is the coward's weapon."

In that Harry was half right and half wrong.

27

A light wind from the southeast raised the temperature into the low seventies. The day sparkled, leaves the color of butter vibrated in the breeze, and the shadows disappeared since it was noon.

Harry, home after cub hunting early in the morning, had rubbed down Poptart, turned her out with the other two horses, and was now scouring her stock trailer. Each year she repacked the bearings, inspected the boards, sanded off any rust, and repainted those areas. Right now her trailer resembled a dalmatian, spots everywhere. She'd put on the primer but didn't finish her task before cub hunting started, which was usually in September. Cubbing meant young hounds joined older ones, and young foxes learned along with the young hounds what was expected of them. With today's good weather she'd hoped to finish the job.

Blair lent her his spray painter. As Blair bought the best of everything, she figured she could get the job done in two hours, tops. She'd bought metallic Superman-blue paint from Art Bushey, who gave her a good deal.

"*That stuff smells awful.*" Tucker wrinkled her nose at the paint cans.

"*She's going to shoot the whole afternoon on this.*" Pewter stretched. "*I'll mosey on up to the house.*"

"*Wimp. You could sleep under the maple tree and soak up the sunshine,*" Mrs. Murphy suggested.

"*Don't start one of your outdoor exercise lectures about how we felines are meant to run, jump, and kill. This feline was meant to rest on silk cushions and eat steak tartare.*"

"*Tucker, let's boogie.*" Mrs. Murphy shook herself, then scampered across the stable yard.

"*I'm not going, and don't you come back here and make up stories about what I've missed,*" Pewter called after them. "*And I don't want to hear about the bobcat either. That's a tall tale if I ever heard one.*" Then she giggled. "*'Cept they don't have tails.*" By now she was heading toward the house, carrying on a conversation with herself. "*Oh, and if it isn't the bobcat, then it's the bear and her two cubs. And if I hear one more time about how Tucker was almost drug under by an irate beaver while crossing the creek . . . next they'll tell me there's an elephant out there. Fine, they can get their pads cut up. I'm not.*" She sashayed into the screened-in porch and through the open door to the kitchen. "*Mmm.*" Pewter jumped onto the counter to gobble up crumbs of Danish. "*What a pity that Harry isn't a cook.*"

She curled up on the counter, the sun flooding through the window over the sink, and fell fast asleep.

The cat and dog trotted toward the northwest. Usually they'd head to the creek that divided Harry's land from Blair Bainbridge's land, but as they'd seen him this morning when he brought over the paint sprayer on his way to cubbing, they decided to sprint in the other direction.

"Pewter cracks me up." Mrs. Murphy laughed.

"Me, too." Tucker stopped and lifted her nose. *"Deer."*

"Close?"

"Over there." The corgi indicated a copse of trees surrounded by high grass.

"Let's not disturb them. It's black-powder season, and there's bound to be some idiot around with a rifle."

"I don't mind a good hunter. They're doing us a favor. But the other ones..." The dog shuddered, then trotted on. *"Mom and Blair didn't have much to say to each other, did they?"*

"She was in a hurry. So was he." Mrs. Murphy continued, *"Sometimes I worry about her. She's getting set in her ways. Makes it hard to mesh with a partner, know what I mean?"*

"She likes living alone. All that time I wanted Fair to come back, which he's tried to do—I really think she likes being her own boss."

"Tucker, she was hardly your typical wife."

"No, but she made concessions."

"So did he." Mrs. Murphy stopped a moment to examine a large fox den. *"Hey, you guys run this morning?"*

"No," came the distant reply.

"Next week they'll leave from Old Greenwood Farm."

"Thanks."

"Since when did you get matey with foxes?" Tucker asked. *"I thought you hated them."*

"Nah, only some of them."

"Hypocrite."

"Stick-in-the-mud. Remember what Emerson said, 'A foolish consistency is the hobgoblin of little minds.'"

"Where are we going?" Tucker ignored Murphy's reference.

"Here, there, and everywhere." Mrs. Murphy swished her tail.

"Goody." The dog loved wandering with no special plan.

They ran through a newly mown hayfield. Grasshoppers flew up in the air, the faint rattle of their wings sounding like thousands of tiny castanets. The last of the summer's butterflies swooped around. Wolf spiders, some lugging egg sacs, hurried out of their way.

At the end of the field a line of large old hickories stood sentinel over a farm road rarely used since the Bowdens put down a better road fifty yards distant.

"Race you!" the cat called over her shoulder as she turned left on the road heading down to a deep ravine and a pond.

"Ha!" The dog bounced for joy, screeching after the cat.

Corgis, low to the ground, can run amazingly fast when stretched out to full body length. Since Mrs. Murphy zigged and zagged when she ran, Tucker soon overtook her.

"I win!" the dog shouted.

"Only because I let you."

They tumbled onto each other, rolling in the sunshine. Springing to their feet, they ran some more, this time with the tiger soaring over the corgi, dipping in front of her and then jumping her from the opposite direction.

The sheer joy of it wore them out. They sat under a gnarled walnut at the base of a small spring.

Mrs. Murphy climbed the tree, gracefully walking out on a limb. *"Hey, there's a car over that rise."*

"No way."

"Wanna bet?"

They hurried up and over the small rise, the ruts in the road deeper than their own height. Stranded in the middle of the road was a 1992 red Toyota Camry with the license plates removed. As they drew closer they could see a figure in the driver's seat.

Tucker stopped and sniffed. *"Uh-oh."*

Mrs. Murphy bounded onto the hood and stared, hair rising all over her body. Quickly she jumped off. *"There's a dead human in there."*

"How dead?"

"Extremely dead."

"That's what I thought. Who is it?"

"Given the condition of the body, your guess is as good as mine. But it was once a woman. There's a blue barrette in her hair with roses on it, little yellow plastic roses."

"We'd better go get Mom."

Mrs. Murphy walked away from the Camry and sat on the rise. She needed to collect her thoughts.

"Tucker, it won't do any good. Mother won't know what we're telling her. The humans don't use this road anymore. It might be days, weeks, or even months before anyone finds this, uh, mess."

"Maybe by that time she'll be bones."

"Tucker!"

"Just joking." The dog leaned next to her dear friend. *"Trying to lighten the moment. After all, you don't know who it is. I can't see that high up. Humans commit suicide, you know. Could be one of those things. They like to shoot themselves in cars or hotel rooms. Drugs are for the wimps, I guess. I mean, how many ways can they kill themselves?"*

"Lots of ways."

"I never met a dog that committed suicide."

"How could you? The dog would be dead."

"Smart-ass." Tucker exhaled. *"Guess we'd better go back home."*

On the way across the mown hayfield Murphy said out loud what they both were thinking. *"Let's hope it's a suicide."*

They reached the farm in twenty minutes, rushing inside to tell Pewter, who refused to believe it.

"Then come with us."

"Murphy, I am not traipsing all over creation. It's soon time for supper. Anyway, what's a dead human to me?"

"You'd think someone would report a missing person, wouldn't you?" Tucker scratched her shoulder.

"So many humans live alone, they aren't missed for a long time. And she's been dead a couple of weeks," Murphy replied.

28

Puce-faced Little Marilyn, hands on hips, stood in the middle of Roscoe Fletcher's office, as angry as April Shively.

"You hand those files over!"

Coolly, relishing her moment of power, April replied, "Roscoe told me not to release any of this information until our Homecoming banquet."

Little Mim, a petite woman, advanced on April, not quite petite but small enough to be described as perky. "I am chair of the fund-raising committee. If I am to properly present St. Elizabeth's to potential donors, I need information. Roscoe and I were to have our meeting today and the files were to be released to me."

"I don't know that. It's not written in his schedule book."

April shoved the book across his desk toward Marilyn, who ignored it.

Marilyn baited her. "I thought you knew everything there was to know about Roscoe."

"What's that supposed to mean?"

"Take it any way you like."

"Don't you dare accuse me of improper conduct with Roscoe! People always say that. They say it behind my back and think I don't know it." Her words were clipped, her speech precise.

"You *were* in love with him."

"I don't have to answer that. And I don't have to give you this file either."

"Then you're hiding something. I will convene the board and request an immediate audit."

"What I'm hiding is something good!" She sputtered. "It's a large donation by Maury McKinchie for the film department."

"Then show it to me. We'll celebrate together." Little Mim reached out her left hand, with the pinkie ring bearing the crest of the Urquharts.

"No! I take his last words to me as a sacred duty."

Exasperated, tired, and ready to bat April silly, Little Mim left, calling over her shoulder, "You will hear from a lawyer selected by the board and from an accounting firm. Good or bad, we must know the financial health of this institution."

"If Roscoe were alive, you wouldn't talk to me this way."

"April, if Roscoe were alive, I wouldn't talk to you at all."

29

Little Mim was as good as her word. She convened an emergency board meeting chaired by Sandy Brashiers. Sandy had the dolorous duty of telling the group that he believed April had removed files from Roscoe's office: she refused to cooperate even with Sheriff Shaw. The suspicion lurked in many minds that she might have taken other items, perhaps valuable ones like Roscoe's Cartier desk clock.

Alum bigwigs blew like bomb fragments. Kendrick Miller called Ned Tucker at home, asking him to represent the board. Ned agreed. Kendrick then handed State Senator Guyot his mobile phone to call the senior partner of a high-powered accounting firm in Richmond, rousing him from a tense game of snooker. He, too, agreed to help the board, waiving his not inconsiderable fee.

Maury McKinchie, the newest member of the board, suggested this unsettling news not be discussed until the Homecoming banquet. He made no mention of his large bequest.

Sandy Brashiers then made a motion to dismiss April from her post.

Fair Haristeen, serving his last year on the board, stood up. "We need time to think this over before voting. April is out of line, but she's overcome by grief."

"That doesn't give her the right to steal school records and God knows what else." Sandy leaned back in his chair. Underneath the table he tapped his foot, thrilled that revenge was so quickly his.

"Perhaps one of us could talk to her," Fair urged.

"I tried."

"Marilyn," Maury folded his hands on the table, "she may resent you because you're a strong supporter of Sandy."

"I am," Little Mim said forthrightly, as Sandy tried not to grin from ear to ear. "We have put our differences behind us."

"I don't want to open a can of worms—after all that has happened—but there had been tension inside the administration, two camps, you might say, and we all know where April's sympathies rest," Fair said.

"As well as her body," Kendrick said, a bit too quickly.

"Come on, Kendrick!" Fair was disgusted. "We don't know that."

"I'm sorry," Kendrick said, "but she's grieving more than Naomi."

"That's inappropriate!" Maury banged the table, which surprised them all.

"She spent more time with him than his wife did."

Kendrick held up his hands before him, palms outward, a calm-down signal.

"Who then will bell the cat?" Sandy returned to business, secretly loving this uproar.

No one raised a hand. An uncomfortable silence hung over the conference room.

Finally Maury sighed. "I can try. I have little history with her, which under the circumstances seems an advantage. And Roscoe and I were close friends."

Little Mim smiled wanly. "Thank you, Maury, no matter what the consequences."

"Hear, hear!"

Sandy noticed the lights were on in the gymnasium after the meeting adjourned. He threw on his scarf and his tweed jacket, crossing the quad to see what activity was in progress. He couldn't remember, but then he had a great deal on his mind.

Ahead of him, striding through the darkness, was Maury McKinchie, hands jammed into the pockets of an expensive lambskin jacket.

"Maury, where are you going?"

"Fencing exhibition." Maury's voice was level but he had little enthusiasm for Sandy Brashiers.

"Oh, Lord, I forgot all about it." Sandy recalled the university fencing club was visiting St. Elizabeth's hoping to find recruits for the future. One of Coach Hallvard's pet projects was to introduce fencing at the secondary-school level. It was her sport. She coached field hockey and lacrosse, and had even played on the World Cup lacrosse team in 1990, but fencing was her true love.

Sandy jogged up to Maury. "I'm starting to feel like the absent-minded professor."

"Goes with the territory," came the flat reply.

"I know how you must feel, Maury, and I'm sorry. Losing a friend is never easy. And I know Roscoe did not favor me. We were just—too different to really get along. But we both wanted the best for St. Elizabeth's."

"I believe that."

"I'm glad you're on the board. We can use someone whose vision and experience is larger than Albemarle County. I hope we can work together."

"Well, we can try. I'm going to keep my eye on things, going to try to physically be here, too—until some equilibrium is achieved."

Both men sidestepped the volatile question of a film department. And neither man yet knew that Roscoe had been poisoned, which would have cast a pall over their conversation.

Sandy smiled. "This must seem like small beer to you—after Hollywood."

Maury replied, "At least you're doing something important: teaching the next generation. That was one of the things I most respected about Roscoe."

"Ah, but the question is, what do we teach them?"

"To ask questions." Maury opened the gym door for Sandy.

"Thank you." Sandy waited as Maury closed the door.

The two men found places in the bleachers.

Sean Hallahan was practicing thrusts with Roger Davis, not quite so nimble as the football player.

Karen Jensen, face mask down, parried with a University of Virginia sophomore.

Brooks and Jody attacked each other with épées.

Jody flipped up her mask. "I want to try the saber."

"Okay." Coach Hallvard switched Roger and Sean from saber to épée, giving the girls a chance at the heavier sword.

"Feels good," Jody said.

Brooks picked up the saber, resuming her position. Jody slashed at her, pressing as Brooks retreated.

Hallvard observed this burst of aggression out of the corner of her eye. "Jody, give me the saber."

Jody hesitated, then handed over the weapon. She walked off the gym floor, taking the bleacher steps two at a time to sit next to Maury.

"How did you like it?" he asked her.

"Okay."

"I never tried fencing. You need quick reflexes."

"Mr. McKinchie." She lowered her voice so Sandy Brashiers wouldn't hear. His attention was focused on the UVA fencers. "Have you seen the BMW Z3, the retro sports car? It's just beautiful."

"It is a great-looking machine." He kept his eyes on the other students.

"I want a bright red one." She smiled girlishly, which accentuated her smashing good looks.

He held his breath for an instant, then exhaled sharply. She squeezed his knee, then jumped up gracefully and rejoined her teammates.

Karen Jensen flipped up her face mask, glaring at Jody, who glared right back. "Did you give out already?"

"No, Coach took away my saber."

Roger, in position, lunged at Brooks. "Power thighs."

"Sounds—uh—" Brooks giggled, not finishing her sentence.

"You never know what's going to happen at St. E's." With Sean in tow, Karen joined them. "At least this is better than shooting those one-minute stories. I hated that."

"If it's not sports, you don't like it," Jody blandly commented on Karen's attitude.

"Took too long." Karen wiped her brow with a towel. "All that worrying about light. I thought our week of film studies was one of the most boring things we ever did."

"When did this happen?" Brooks asked.

"First week of school," Karen said. "Lucky you missed it."

"That's why Mr. Fletcher and Mr. McKinchie are, I mean, were, so tight," Sean said. " 'Cause Mr. Fletcher said if we are to be a modern school, then we have to teach modern art forms."

"Stick with me, I'll make you a star." Jody mimicked the dead headmaster.

"Mr. McKinchie said he'd try to get old equipment donated to the school."

"I didn't think it was boring," Sean told Brooks.

"Mr. Fletcher said we'd be the only prep school in the nation with a hands-on film department," Karen added. "Hey, see you guys in a minute." She left to talk to one of the young men on the fencing team. Sean seethed.

"She likes older men," Jody tormented him.

"At least she likes men," Sean, mean-spirited, snarled at her.

"Drop dead, Hallahan," Roger said.

Jody, surprisingly calm considering her behavior the last two weeks, replied, "He can call me anything he wants, Roger. I couldn't care less. This dipshit school is not the world, you know. It's just his world."

"What's that supposed to mean?" Sean, angry, took it out on Jody.

"You're a big frog in a small pond. Like—who cares?" She smiled, a hint of malice in her eyes. "Karen's after bigger game than a St. Elizabeth halfback."

Sean's eyes followed Karen.

"She's not the only woman in the world." He feigned indifference.

"No, but she's the one you want," Jody said, needling him more.

Roger gently put his hand under Brooks's elbow, wheeling her away from the squabbling Jody and Sean. "Would you go with me to the Halloween dance?"

"Uh—" She brightened. "Yes."

30

Harry dropped the feed scoop in the sweet feed when the phone rang in the tack room.

She hurried in and picked up the phone. It was 6:30 A.M.

"Miranda, it had to be you."

"Just as Rick Shaw said, the story of Roscoe's poisoning is finally in the paper. But no one is using the word 'murder.'"

"Huh—well, what does it say?"

"There's the possibility of accidental ingestion, but deliberate poisoning can't be ruled out. Rick's soft-pedaling it."

"What has me baffled is the motive. Roscoe was a good headmaster. He liked the students. They liked him, and the parents did, too. There's just something missing—or who knows, maybe it was random, like when a disgruntled employee put poison in Tylenol."

"That was heinous."

"Except—I don't know—I'm just lost. I can't think of any reason for him to be killed."

"He wasn't rich. He appeared to have no real enemies. He had disagreements with people like Sandy Brashiers, but"—Miranda stopped to cough—"well, I guess that's why we have a sheriff's department. If there is something, they'll find it."

"You're right," Harry responded with no conviction whatsoever.

31

The repeated honking of a car horn brought Harry to the front window of the post office. Tucker, annoyed, started barking. Mrs. Murphy opened one eye. Then she opened both eyes.

"Would you look at that?" Harry exclaimed.

Miranda, swathed in an old cashmere cardigan—she was fighting off the sniffles—craned her neck. "Isn't that the cutest thing you ever saw?"

Pewter bustled out of Market's store. She had put in an appearance today, primarily because she knew sides of pork would be carried in to hang in the huge back freezer.

Jody Miller, her black eye fading, emerged from a red BMW sports car. The fenders were rounded, the windshield swept back at an appealing angle. She hopped up the steps to the post office.

Harry opened the door for her. "What a beautiful car!"

"I know." The youngster shivered with delight.

"Did your father buy you that?" Miranda thought of her little Ford Falcon. As far as she was concerned, the styling was as good as this far more expensive vehicle's.

"No, I bought it myself. When Grandpa died, he left money for me, and it's been drawing interest. It finally made enough to buy a new car!"

"Has everyone at school seen it?" Harry asked.

"Yeah, and are they jealous."

Since she was the first student to come in to pick up mail that day, neither woman knew what the kids' responses were to the newspaper story.

"How are people taking the news about Mr. Fletcher?" Miranda inquired.

Jody shrugged. "Most people think it was some kind of accident. People are really mad at Sean, though. A lot of kids won't talk to him now. I'm not talking to him either."

"Rather a strange accident," Miranda mumbled.

"Mr. Fletcher was kind of absentminded." Jody bounced the mail on the counter, evening it. "I liked him. I'll miss him, too, but Dad says people have a shelf life and Mr. Fletcher's ran out. He said there really aren't accidents. People decide when to go."

"Only the Lord decides that." Miranda firmly set her jaw.

"Mrs. Hogendobber, you'll have to take that up with Dad. It's"—she glanced at the ceiling, then back at the two women—"too deep for me. 'Bye." She breezed out the door.

"Kendrick sounds like a misguided man—and a cold-blooded one." Miranda shook her head as Pewter popped through the animal door, sending the flap whapping.

"Hey, I'd look good in that car."

"Pewter, you need a station wagon." Mrs. Murphy jabbed at her when she jumped on the counter.

"I am growing weary, very weary, of these jokes about my weight. I am a healthy cat. My bones are different from yours. I don't say anything about your hair thinning on your belly."

"Is not!"

"Mmm." The gray cat was noncommittal, which infuriated the tiger.

"Do cats get bald?" Tucker asked.

"She is."

"Pewter, I am not." Mrs. Murphy flopped on her back, showing the world her furry tummy.

Harry noticed this brazen display. "Aren't you the pretty puss?"

"Bald."

"Am not." Mrs. Murphy twisted her head to glare at Pewter.

"Wouldn't you love to know what this is about?" Harry laughed.

"Yes, I would." Miranda looked at the animals pensively. "How do I know they aren't talking about us?"

"And this coming from a woman who didn't like cats."

"Well—"

"You used to rail at me for bringing Mrs. Murphy and Tucker to work, and you said it was unclean for Market to have Pewter in the store."

Mrs. Hogendobber tickled Mrs. Murphy's stomach. "I have repented of my ways. 'O Lord, how manifold are thy works! In wisdom hast thou made them all: the earth is full of thy riches.' Psalm one hundred four." She smiled. "Cats and dogs are part of His riches."

As if on cue, the Reverend Herbert Jones strolled in. "Girls."

"Herb, how are you?"

"Worried." He opened his mailbox, the metal rim clicking when it hit the next box because he opened it hard. "Roscoe Fletcher murdered..." He shook his head.

"The paper didn't say he was murdered—just poisoned," Harry said.

"Harry, I've known you all your life. You think he was murdered, just as I do."

"I do. I wanted to see if you knew something I didn't," she replied sheepishly.

"You think his wife killed him?" Herb closed the mailbox, ignoring her subterfuge.

"I don't know," Harry said slowly.

"Fooling around, I'll bet you," Miranda commented.

"A lot of men fool around. That doesn't mean they're killed for it." Herb lightly slapped the envelopes against his palm.

Miranda shook her head. "Perhaps retribution is at work, but there's something eerie about Roscoe's obituary appearing in the paper. The murderer was advertising!"

"Some kind of power trip." He paused, staring at Mrs. Murphy. "And Sean Hallahan is the cat's-paw."

"Yes, Herb, just so." Miranda removed her half glasses to clean them. "I know I've harped to Harry about the obituary, but it upsets me so much. I can't get it out of my mind."

"So the killer, who I still say is a coward, is taunting us?"

"No, Harry, the killer was taunting Roscoe, although I

doubt he recognized that. He thought it was a joke, I really believe that. The killer was someone or is someone he discounted." Herb waved his envelopes with an emphatic flourish. "And Sean Hallahan was the fall guy."

"In that case I wouldn't want to be in Maury McKinchie's shoes or Sean's."

"Me neither." Harry echoed Miranda.

"Then perhaps the killer is someone *we've* discounted." The Reverend Jones pointed his envelopes at Harry.

"You've got to be pushed to the edge to kill. Being ignored or belittled isn't a powerful enough motive to kill," Harry said sensibly.

"I agree with you there." Herb's deep voice filled the room. "There's more to it. You think Rick is guarding McKinchie?"

"I'll ask him." Miranda picked up the phone. She explained their thinking to Rick, who responded that he, too, had considered that Maury and Sean might be in jeopardy. He didn't have enough people in the department for a guard, but he sent officers to cruise by the farm. Maury himself had hired a bodyguard. Rick requested that Miranda, Harry, and Herb stop playing amateur detective.

Miranda then replayed this information minus the crack about being amateurs.

"Cool customer," Herb said.

"Huh?"

"Harry, Maury never said anything about a bodyguard."

"I'd sure tell—if for no other reason than hoping it got back to the killer. It'd put him on notice."

"Miranda, the killer could be in Paris by now," Herb said.

"No." Miranda pushed aside the mail cart. "We'd know

who it is then. The killer can't go, and furthermore, he or she doesn't want to go."

"The old girl is cooking today, isn't she?" Pewter meowed admiringly.

"That body in the Toyota has something to do with this," Mrs. Murphy stated firmly.

"Nah."

"Pewter, when we get home tonight, I'll take you there," Mrs. Murphy promised.

"I'm not walking across all those fields in the cold."

"Fine." Mrs. Murphy stomped away from her.

Susan walked in the backdoor. "Harry, you've got to help me."

"Why?"

"Danny's in charge of the Halloween maze at Crozet High this year. I forgot and like an idiot promised to be a chaperon at the St. Elizabeth's Halloween dance."

"You still haven't figured out how to be in two places at the same time?" Harry laughed at her. As they had exhaustively discussed Roscoe's demise over the phone, there was no reason to repeat their thoughts.

"All the St. Elizabeth's kids will go through the maze and then go on to their own dance." Susan paused. "I can't keep everyone's schedules straight. I wouldn't even remember my own name if it wasn't sewn inside my coat."

"I'll do it"—Harry folded her arms across her chest—"and extract my price later."

"I do not have enough money to buy you a new truck." Susan caught her mail as Harry tossed it to her, a blue nylon belt wrapped around it. "Actually, your truck looks new now that you've painted it."

"Everything on our farm is Superman blue," Murphy cracked, *"even the manure spreader."*

That evening Mrs. Murphy and Tucker discussed how to lure a human to the ditched car. They couldn't think of a way to get Harry to follow them for that great a distance. A human might go one hundred yards or possibly even two hundred yards, but after that their attention span wavered.

"I think we'll have to trust to luck." Tucker paced the barn center aisle.

"You know, they say that killers return to the scene of the crime." Mrs. Murphy thought out loud.

"That's stupid," Pewter interjected. *"If they had a brain in their head, they'd get out of there as fast as they could."*

"The emotion. Murder must be a powerful emotion for them. Maybe they go back to tap into that power." The tiger, on the rafters, passed over the top of Gin Fizz's stall.

Pewter, curled on a toasty horse blanket atop the tack trunk, disagreed. *"Powerful or not, it would be blind stupid to go down Bowden's Lane. Think about it."*

"I am thinking about it! I can't figure out how to get somebody out there."

"You really don't want Mother to see it, do you?" Tucker saw a shadowy little figure zip into a stall. *"Mouse."*

"I know." Mrs. Murphy focused on the disappearing tail. *"Does it to torment. Anyway, you're right. It's a grisly sight, and it would give Mother nightmares. Didn't like it much myself, and we're tougher about those things than humans."*

"In the old days humans left their criminals hanging from gibbets or rotting in cages. They put heads on the gates in London." Tucker imagined a city filled with the aroma of decay, quite pleasing to a dog.

"Those days are long gone. Death is sanitized now." Pewter watched the mouse emerge and dash in the opposite direction. *"What is this, the Mouse Olympics?"*

A squeaky laugh followed this remark.

"Those mice have no respect," Tucker grumbled.

32

Hands patiently folded in his lap, Rick sat in the Hallahan living room. Sean, his mother, father, and younger brother sat listening.

Cynthia had perched on the raised fireplace hearth and was taking notes.

"Sean, I don't want to be an alarmist, but if you did not act alone in placing that obituary, you've got to tell me. The other person may have pertinent information about Mr. Fletcher's death."

"So he was murdered?" Mr. Hallahan exclaimed.

Rick soothingly replied, opening his hands for effect, "I'm a sheriff. I have to investigate all possibilities. It could have been an accident."

Sean, voice clear, replied, "I did it. Alone. I wish I hadn't done it. Kids won't talk to me at school. I mean, some will, but others are acting like I killed him. It's like I've got the plague."

Sympathetically Cooper said, "It will pass, but we need your help."

Rick looked at each family member. "If any of you know anything, please, don't hold back."

"I wish we did," Mrs. Hallahan, a very pretty brunette, replied.

"Did anyone ever accompany your son on his paper route?"

"Sheriff, not to my knowledge." Mr. Hallahan crossed and uncrossed his legs, a nervous habit. "He lost the route, as I'm sure you know."

"Sean?" Rick said.

"No. No one else wanted to get up that early."

Rick stood up. "Folks, if anything comes to mind—anything—call me or Deputy Cooper."

"Are we in danger?" Mrs. Hallahan asked sensibly.

"If Sean is telling the truth—no."

33

Later that evening Sean walked into the garage to use the telephone. His father had phones in the bathrooms, bedrooms, kitchen, and in his car. Sean felt the garage was the most private place; no one would walk in on him.

He dialed and waited. "Hello."

"What do you want?"

"I don't appreciate you not talking to me at school. That's a crock of shit."

Jody seethed on the other end of her private line. "That's not why I'm ignoring you."

"Oh?" His voice dripped sarcasm.

"I'm ignoring you because you've got a crush on Karen Jensen. I was just convenient this summer, wasn't I?"

A pause followed this astute accusation. "You said we were friends, Jody. You said—"

"I know what I said, but I hardly expected us to go back to school and you try to jump Karen's bones. Jeez."

"I am not trying to jump her bones."

"You certainly jumped mine. I can't believe I was that stupid."

"Stupid? You wanted to do it as much as I did."

"Because I liked you."

"Well, I liked you, too, but we were friends. It wasn't a"— he thought for a neutral word—"like a hot romance. Friends."

"Friends don't sleep with each other's best friends . . . and besides, you wouldn't be the first."

"First what?"

"First guy to sleep with Karen. She tells me *everything*."

"Who did she sleep with?" Tension and a note of misery edged his voice.

"That's for me to know and for you to find out," she taunted. "I'm never letting you touch me again." As an after-thought she added, "And you can't drive my BMW either!"

"Do your parents know about the car?" he asked wearily, his brain racing for ways to get the information about Karen from Jody.

"No."

"Jody, if you had wanted . . . more, I wish you'd told me then, not now. And if you don't speak to me at school, people will think it's because of the obit."

"All you think about is yourself. What about me?"

"I like you." He wasn't convincing.

"I'm convenient."

"Jody, we have fun together. This summer was—great."

"But you've got the hots for Karen."

"I wouldn't put it like that."

"You'd better forget all about Karen. First of all, she knows you've slept with me. She's not going to believe a word you say. And furthermore, I can make life really miserable for you if I feel like it. I'll tell everyone you gave me my black eye."

"Jody, I never told anyone I slept with you. Why would you tell?" He ignored the black-eye threat. Jody had told him her father gave her the black eye.

"Because I felt like it." Exasperated, she hung up the phone, leaving a dejected Sean shivering in the garage.

34

Larry Johnson removed his spectacles, rubbing the bridge of his nose where they pinched it. He replaced them, glanced over Jody Miller's file, and then left his office, joining her in an examining room.

"How are you?"

"I'm okay, I think." She sat on the examining table when he motioned for her to do so.

"You were just here in August for your school physical."

"I know. I think it's stupid that I have to have a physical before every season. Coach Hallvard insists on it."

"Every coach insists on it." He smiled. "Now what seems to be the problem?"

"Well"—Jody swallowed hard—"I, uh, I've missed my period for two months in a row."

"I see." He touched his stethoscope. "Have you been eating properly?"

"Uh—I guess."

"The reason I ask that is often female athletes, especially the ones in endurance sports, put the body under such stress that they go without their period for a time. It's the body's way of protecting itself because they couldn't bring a baby to term. Nature is wise."

"Oh." She smiled reflexively. "I don't think field hockey is one of those sports."

"Next question." He paused. "Have you had sexual relations?"

"Yes—but I'm not telling."

"I'm not asking." He held up his hand like a traffic cop. "But there are a few things I need to know. You're seventeen. Have you discussed this with your parents?"

"No," she said quickly.

"I see."

"I don't talk to them. I don't want to talk to them."

"I understand."

"No, you don't."

"Let's start over, Jody. Did you use any form of birth control?"

"No."

"Well, then"—he exhaled—"let's get going."

He took blood for a pregnancy test, at the same time pulling a vial of blood to be tested for infectious diseases. He declined to inform Jody of this. If something turned up, he'd tell her then.

"I hate that." She turned away as the needle was pulled from her arm.

"I do, too." He held the small cotton ball on her arm. "Did your mother ever talk to you about birth control?"

"Yes."

"I see."

She shrugged. "Dr. Johnson, it's not as easy as she made it sound."

"Perhaps not. The truth is, Jody, we don't really understand human sexuality, but we do know that when those hormones start flowing through your body, a fair amount of irrationality seems to flow with them. And sometimes we turn to people for comfort during difficult times, and sex becomes part of the comfort." He smiled. "Come back on Friday." He glanced at his calendar. "Umm, make it Monday."

"All right." She paled. "You won't tell anyone, will you?"

"No. Will you?"

She shook her head no.

"Jody, if you can't talk to your mother, you ought to talk to another older woman. Whether you're pregnant or not, you might be surprised to learn that you aren't alone. Other people have felt what you're feeling."

"I'm not feeling much."

He patted her on the back. "Okay, then. Call me Monday."

She mischievously winked as she left the examining room.

35

Not wishing to appear pushy, Sandy Brashiers transferred his office to the one next to Roscoe Fletcher's but made no move to occupy the late headmaster's sacred space.

April Shively stayed just this side of rude. If Naomi asked her to perform a chore, retrieve information, or screen calls, April complied. She and Naomi had a cordial, if not warm, relationship. If Sandy asked, she found a variety of ways to drag her heels.

Although the jolt of Roscoe's death affected her every minute of the day, Naomi Fletcher resumed her duties as head of the lower school. She needed the work to keep her mind from constantly returning to the shock, and the lower school needed her guidance during this difficult time.

During lunch hour, Sandy walked to Naomi's office, then both of them walked across the quad to the upper-school administration building—Old Main.

"Becoming the leader is easier than being the teacher, isn't it?" Naomi asked him.

"I guess for these last seven years I've been the loyal opposition." He tightened the school scarf around his neck. "I'm finding out that no matter what decision I make there's someone to 'yes' me, someone to 'no' me, and everyone to second-guess me. It's curious to realize how people want to have their own way without doing the work."

She smiled. "Monday morning quarterbacks. Roscoe used to say that they never had to take the hits." She wiggled her fingers in her fur-lined gloves. "He wasn't your favorite person, Sandy, but he was an effective headmaster."

"Yes. My major disagreement with Roscoe was not over daily operations. You know I respected his administrative skills. My view of St. Elizabeth's curriculum was one hundred eighty degrees from his, though. We must emphasize the basics. Take, for instance, his computer drive. Great. We've got every kid in this school computer literate. So?" He threw up his hands. "They stare into a lighted screen. Knowing how to use the technology is useless if you have nothing to say, and the only way you can have something to say is by studying the great texts of our culture. The computer can't read and comprehend *The Federalist Papers* for them."

"Teaching people to think is an ancient struggle," she said. "That's why I love working in the lower school . . . they're so young . . . their minds are open. They soak up everything."

He opened the door for her. They stepped into the administration building, which also had some classrooms on the first floor. A blast of warm radiator heat welcomed them.

They climbed the wide stairs to the second floor, entering Roscoe's office from the direction that did not require them to pass April's office.

She was on her hands and knees putting videotapes into a cardboard box. The tapes had lined a bottom shelf of the bookcase.

"April, I can do that," Naomi said.

Not rising, April replied, "These are McKinchie's. I thought I'd return them to him this afternoon." She held up a tape of *Red River*. "He lent us his library for film history week."

"Yes, he did, and I forgot all about it." Naomi noticed the girls of the field hockey team leaving the cafeteria together. Karen Jensen, in the lead, was tossing an apple to Brooks Tucker.

"April, I'll be moving into this office next week. I can't conduct meetings in that small temporary office. Will you call Design Interiors for me? I'd like them to come out here." Sandy's voice was clear.

"What's wrong with keeping things just as they are? It will save money." She dropped more tapes into the box, avoiding eye contact.

"I need this office to be comfortable—"

"This is comfortable," she interrupted.

"—for me," he continued.

"Well, you might not be appointed permanent headmaster. The board will conduct a search. Why spend money?"

"April, that won't happen before this school year is finished." Naomi stepped in, kind but firm. "Sandy needs our support in order to do the best job he can for St. Elizabeth's. Working in Roscoe's shadow"—she indicated the room, the paintings—"isn't the way to do that."

April scrambled to her feet. "Why are you helping him He dogged Roscoe every step of the way!"

Naomi held up her hands, still gloved, in a gesture o peace. "April, Sandy raised issues inside our circle that al lowed us to prepare for hard questions from the board. H wasn't my husband's best friend, but he has always had th good of St. Elizabeth's at heart."

April clamped her lips shut. "I don't want to do it, but I' do it for you." She picked up the carton and walked by Sandy closing the door behind her.

He exhaled, jamming his hands in his pockets. "Naomi, don't ask that April be fired. She's given long years of service but there's absolutely no way I can work with her or her wit me. I need to find my own secretary—and that will bump u the budget."

She finally took off her gloves to sit on the edge of Roscoe' massive desk. "We'll have to fire her, Sandy. She'll foment re bellion from wherever she sits."

"Maybe McKinchie could use her. He has enough money and she'd be happy in his little home office."

"She won't be happy anywhere." Naomi hated this whol subject. "She was so in love with Roscoe—I used to tease hir about it. No one will ever measure up to him in her eyes. Yo know, I believe if he had asked her to walk to hell and back she would have." She smiled ruefully. "Of course, she didn' have to live with him."

"Well, I won't ask her to walk that far, but I guess you'r right. She'll have to go."

"Let's talk to Marilyn Sanburne first. Perhaps she'll have a idea—or Mim."

"Good God, Mim will run St. Elizabeth's if you let her."

"The world." Naomi swung her legs to and fro. "St. Elizabeth's is too small a stage for Mim the Magnificent."

April opened the door. "I know you two are talking about me."

"At this precise moment we were talking about Mim."

Sourly, April shut the door. Sandy and Naomi looked at each other and shrugged.

36

"How did I get roped into this?" Harry complained.

Her furry family said nothing as she fumbled with her hastily improvised costume. Preferring a small group of friends to big parties, Harry had to be dragged to larger affairs. Even though this was a high school dance and she was a chaperon, she still had to unearth something to wear, snag a date, stand on her feet, and chat up crashing bores. She thought of the other chaperons. One such would be Maury McKinchie, fascinating to most people but not to Harry. Since he was a chaperon, she'd have to gab with him. His standard fare, those delicious stories of what star did what and to whom on his various films, filled her with ennui. Had he been a hunting man she might have endured him, but he was not. He also appeared much too interested in her breasts. Maury was one of those men who didn't look you in the eye when he spoke to you—he spoke to your breasts.

Sandy Brashiers she liked until he grew waspish about the other faculty at St. Elizabeth's. With Roscoe dead he would need to find a new whipping boy. Still, he looked her in the eye when he spoke to her, and that was refreshing.

Ed Sugarman collected old cigarette advertisements. He might expound on the chemical properties of nicotine, but if she could steer him toward soccer, he proved knowledgeable and entertaining.

Coach Hallvard could be lively. Harry then remembered that the dreaded Florence Rubicon would be prowling the dance floor. Harry's Latin ebbed away with each year but she remembered enough Catullus to keep the old girl happy.

Harry laughed to herself. Every Latin teacher and subsequent professor she had ever studied under had been an odd duck, but there was something so endearing about them all. She kept reading Latin partly to bask in the full bloom of eccentricity.

"I can't wear this!" Harry winced, throwing off a tight pump. The patent leather shoe scuttled across the floor. She checked the clock, groaning anew.

"There's time," Mrs. Murphy said. *"Can the tuxedo. It isn't you."*

"I fed you."

"Don't be obtuse. Get out of the tuxedo." Murphy spoke louder, a habit of hers when humans proved dense. *"You need something with imagination."*

"Harry doesn't have imagination," Tucker declared honestly.

"She has good legs," Pewter replied.

"*What does that have to do with imagination?*" Tucker wanted to know.

"*Nothing, but she should wear something that shows off her legs.*"

Mrs. Murphy padded into the closet. "*There's one sorry skirt hanging in here.*"

"*I didn't even know Mom owned a skirt.*"

"*This has to be a leftover from college.*" The tiger inspected the brown skirt.

Pewter joined her. "*I thought she was going to clean out her closet.*"

"*She organized her chest of drawers; that's a start.*"

The two cats peered upward at the skirt, then at each other.

"*Shall we?*"

"*Let's.*" Pewter's eyes widened.

They reached up, claws unsheathed, and shredded the skirt.

"*Wheee!*" They dug in.

Harry, hearing the sound of cloth shredding, poked her head in the closet, the single light bulb swaying overhead. "Hey!"

With one last mighty yank, Mrs. Murphy scooted out of the closet. Pewter, a trifle slower, followed.

Harry, aghast, took out the skirt. "I could brain you two. I've had this skirt since my sophomore year at Crozet High."

"*We know,*" came the titters from under the bed.

"*Cats can be so destructive.*" Tucker's soulful eyes brimmed with sympathy.

"*Brownnoser!*" Murphy accused.

"*I am a mighty cat. What wondrous claws have I. I can rip and tear and even shred the sky,*" Pewter sang.

"Great. Ruin my skirt and now caterwaul underneath the bed." Harry knelt down to behold four luminous chartreuse eyes peeking at her. "Bad kitties."

"*Hee hee.*"

"I mean it. No treats for you."

Pewter leaned into Murphy. "*This is your fault.*"

"*Sell me out for a treatie.*" Mrs. Murphy bumped her.

Harry dropped the dust ruffle back down. She stared at the ruined skirt.

Murphy called out from her place of safety, "*Go as a vagabond. You know, go as one of those poor characters from a Victor Hugo novel.*"

"Wonder if I could make a costume out of this?"

"*She got it!*" Pewter was amazed.

"*Don't count your chickens.*" Mrs. Murphy slithered out from under the bed. "*I'll make sure she puts two and two together.*"

With that she launched herself onto the bed and from the bed she hurtled toward the closet, catching the clothes. She hung there, swaying, then found the tattiest shirt she could find. She sank her claws in and slid down to the floor, the intoxicating sound of rent fabric heralding her descent.

"You're crazy!" Harry dashed after her, but Murphy blasted into the living room, jumped on a chair arm, then wiggled her rear end as though she was going to leap into the bookshelves filled not only with books but with Harry's ribbons and trophies. "Don't you dare."

"*Then leave me alone,*" Murphy sassed, "*and put together your vagabond costume. Time's a-wasting.*"

The human and the cat squared off, eye to eye. "You're in a mood, pussycat."

Tucker tiptoed out. Pewter remained under the bed, straining to hear.

"What's got into you?"

"It's Halloween," Murphy screeched.

Harry reached over to grab the insouciant feline, but Mrs. Murphy easily avoided her. She hopped to the other side of the chair, then ran back into the bedroom where she leapt into the clothes and tore them up some more.

"Yahoo! Banzai! Death to the Emperor!"

"Have you been watching those World War Two movies again?" Tucker laughed.

"Don't shoot until you see the whites of their eyes." Murphy leapt in the air, turning full circle and landing in the middle of the clothes.

"She's on a military kick." Pewter snuck out from under the bed. *"If you get us both punished, Murphy, I will be really upset."*

Murphy catapulted off the bed right onto Pewter. The two rolled across the bedroom floor, entertaining Harry with their catfight.

Finally Pewter, put out, extricated herself from the grasp of Murphy. She stalked off to the kitchen.

"Fraidycat."

"Mental case," Pewter shot back.

"Anything that happens tonight will be dull after this," Harry said with a sigh.

Boy, did she have a wrong number.

37

Little Mim, taut under her powdered face, wig bobbling, wandered across the highly polished gym floor to Harry. At least she thought it was Harry because the vagabond's escort, a pirate, was too tall to be anyone but Fair.

The dance was turning into a huge success, thanks to the band, Yada Yada Yada.

The curved sword, stuck through his sash, gave Fair a dangerous air. Other partyers wore swords. There was Stonewall Jackson and Julius Caesar. A few wore pistols that upon close examination turned out to be squirt guns.

Karen Jensen, behind a golden mask, drove the boys wild because she came as a golden-haired Artemis. Quite a bit of Karen was showing, and it was prime grade.

But then, quite a bit of Harry was showing, and that wasn't bad either.

Little Mim put her hand on Harry's forearm. "Could I have a minute?"

"Sure. Fair, I'll be right back."

"Okay," he replied from under his twirling mustache.

Marilyn pulled Harry into a corner of the auditorium. Madonna and King Kong were making out behind them. King Kong was having a hard time of it.

"I hope you aren't cross with me. I should have called you."

"About what?"

"I asked Blair to the dance. Well, it wasn't just that I needed an escort, but I thought I might interest him in the school and—"

"I have no claim on him. Anyway, we're just friends," Harry said soothingly.

"Thanks. I'd hoped you'd understand." Her wig wobbled. "How did they manage with these things?" She glanced around. "Can you guess who Stonewall Jackson is?"

"Mmm, the paunch means he's a chaperon," Harry stated.

"Kendrick Miller."

"Where's Irene? It isn't World War Three yet with those two, is it?"

"Irene's over there. It'd be a perfect costume if she were twenty years younger. Some women can't accept getting old, I guess." She indicated the woodland fairy, the wings diaphanous over the thin wire. Then, lowering her voice, "Did you see April Shively? Dressed as a witch. How appropriate."

"I thought you liked April."

Realizing she might have said too much, Little Mim back-tracked. "She's not herself since Roscoe's death, and she's making life difficult for everyone from the board on down to the faculty. It will pass."

"Or she will," Harry joked.

"Two bewitching masked beauties." Maury McKinchie complimented them from behind his Rhett Butler mask.

"What a line!" Harry laughed, her voice giving her away.

"May I have this dance?" Maury bowed to Harry, who took a turn on the floor.

Little Mim, happy she wasn't asked, hastened to Blair as fast as her wig would allow.

Sean Hallahan, dressed as a Hell's Angel, danced with Karen Jensen. After the dance ended, he escorted her off the floor. "Karen, is everyone mad at me?"

Jody, dragged along by her mother, glared at Sean. She was in a skeleton outfit that concealed her face, but Sean knew it was Jody.

"Jody is."

"Are you mad at me?"

"No."

"I feel like you've been avoiding me."

"Field hockey practice takes up as much time as football practice." She paused, clearing her throat. "And you've been a little weird lately—distant."

"Yeah, I know."

"Sean, you couldn't help the way things turned out—Mr. Fletcher's dying—and until then it was pretty funny. Even the phony obituary for Mr. McKinchie was funny."

"I didn't do that."

"I know, it was on Roger's paper route, and he says he didn't do it either."

"But I *really* didn't." He sensed her disbelief.

"Okay, okay."

"That's an incredible costume," he said admiringly.

"Thanks."

"Karen—do you like me a little?"

"A little," she said teasingly, "but what about Jody?"

"It's not—well, you know. We're close but not that way. We practiced a lot this summer and—"

"Practiced what?"

"Tennis. It's our spring sport." He swallowed hard.

"Oh." She remembered Jody's version of the summer.

"Will you go out with me next Friday after the game?"

"Yes," she said without hesitation.

He smiled, pushing her back out on the dance floor.

Coach Renee Hallvard, dressed as Garfield the cat, sidled up next to Harry.

"Harry, is that you?"

"Coach?"

"Yes, or should I say 'Meow'?"

"Wonder what Mrs. Murphy would say about this."

Coach reached back, draping her tail over her arm. "Get a life."

They both laughed.

"She probably would say that."

"If you don't mind, I'll drop off this year's field hockey rule book on Monday."

"Why?" Harry murmured expectantly.

"I need a backup referee—just in case. You know the game."

"Oh, Coach. Make Susan do it."

"She can't." Coach Hallvard laughed at Harry. "Brooks is on the team."

"Well—okay."

Coach Hallvard clapped her on the back. "You're a good sport."

"Sucker is more like it."

Rhett Butler asked Harry to dance a second time. "You've got beautiful legs."

"Thank you," she murmured.

"I ought to give you a screen test."

"Get out of here." Harry thumped his back with her left hand.

"You're very attractive. The camera likes some people. It might like you." He paused. "What's so curious is that even professionals don't know who will be good on-screen and who won't."

"Rhett," she joked because she knew it was Maury, "I bet you say that to all the girls."

"Ha." He threw his head back and laughed. "Just the pretty ones."

"In fact, I heard you have a car full of vital essences, so you must have said something to BoomBoom."

"Oh!" His voice lowered. "What was I thinking?"

Part of Maury's charm was that he never pretended to be better than he was.

"Hey, I'll never tell."

"You won't have to. She will." He sighed. "You see, Harry, I'm a man who needs a lot of attention, female attention. I admit it."

Stonewall and Garfield, dancing near them, turned their heads. "You don't give a damn who you seduce and who you hurt. You don't need attention, you need your block knocked off," Kendrick Miller, as Stonewall, mumbled.

Rhett danced on. "Kendrick Miller, you're a barrel of

laughs. I say what I think. You think being a repressed Virginian is a triumph. I think you're pathetic."

Kendrick stopped. Coach Hallvard stepped back.

"Guys. Chill out," Harry told them.

"I'll meet you after the dance, McKinchie. You say where and when."

"Are we going to fight a duel, Kendrick? Do I get the choice of weapons?"

"Sure."

"Pies. You need a pie in the face."

Harry dragged Maury backward. She had heard about Kendrick's flash temper.

"Since we can't use guns, we can start with fists," Kendrick called after him as Renee Hallvard pulled him in the direction opposite Maury.

As the dancers closed the spaces left by the vacating couples, a few noticed the minor hostilities. Fortunately, most of the students were wrapped up in the music and one another.

Jody put her hands on her hips, turned her back on her father, and walked to the water fountain. She had to take off the mask to drink.

"What a putz!" Maury shook his head.

"No one has ever accused Kendrick of having a good time or a sense of humor." Harry half laughed.

"Totally *humorless*." Maury emphasized the word. "Thank God his kid doesn't take after him. Funny thing, though, the camera liked Jody, and yet Karen Jensen is the more beautiful girl. I noticed that when we had our one-day film clinic."

"Hmm."

"Ah, the camera... it reveals things the naked eye can't see." He bowed. "Thank you, madam. Don't forget your screen test."

She curtseyed. "Sir." Then she whispered, "Where's your bodyguard?"

He winked. "I made that up."

Fair ambled over when he'd gone. "Slinging the bull, as usual?"

"Actually, we were talking about the camera... after he had a few words with Kendrick Miller. Testosterone poisoning."

"If you keep saying that, I'll counter with 'raging hormones.'"

"You do, anyway, behind our backs."

"I do not."

"Most men do."

"I'm not most men."

"No, you aren't." She slipped her arm through his.

The evening progressed without further incident, except that Sean Hallahan had a flask of booze in his motorcycle jacket. No one saw him drinking from it, but he swayed on his feet after each return from outside.

He got polluted, and when someone dressed as a Musketeer showed up at the party, sword in hand, and knocked him down, he couldn't get up.

As Yada Yada Yada played the last song of the evening, some of the kids began sneaking off. Roger and Brooks danced the last dance. They were a hit as Lucy and Desi.

A piercing scream didn't stop the dancers. After all, ghosts and goblins were about.

The piercing scream was followed by moans that seemed

frightening enough. Finally, Harry and Fair left the dance to investigate. They found Rhett Butler lying bleeding on the hall floor, gasping for breath as the blood spurted from his throat and his chest. Bending over him, sword in hand, was a paunchy Stonewall Jackson.

38

Maury McKinchie died before the rescue squad arrived at St. Elizabeth's. Rick Shaw, sirens blaring, arrived seconds after his final gurgle.

Rick lifted Kendrick's bloodied sword from his hand.

"It wasn't me, it was the Musketeer. I fought him off, but it was too late," Kendrick babbled.

"Kendrick Miller, I am booking you under suspicion of murder. You have the right to remain silent..." Rick began.

Harry, Fair, Little Mim, and the other chaperons quickly cordoned off the hallway leading to the big outside doors, making sure that Irene was hurried out of the gym. Florence Rubicon ushered the dancers out by another exit at the end of the gym floor. Still, a few kids managed to creep in to view the corpse.

Karen and Sean, both mute, simply stared.

Jody walked up behind them, her mask off, her hair tousled, the horror of the scene sinking in. "Dad? Dad, what's going on?"

Cynthia flipped open her notebook and started asking questions.

Sandy Brashiers, in a low voice, said to Little Mim, "People are going to yank their kids out of here. By Monday this school will be a ghost town."

39

A light brown stubble covered Rick Shaw's square chin. As his thinning hair was light brown, the contrast amused Cynthia Cooper, although little was amusing at the moment.

The ashtray in the office overflowed. The coffee machine pumped out cup after cup of the stimulant.

Cynthia regretted Maury McKinchie's murder, not just because a man was cut down, literally, but because Sunday, which would dawn in a couple of hours, was her day off. She had planned to drive over to the beautiful town of Monterey, almost on the West Virginia border. She'd be driving alone. Her job prevented her from having much of a social life. It wasn't that she didn't meet men. She did. Usually they were speeding seventy-five miles per hour in a fifty-five zone. They rarely smiled when they saw her, even though she was easy on the eyes. The roundup of drunks at the mall furnished her with scores of men, and they fell all over her—literally. The occasional white-collar criminal enlivened her harvest of captive males.

Over the last years of working together she and Rick had grown close. As he was a happily married man, not a hint of impropriety tainted their relationship. She relied on his friendship, hard won because when she joined the force as the first woman Rick was less than thrilled.

The one man she truly liked, Blair Bainbridge, set many hearts on fire. She felt she didn't have a chance.

Rick liked to work from flow charts. He'd started three, ultimately throwing out each of them.

"What time is it?"

"Five thirty."

"It's always darkest before the dawn." Rick quoted the old saw. He swung his feet onto his desktop. "I hate to admit that I'm stumped, but I am."

"We've got Kendrick Miller in custody."

"Not for long. He'll get a big-money lawyer, and that will be that. And it had occurred to me that Kendrick isn't the kind of man to get caught committing a murder. Standing over a writhing victim doesn't compute."

"Could have lost his head." She emptied her cup. She couldn't face another swig of coffee. "But you're not buying, are you?"

"No." He paused. "We deal in the facts. The facts are, he had a bloody sword in his hand."

"And there were two other partyers wearing swords. One of whom vanished into thin air."

"Or knew where to hide."

"Not one kid there knew who the Musketeer was or had heard him speak." Cooper leaned against the small sink in the corner of the old room. She held her fingers to her temples, which throbbed. "Boss, let's back up. Let's start with Roscoe Fletcher."

"I'm listening."

"Sandy Brashiers coveted Roscoe's job. They never saw eye to eye."

He held up his hand. "Granted, but killing to become headmaster of St. Elizabeth's—is the game worth the candle?"

"People have killed for less."

"You're right. You're right." He folded his hands over his chest and made a mental note to dig into Sandy's past.

"Anyone could have poisoned Roscoe. He left his car unlocked, his office unlocked. It wouldn't take a rocket scientist to put a hard candy drenched in poison in his car or in his pocket or to hand it to him. Anyone could do it."

"Who would want to do it, though?" She put her hands behind her head. "Not one trace of poison was found in the tin of strawberry hard candies in his car. And the way he handed out candy, half the county would be dead. So we know the killer had a conscience, sort of."

"That's a quaint way of looking at it."

"I have a hunch Roscoe was sleeping with Irene Miller." Cynthia shook her feet, which were falling asleep in her regulation shoes. "That would be a motive for the first murder."

"We have no proof that he was carrying on an extramarital affair."

Cynthia smirked. "This is Albemarle County."

Rick half laughed, then stood up to stretch. "Everyone's got secrets, Coop. The longer I work this show, the more I realize that every single person harbors secrets."

"What about that money in the Jiffy bag?" Cynthia said.

"Too many prints on the bag and not a single one on the money." Rick sighed. "I am flat running into walls. The obvious conclusion is drug money, but we haven't got one scrap of evidence."

Cynthia shot a rubber band in the air. It landed with a flop on Rick's desk. "These murders are tied together, I'll bet my badge on that, but what I can't figure out is what an expensive school like St. Elizabeth's has to do with it. All roads lead back to that school."

"Roscoe's murder was premeditated. Maury's was not—or so it appears. Kendrick Miller has a tie to St. Elizabeth's, but—" He shrugged.

"But"—Cooper shot another rubber band straight in the air—"while we're just postulating—"

"Postulating? I'm pissing in the wind."

"You do that." She caught the rubber band as it fell back. "Listen to me. St. Elizabeth's is the tie. What if Fletcher and McKinchie were filching alumni contributions?"

"Kendrick Miller isn't going to kill over alumni misappropriations." He batted down her line of thought.

The phone rang. The on-duty operator, Joyce Thomson, picked it up.

Cynthia said, "I've always wanted to pick up the phone and say, 'Cops and Robbers.'"

Rick's line buzzed. He punched in the button so Cynthia could listen. "Yo."

"Sheriff," Joyce Thomson said, "it's John Aurieano. Mrs. Berryhill's cows are on his land, and he's going to shoot them if you don't remove them."

Rick punched the line and listened to the torrent of outrage. "Mrs. Berryhill's a small woman, Mr. Aurieano. She can't round up her cattle without help, and it will take me hours to send someone over to help. We're shorthanded."

More explosions.

"Tell you what, I'll send someone to move them, but let me give you some friendly advice.... This is the country. Cows are part of the country, and I'll let you in on something quite shocking—they can't read 'No Trespassing' signs. You shoot the cows, Mr. Aurieano, and you're going to be in a lot more trouble than you can imagine. If you don't like the way things are, then move back to the city!" He put the phone down. "You know, there are days when this job is a real pain in the ass."

40

A subdued congregation received early-morning mass. Jody Miller and her mother, Irene, sat in a middle pew. The entire Hallahan family occupied a pew on the left. Samson Coles made a point of sitting beside Jody. Lucinda squeezed next to Irene. Whatever Kendrick Miller may or may not have done, the opprobrium shouldn't attach to his wife and child.

Still, parishioners couldn't help staring.

Rick and Cooper knelt in the back row. Rick's head bobbed as he started to drift off, and his forehead touched his hand. He jerked his head up. "Sorry," he whispered.

He and Cynthia waited in the vestibule while people shuffled out after the service. Curious looks passed among the churchgoers as everyone watched to see if the police would stop Irene. She and Jody passed Rick without looking right or left. The Hallahans nodded a greeting but kept moving.

Finally, disappointed, the rest of the congregation walked into the brisk air, started their cars, and drove away.

Rick checked his watch, then knocked on the door at the left of the vestibule.

"Who's there?" Father Michael called out, hearing the knock.

"Rick Shaw and Deputy Cooper."

Father Michael, wearing his robe and surplice, opened the door. "Come in, Sheriff, Deputy."

"I don't mean to disturb you on Sunday. I have a few quick questions, Father."

He motioned. "Come in. Sit down for a minute."

"Thanks." They stepped inside, collapsing on the old leather sofa. "We're beat. No sleep."

"I didn't sleep much myself. . . ."

"Have you been threatened, Father?" Rick's voice cracked from fatigue.

"No."

"In your capacity as chaplain to St. Elizabeth's, have you noticed anything unusual, say, within the faculty? Arguments with Roscoe? Problems with the alumni committee?"

Father Michael paused a long time, his narrow but attractive face solemn. "Roscoe and Sandy Brashiers were inclined to go at it. Nothing that intense, though. They never learned to agree to disagree, if you know what I mean."

"I think I do." Rick nodded. "Apart from the inviolate nature of the confessional, do you know or have you heard of any sexual improprieties involving Roscoe?"

"Uh—" The middle-aged man paused a long time again.

"There was talk. But that's part and parcel of a small community."

"Any names mentioned?" Cynthia said. "Like Irene Miller, maybe?"

"No."

"What about Sandy Brashiers and Naomi Fletcher?"

"I'd heard that one. The version goes something like, Naomi tires of Roscoe's infidelities and enlists his enemy, or shall we say rival, to dispose of him."

Rick stood up. "Father, thank you for your time. If anything occurs to you or you want to talk, call me or Coop."

"Sheriff"—Father Michael weighed his words—"am I in danger?"

"I hope not," Rick answered honestly.

41

April Shively was arrested Monday morning at the school. She was charged with obstructing justice since she had consistently refused to hand over the school records, first to Sandy, then to the police. As she and Roscoe had worked hand in glove, not even Naomi knew how much April had removed and hidden.

Sandy Brashiers wasted no time in terminating her employment. On her way out of the school, April turned and slapped his face. Cynthia Cooper hustled her to the squad car.

St. Elizabeth's, deserted save for faculty, stood forlorn in the strong early November winds. Sandy and Naomi convened an emergency meeting of faculty and interested parties.

Neither could answer the most important question: What was happening at St. Elizabeth's?

The Reverend Herbert C. Jones received an infuriating phone call from Darla McKinchie. No, she would not be returning to Albemarle County for a funeral service. She would be shipping her late husband's body to Los Angeles immediately. Would the Reverend please handle the arrangements with Dale and Delaney Funeral Home? She would make a handsome contribution to the church. Naturally, he agreed, but was upset by her high-handed manner and the fact that she cared so little for Maury's local friends, but then again, she seemed to care little for Maury himself.

Blue Monday yielded surprises every hour on the hour, it seemed. Jody Miller learned that yes, she was pregnant. She begged Dr. Larry Johnson not to call her mother. He wouldn't agree since she was under twenty-one, so she pitched a hissy fit right there in the examining room. Hayden McIntire, the doctor's much younger partner, and two nurses rushed in to restrain Jody.

The odd thing was that when Irene Miller arrived it was she who cried, not Jody. The shame of an out-of-wedlock pregnancy cut Irene to the core. She was fragile enough, thanks to the tensions inside her house and now outside it as well. As for Jody, she had no shame about her condition, she simply didn't want to be pregnant. Larry advised mother and daughter to have a heart-to-heart but not in his examining room.

At twelve noon Kendrick Miller was released on $250,000 bail into the custody of his lawyer, Ned Tucker. At one in the afternoon, he told his divorce lawyer not to serve papers on Irene. She didn't need that crisis on top of this one, he said. What he really wanted was for Irene to stand beside him, but

Kendrick being Kendrick, he had to make it sound as though he were doing his wife a big favor.

At two thirty he blasted Sandy Brashiers on the phone and said he was taking his daughter out of that sorry excuse for a school until things got straightened out over there. By three thirty the situation was so volatile that Kendrick picked up the phone and asked Father Michael for help. For him to admit he needed help was a step in the right direction.

By four forty-five the last surprise of the day occurred when BoomBoom Craycroft lost control of her shiny brand-new 7 series BMW. She had roared up the alleyway behind the post office where she spun in a 360-degree turn, smashing into Harry's blue Ford.

Hearing the crash, the animals rushed out of the post office. BoomBoom, without a scratch herself, opened the door to her metallic green machine, put one foot on the ground, and started to wail.

"Is she hurt?" Tucker ran over.

Mrs. Murphy, moving at a possum trot, declared, *"Her essences are shaken."*

In the collision the plastic case in which BoomBoom kept her potions slammed up against the dash, cracking and spilling out a concoction of rose, sage, and comfrey.

Harry opened the backdoor. "Oh, no!"

"I couldn't help it! My heel got stuck in the mat." Boom-Boom wept.

Mrs. Hogendobber stuck her head out the door. Her body immediately followed. "Are you all right?"

"My neck hurts."

"Do you want me to call the rescue squad?" Harry asked, dubious but giving BoomBoom the benefit of the doubt.

"No. I'll go over to Larry's. It's probably whiplash." She

viewed the caved-in side of the truck. "I'm insured, Harry, don't worry."

Harry sighed. Her poor truck. Tucker ran underneath to inspect the frame, which was undamaged. The BMW had suffered one little dent in the right fender.

Pewter, moving at a slower pace, walked around the truck. *"We can still drive home in it. It's only the side that's bashed in."*

"I'll call the sheriff's department." Miranda, satisfied that BoomBoom was fine, walked back into the post office.

Market Shiflett opened his backdoor. "I thought I heard something." He surveyed the situation.

Before he could speak, BoomBoom said, "No bones broken."

"Good." He heard the front door ring and ducked back into his store.

"Come inside." Harry helped her former rival out of the car. "It's cold out here."

"My heel stuck in that brand-new mat I bought." She pointed to a fuzzy mat with the BMW logo on it.

"BoomBoom, why wear high heels to run your errands?"

"Oh—well—" Her hand fluttered.

"Where have you been? You always come down to pick up your mail."

"I've been under the weather. These murders upset me."

Once inside, Mrs. Hogendobber brewed a strong cup of tea while they waited for someone to appear from the sheriff's department.

"I think it's dreadful that Darla McKinchie, that self-centered nothing of an actress, isn't having the service here." BoomBoom, revived by the tea, told them about Herb's phone call. She'd seen Herbie Jones at the florist.

"That is pretty cold-blooded." Harry bent down to tie her shoelaces. Mrs. Murphy helped.

"Someone should sponsor a service here."

"That would be lovely, BoomBoom, why don't you do it?" Miranda smiled, knowing she'd told BoomBoom to do what she wanted to do anyway.

After the officer left, having asked questions about the accident and taken pictures, the insurance agent showed up and did the same. Then he was gone, and finally BoomBoom herself left, which greatly relieved Harry, who strained to be civil to a woman she disliked. BoomBoom said she was too rattled to drive her car, so Lucinda Coles picked her up. BoomBoom left her car at the post office, keys in the ignition.

42

"April, cooperate, for Christ's sake." Cooper, exasperated, rapped her knuckles on the table.

"No, I'll stay here and live off the county for a while. My taxes paid for this jail." She pushed back a stray forelock.

"Removing documents pertinent to the murder of Roscoe Fletcher—"

April interrupted. "But they're not! They're pertinent to the operations of St. Elizabeth's, and that's none of your business."

Cooper slapped her hand hard on the table. "Embezzlement *is* my business!"

April, not one to be shaken by an accusation, pursed her lips. "Prove it."

Cynthia stretched her long legs, took a deep breath, counted to ten, and started anew. "You have an important place in this community. Don't throw it away to protect a dead man."

Folding her arms across her chest, April withdrew into hostile silence.

Cooper did likewise.

Twenty minutes later April piped up, "You can't prove I had an affair with him either. That's what everyone thinks. Don't give me this baloney about having an important place in the community."

"But you do. You're important to St. Elizabeth's."

April leaned forward, both elbows on the table. "I'm a secretary. That's nothing"—she made a gesture of dismissal with her hand—"to people around here. But I'm a damned good secretary."

"I'm sure you are."

"And"—she lurched forward a bit more—"Sandy Brashiers will ruin everything we worked for, I guarantee it. That man lives in a dream world, and he's sneaky. Well, he may be temporary headmaster, but headmaster of what! No one was at school today."

"You were."

"That's my job. Besides, no one is going to kill me—I'm too low on the totem pole."

"If you know why Roscoe was killed, they might."

"I don't know."

"If you did, would you tell me?"

A brief silence followed this question as a clap of thunder follows lightning.

Looking Cynthia square in the eye, April answered resolutely. "Yes. And I'll tell you something else. Roscoe had something on Sandy Brashiers. He never told me what it was, but it helped him keep Sandy in line."

"Any ideas—any ideas at all?"

"No." She gulped air. "I wish I knew. I really do."

43

Kendrick stared at Jody's red BMW as she exploded. "No! I paid for it with Grandpa K's money. He left the money to me, not you."

"He left it to pay for college, and you promised to keep it in savings." His face reddened.

Irene, attempting to defuse a full-scale blowup, stepped in. "We're all tired. Let's discuss this tomorrow." She knew perfectly well this was not the time to bring up the much larger issue of Jody's pregnancy.

"Stop protecting her," Kendrick ordered.

"You know, Dad, we're not employees. You can't order us around."

He slammed the side door of the kitchen, returning inside

with the BMW keys in his hand. He dangled them under his daughter's nose. "You're not going anywhere."

She shrugged since she'd stashed away the second set of keys.

Kendrick calmed down for a moment. "Did you pick the car up today?"

"Uh—"

"No, she's had it for a few days."

"Three days."

Irene didn't know how long Jody had had the car, but that was hardly a major worry. She'd become accustomed to her daughter's lying to her. Other parents said their children did the same, especially in the adolescent years, but Irene still felt uneasy about it. Getting used to something didn't mean one liked it.

"If you've had this car three days, where was it?"

"I lent it to a friend."

"Don't lie to me!" The veins stood out in Kendrick's neck.

"Isn't it a little late to try and be a dad now?" she mumbled.

He backhanded her across the face hard. Tears sprang into her eyes. "The car goes back!"

"No way."

He hit her again.

"Kendrick, please!"

"Stay out of this."

"She's my daughter, too. She's made a foolish purchase, but that's how we learn, by making foolish mistakes," Irene pleaded.

"Where did you hide the car?" Kendrick bellowed.

"You can beat me to a pulp. I'll never tell you."

He raised his hand again. Irene hung on to it as Jody ducked. He threw his wife onto the floor.

"Go to your room."

Jody instantly scurried to her room.

Kendrick checked his watch. "It's too late to take the car back now. You can follow me over tomorrow."

Irene scrambled to her feet. "She'll lose a lot of money, won't she?"

"Twenty-one percent." He turned from Irene's slightly bedraggled form to walk into the kitchen, where he turned on the television to watch CNN.

He forgot or didn't care that Jody had a telephone in her room, which she used the second she shut her door.

"Hello, is Sean there?"

Moments later Sean picked up the phone.

"It's Jody."

"Oh, hi." He was wary.

"I just found out today that I'm pregnant."

A gasp followed. "What are you going to do?"

"Tell everyone it was you."

"You can't do that!"

"Why not? You didn't find me that repulsive this summer."

A flash of anger hit him. "How do you know it was me?"

"You asshole!" She slammed down the receiver.

A shaken, lonely Sean Hallahan put the receiver back on the cradle.

44

The front-office staff at Crozet High, frazzled by parental requests to accept transfers from St. Elizabeth's, stopped answering the phone. The line in the hall took precedence.

The middle school and grammar school suffered the same influx.

Sandy Brashiers took out an ad in the newspaper. He had had the presence of mind to place the full-page ad the moment Maury was killed. Given lag time, it ran today.

The ad stated that the board of directors and temporary headmaster regretted the recent incidents at St. Elizabeth's, but these involved adults, not students.

He invited parents to come to his office at Old Main

Building or to visit him at home... and he begged parents not to pull their children out of the school.

A few parents read the ad as they stood in line.

Meanwhile, the St. Elizabeth's students were thoroughly enjoying their unscheduled vacation.

Karen Jensen had called Coach Hallvard asking that the hockey team be allowed to practice with Crozet High in the afternoon until things straightened out.

Roger Davis used the time to work at the car wash. Jody said she needed money, so she was there, too.

Karen borrowed her daddy's car, more reliable than her own old Volvo, and took Brooks with her to see Mary Baldwin College in Staunton. She was considering applying there but wanted to see it without her mom and dad.

The college was only thirty-five miles from Crozet.

"I'd rather finish out at St. Elizabeth's than go to Crozet High." Karen cruised along, the old station wagon swaying on the highway. "Transferring now could mess up my grade-point average, and besides, we're not the ones in danger. So I'd just as soon go back."

"My parents are having a fit." Brooks sighed and looked out the window as they rolled west down Waynesboro's Main Street.

"Everybody's are. Major weird. BoomBoom Craycroft said it's karma."

"Karma is celestial recycling," Brooks cracked.

"Three points."

"I thought so, too." She smiled. "It *is* bizarre. Do you think the killer is someone at St. Elizabeth's?"

"Sean." Karen giggled.

"Hey, some people really think he did kill Mr. Fletcher. And everyone thinks Mr. Miller skewered Mr. McKinchie.

He just got out of jail because he's rich. He was standing over him, sword in hand."

Brooks stared at the sumac, reddening, by the side of the road as they passed the outskirts of Waynesboro. "Did you hear April Shively's in jail? Maybe she did it."

"Women don't kill," Karen said.

"Of course they do."

"Not like men. Ninety-five percent of all murders are committed by men, so the odds are it's a man."

"Karen, women are smarter. They don't get caught."

They both laughed as they rolled into Staunton on Route 250.

45

November can be a tricky month. Delightful warm interludes cast a soft golden glow on tree limbs, a few still sporting colorful leaves. The temperature hovers in the high fifties or low sixties for a few glorious days, then cold air knifes in, a potent reminder that winter truly is around the corner.

This was one of those coppery, warm days, and Harry sat out back of the post office eating a ham sandwich. Sitting in a semicircle at her feet, rapturous in their attentions, were Mrs. Murphy, Pewter, and Tucker.

Mrs. Hogendobber stuck her head out the backdoor. "Take your time with lunch. Nothing much is going on."

Harry swallowed so she wouldn't be talking with her

mouth full. "It's a perfect, perfect day. Push the door open and sit out here with me."

"Bring a sandwich," Pewter requested.

"Later. I am determined to reorganize the back shelves. Looks like a storm hit them."

"Save it for a rainy day. Come on," Harry cajoled.

"Well, it is awfully pretty, isn't it?" She disappeared quickly, returning with a sandwich and two orange-glazed buns, her specialty.

Although Mrs. Hogendobber's house was right across the alley from the post office, she liked to bring her lunch and pastries to work with her. A small refrigerator and a hot plate in the back allowed the two women to operate Chez Post, as they sometimes called it.

"The last of my mums." Miranda pointed out the deep russet-colored flowers bordering her fall gardens. "What is there about fall that makes one melancholy?"

"Loss of the light." Harry enjoyed the sharp mustard she'd put on her sandwich.

"And color, although I battle that with pyracantha, the December-blooming camellias, and lots of holly in strategic places. Still, I miss the fragrance of summer."

"Hummingbirds."

"Baby snakes." Mrs. Murphy offered her delectables.

"Baby mice," Pewter chimed in.

"You have yet to kill a mouse." Mrs. Murphy leaned close to Harry just in case her mother felt like sharing.

Pewter, preferring the direct approach, sat in front of Harry, chartreuse eyes lifted upward in appeal. *"Look who's talking. The barn is turning into Mouse Manhattan."*

Tucker drooled. Mrs. Hogendobber handed her a tidbit of

ham, to the fury of the two cats. She tore off two small pieces for them, too.

"Mine has mustard on it," Mrs. Murphy complained.

"I'll eat it," Tucker gallantly volunteered.

"In a pig's eye."

"Aren't we lucky that Miranda makes all these goodies?" Pewter nibbled. *"She's the best cook in Crozet."*

Cynthia Cooper slowly rolled down the alleyway, pulling in next to BoomBoom's BMW. "Great day."

"Join us."

She checked her watch. "Fifteen minutes."

"Make it thirty, and leave your radio on." Harry smiled.

"Good idea." Cynthia cut off the ignition, then turned the volume up on the two-way radio. "Mrs. H., did you make sandwiches for Market today?"

"Indeed, I did."

Cynthia sprinted down the narrow alley between the post office and the market. Within minutes she returned with a smoked turkey sandwich slathered in tarragon mayonnaise, Boston lettuce peeping out from the sides of the whole wheat bread.

The three sat on the back stoop. Every now and then the radio squawked, but no calls for Coop.

"Why did you paint your fingernails?" Harry noticed the raspberry polish.

"Got bored."

"Isn't it funny how Little Mim changes her hairdo? Each time it's a new style or color, you know something is up," Miranda noted.

Sean Hallahan ambled down the alleyway.

"You look like the dogs got at you under the porch." Harry laughed at his disheveled appearance.

"Oh"—he glanced down at his wrinkled clothes—"guess I do."

"Is the football team going to practice at Crozet High? Field hockey is," Harry said.

"Nobody's called me. I don't know what we're going to do. I don't even know if I'm going back to St. Elizabeth's."

"Do you want to?" Cynthia asked.

"Yeah, we've got a good team this year. And it's my senior year. I don't want to go anywhere else."

"That makes sense," Mrs. Hogendobber said.

He ran his finger over the hood of the BMW. "Cool."

"Ultra," Harry replied.

"Just a car." Pewter remained unimpressed by machines.

He bent over, shading his eyes, and peered inside. "Leather. Sure stinks, though."

"She spilled her essences," Harry said.

"Don't be squirrelly," Mrs. Murphy advised.

Sean opened the door, and the competing scents rolled out like a wave. "I hope I get rich."

"Hope you do, too." Harry gave the last of her sandwich to the animals.

He turned on the ignition, rolled down the windows, and clicked on the radio. "Too cool. This is just too cool."

"Where is BoomBoom, anyway?" Cynthia drank iced tea out of a can.

"Who knows? She needs someone to follow her to the BMW dealer. She slightly dented her bumper, not even a dent actually—she rubbed off some of the finish." Harry indicated the spot.

Sean, paying no attention to the conversation, leaned his head back and turned up the radio a bit. He was surrounded by speakers. Then he let off the emergency brake, popped her in reverse, and backed out into the alleyway. He waved at the three women and three animals and carefully rolled forward.

"Should I yank his chain?" Cynthia craned her neck.

"Nah."

They waited a few moments, expecting him to go around the block and reappear. Then they heard the squeal of rubber.

Cooper put down what was left of her sandwich. She stood up. The car was pulling away.

Mrs. Hogendobber listened. "He's not coming back."

"I don't believe this!" Cooper hurried to the squad car as Tucker scarfed down the sandwich remains. She pulled out the speaker, telling the dispatcher where she was and what she was doing. She didn't ask for assistance yet because she thought he was taking a joyride. She hoped to catch him and turn him back before he got into more trouble—he was in enough as it was.

"Can I come?" Harry asked.

"Hop in."

Harry opened the door. Mrs. Murphy and Tucker jumped in with her. "Miranda, do you care?"

"Go on." She waved her off, then glanced down. "Pewter, are you staying with me?"

"*Yes, I am.*" The gray cat followed her back into the post office.

Cynthia turned left, heading toward Route 250. "Sounded like he was heading this way."

"Don't you think he'll make a big circle and come back?"

"Yeah, I do. Right under my nose.... Jeez, what a dumb thing to do." She shook her head.

"He hasn't shown the best judgment lately."

Mrs. Murphy settled in Harry's lap while Tucker sat between the humans.

As they reached Route 250, they noticed a lumber truck pulling off to the right side of the road. Cynthia slowed, putting on her flashers. "Stay here." She stepped out. Harry watched as the driver spoke to her and pointed toward the west. A few choice words escaped his tobacco-stained lips. Coop dashed back to the car.

She hit the accelerator and the sirens.

"Trouble?"

"Yep."

Other cars pulled off to the right as Cynthia's car screeched down Route 250 to the base of Afton Mountain. Then they started the climb to the summit, some 1,850 feet.

"You think he got on Sixty-four?"

"Yeah. A great big four-lane highway. He's gonna bury the speedometer."

"Shit, Cooper, he's going to bury himself."

"That thought has occurred to me."

Mrs. Murphy leaned over Harry and said to Tucker, *"Fasten your seat belt."*

"Yeah," the dog replied, wishing there were seat belts made for animals.

Cynthia hurtled past the Howard Johnson's at the top of the mountain, turning left, then turning right to get onto Interstate 64. Vehicles jerked to the right as best they could but in some places on the entrance ramp the shoulder was inadequate. She swerved to avoid the cars.

The Rockfish Valley left behind was supplanted by the Shenandoah Valley. There was a glimpse of Waynesboro off to the right as they got onto I 64.

Remnants of fall foliage blurred. Cynthia negotiated the large sweeping curves on top of the Blue Ridge Mountains.

"What if he took the Skyline Drive?" Harry asked.

"I'm going to have to call in the state police and Augusta County's police, too. Damn!"

"He asked for it," Harry replied sensibly.

"Yes, he did." Cooper called the dispatcher, gave her location, and requested assistance as well as help on the Skyline Drive.

"Doesn't compute." Mrs. Murphy snuggled as Harry held her in the curves.

"That he stole the car?"

"That he did it right in front of them. He wants to get caught." Her eyes widened as they hung another curve. *"He's in on it, or he knows something."*

"Then why steal a car in front of Coop?" Tucker asked the obvious question.

"That's what I mean—something doesn't compute," Murphy replied.

Up ahead they caught sight of Sean. Cynthia checked her speedometer. She was hitting ninety, and this was not the safest stretch of road in the state of Virginia.

She slowed a bit. "He's not only going to hurt himself, he's going to hurt someone else." She clicked on the black two-way radio button. "Subject in sight. Just past Ninety-nine on the guardrail." She repeated a number posted on a small metal sign. "Damn, he's going one hundred." She shook her head.

As good as the BMW was, Sean was not accustomed to driving a high-performance machine in challenging circumstances. The blue flashing lights behind him didn't scare him as much as the blue flashing lights he saw in the near distance, coming from the opposite direction. He took his eyes off the road for a split second, but a split second at 100 miles an hour is a fraction too long. He spun out, steered hard in the other direction, and did a 360, blasting through the guardrail and taking the metal with him as he soared over the ravine.

"Oh, my God!" Harry exclaimed.

Cynthia screeched to a stop. The BMW seemed airborne for an eternity, then finally crashed deep into the mountain laurels below.

Both Cynthia and Harry were out of the squad car when it stopped. Mrs. Murphy and Tucker could run down the mountainside much better than the two humans could as they stumbled, rolled, and got up again.

"We've got to get him before the car blows up!" Mrs. Murphy shouted to the corgi, who realized the situation also.

The BMW had landed upside down. The animals reached it, and Tucker tried to open the door by standing on her hind legs.

"Impossible."

The tiger raced around the car, hoping windows would have been smashed to bits on the other side.

Harry and Cooper, both covered in mud, scratched, and torn, reached the car. Cooper opened the door. Sean was held in place upside down by the safety belt. She reached in and clicked the belt. Both she and Harry dragged him out.

"Haul," Cynthia commanded.

Harry grabbed his left arm, Cynthia his right, and Tucker grabbed the back of his collar. They struggled and strained but managed to get the unconscious, bloodied boy fifty yards up the mountainside. Mrs. Murphy scampered ahead.

The BMW made a definite clicking sound and then *boom,* the beautiful machine was engulfed in flames.

The two women sat for a moment, holding Sean so he wouldn't slide back down. Mrs. Murphy walked ahead, searching for the easiest path up. Tucker, panting, sat for a moment, too.

They heard more sirens and a voice at the lip of the ravine. Tucker barked. *"We're down here!"*

Harry, still holding Sean, turned around to see rescue workers scrambling down to help. She felt for the vein in his neck; a faint pulse rippled underneath her fingertips. "He's alive."

Mrs. Murphy said under her breath, *"For how long?"*

46

The cherry wood in the fireplace crackled, releasing the heavy aroma of the wood. Tucker, asleep in front of the fire, occasionally chattered, dreaming of squirrels.

Mrs. Murphy curled up in Harry's lap as she sat on the sofa while Pewter sprawled over Fair's bigger lap in the other wing chair. Exhausted from the trauma as well as the climb back up the deep ravine, Harry pulled the worn afghan around her legs, her feet resting on a hassock.

Fair broke the stillness. "I know Rick told you not to reveal Sean's condition, but you can tell me."

"Fair, the sheriff has put a guard in his hospital room. And to tell the truth, I don't know his condition."

"He was mixed up in whatever is going on over at St. Elizabeth's?"

"I guess he is." She leaned her head against a needlepoint pillow. "In your teens you think you know everything. Your parents are out of it. You're invincible. Especially Sean, the football star. I wonder how he got mixed up in this mess, and I wonder what's really behind it."

"I heard April was released from jail today, and she didn't want to leave," Fair remarked. "She must know what's going on, too."

"That's so strange. She doesn't look like a criminal, does she?"

"I always thought she was in love with Roscoe and that he used her," Fair said.

"Slept with her?"

"I don't know. Maybe"—he thought a moment—"but more than that, he used her. She jumped through all his hoops. April was one of the reasons that St. E's ran so smoothly. Sure as hell wasn't Roscoe. His talents rested in directions other than details." He rose and tossed another log on the fire. "He ever offer you candy?"

"Every time he saw me."

"Never offered me catnip," Pewter grumbled.

"Mom's got that look on her face. She's having a brainstorm." Tucker closely observed Harry.

"Humans are fundamentally irrational. They use what precious rationality they have justifying their irrational behavior. A brainstorm is an excuse not to be logical," Pewter said.

"Amen." Murphy laughed.

Harry tickled Murphy's ears. "Aren't we verbal?"

"I can recite entire passages from Macbeth, *if you'd care to hear it. 'Tomorrow and tomorrow and tomorrow creeps—'"*

"Show-off." Pewter swished her tail once. *"Quoting Shakespeare is no harder than quoting 'Katie went to Haiti looking for a thrill.'"*

"Cole Porter." Mrs. Murphy sang the rest of the song with Pewter.

"What's going on with these two?" Harry laughed.

"Mrs. Murphy's telling her about her narrow escape from death."

"That's the first thing I did when we got home." Mrs. Murphy sat up now and belted out the chorus from "Katie Went to Haiti."

"Jesus," Tucker moaned, flattening her ears, *"you could wake the dead."*

Pewter, on a Cole Porter kick, warbled, *"When They Begin the Beguine."*

The humans shook their heads, then returned to their conversation.

"Maybe the link is Sean's connection to Roscoe and Maury." Harry's eyes brightened. "He could easily have stuffed Roger's newspapers with the second obituary. Those kids all know one another's schedules. They must have been using Sean for something—" Her brow wrinkled; for the life of her she couldn't figure out what a teenage boy might have that both men wanted.

"Not necessarily." Fair played devil's advocate. "It really could be coincidence. Just dumb luck."

Harry shook her head, "No, I really don't think so. Sean is up to his neck in this mess."

Fair cracked his knuckles, a habit Harry had tried to forget. "Kendrick Miller stabbed Maury. Maury's murder has nothing to do with Roscoe's. And the kid liberated the BMW, so to speak, and just got carried away. Started something he didn't know how to finish."

"But Rick Shaw's guarding him in the hospital." Harry came back to that very important fact.

"You're right—but connecting him to Roscoe's murder and Maury's seems so far-fetched."

Harry leapt off the sofa. "Sorry, Murphy."

"*I was so-o-o comfortable,*" Murphy moaned angrily. "*Pewter, let's give it to them. Let's sing 'Dixie.'*"

The two cats blended their voices in a rousing version of the song beloved of some folks south of the Mason-Dixon Line.

"*You're a veterinarian. You shut them up,*" Tucker begged.

Fair shrugged, laughing at the two performers.

"Here." Harry tossed Fair a bag of treats. "I know this works." It did, and she dialed Susan. "Hey, Suz."

"Miranda's here. Why didn't you tell me!"

"I am."

"How long have you been home? Oh, Harry, you could have been barbecued."

"I've been home an hour. Fair's here."

"Tell me what happened."

"I will, Susan, tomorrow. I promise. Right now I need to talk to Brooks. Are you sending her to St. Elizabeth's tomorrow?"

"No. Although she wants to go back." Susan called her daughter to the phone.

Harry got right to the point. "Brooks, do you remember who Roscoe Fletcher offered candy to when he waited in line at the car wash?"

"Everybody."

"Try very hard to remember, Brooks."

"Uh, okay...when I first saw him he was almost out on Route Twenty-nine. I don't think he talked to anyone unless it was the guys at the Texaco station. I didn't notice him again until he was halfway to the entrance. Uh—" She strained to picture the event. "Mrs. Fletcher beeped her horn at him. He got out to talk to her, I think. The line was that slow. Then he got back in. Mrs. Miller talked to him. Karen walked over for a second. He called her over. Jody, when she saw him, hid back in the office. She'd been reamed out, remember, 'cause of losing her temper after the field hockey game. Uh—this is hard."

"I know, but it's extremely important."

"Roger, once Mr. Fletcher reached the port—we call it the port."

"Can you think of anyone else?"

"No. But, I was scrubbing down bumpers. Someone else could have walked over for a second and I might not have seen them."

"I realize that. You've done a good job remembering."

"Want Mom back?"

"Sure."

"What are you up to?" Susan asked.

"Narrowing down who was offered candy by Roscoe at the car wash."

Susan, recognizing Harry was obsessed, told her she would see her in the morning.

Harry then dialed Karen Jensen's number. She asked Karen the same questions and received close to the same answers, although Karen thought Jody had been off the premises of the car wash, had walked back, seen Roscoe and ducked inside Jimbo's office. She remembered both Naomi and Irene waiting in line, but she couldn't recall if they got out of their cars. She wanted to know if Sean was all right.

"I don't know."

Karen's voice thickened. "I really like Sean—even if he can be a jerk."

"Can you think of any reason why he'd take Mrs. Craycroft's car?"

"No—well, I mean, he's sort of a cutup. He would never steal it, though. He just wouldn't."

"Thanks, Karen." Harry hung up the phone. She didn't think Sean would steal a car either. Joyride, yes. Steal, no.

She called Jimbo next. He remembered talking to Roscoe himself, then going back into his office to take a phone call. Harry asked if Jody was in the office with him. He said yes, she came in shortly after he spoke to Roscoe, although he couldn't be precise as to the time.

She next tried Roger, who thought Roscoe offered candy to one of the gas jockeys at the Texaco. He had glanced up to count the cars in the line. He remembered both Naomi and Irene getting out of their cars and talking to Roscoe as opposed to Roscoe getting out to talk to his wife. He was pretty sure that was what he saw, and he affirmed that Jody emphatically did not want to talk to Roscoe. He didn't know when Jody first caught sight of Roscoe. She was supposed to be picking up their lunch, but she never made it.

The last call was to Jody. Irene reluctantly called her daughter to the phone.

"Jody, I'm sorry to disturb you."

"That's okay." Jody whispered, "How's Sean? It's all over town that he wrecked BoomBoom Craycroft's new car."

"I don't know how he is."

"Did he say anything?"

"I can't answer that."

"But you pulled him out of the vehicle. He must have said something . . . like why he did it."

"Sheriff Shaw instructed me not to say anything, Jody."

"I called the hospital. They won't tell me anything either." A note of rising panic crept into her voice.

"They always do that, Jody. It's standard procedure. If you were in there with a hangnail, they wouldn't give out information."

"But he's all right, isn't he?"

"I can't answer that. I honestly don't know." Harry paused. "You're good friends, aren't you?"

"We got close this summer, playing tennis at the club."

"Did you date?"

"Sort of. We both went out with other people." She sniffed. "He's got to be okay."

"He's young and he's strong." Harry waited a beat, then switched the subject. "I'm trying to reconstruct how many people Mr. Fletcher offered strawberry drops to since, of course, anyone might have been poisoned." Harry wasn't telling the truth of what she was thinking, although she *was* telling the truth, a neat trick.

"Everyone."

Harry laughed. "That's the general consensus."

"Who else have you talked to?"

"Roger, Brooks, Karen, and Jimbo. Everybody says about the same thing although the sequence is scrambled."

"Oh."

"Did Mr. Fletcher offer you candy?"

"No. I chickened out and ran into Mr. Anson's office. I was in the doghouse."

"Yeah. Well, it was still a great game, and you played superbly."

"Really?" She brightened.

"You could make All-State. That is, if St. Elizabeth's has a season. Who knows what will happen with so many people taking their kids out of there."

"School's school." Jody confidently predicted, "I'm going back, others will, too. I'd rather be there than"—she whispered again—"here."

"Uh, Jody, are your mother and father near?"

"No, but I don't trust them. Dad's truly weird now that he's out on bail. Mom could be on the extension for all I know."

"Only because she's worried about you."

"Because she's a snoop. Hear that, Mom? If you're on the line, get off!"

Harry ignored the flash of bad manners. "Jody, can you tell me specifically who Mr. Fletcher offered candy to, that is, if you were watching from Jimbo's office?"

"Mr. Anson went out to talk to him. I sat behind the desk. I didn't really notice."

"Did you see Mrs. Fletcher or your mom get out of their cars and talk to Mr. Fletcher?"

"I don't remember Mom doing anything—but I wasn't really watching them."

"Oh, hey, before I forget it, 'cause I don't go over there much, the kids said you were on lunch duty that day. Where do you get good food around there?"

"You don't."

"You were on lunch duty?" Harry double-checked.

"Yeah, and Roger got pissed at me because he was starving and I saw Mr. Fletcher before I crossed the road so I ran back.

If I'd crossed the road he would have seen me. The line was so long he was almost out at the stoplight."

"Did he see you?"

"I don't think so. He saw me in the office later. He wasn't even mad. He waved."

"Did you give Jim his money back?" Harry laughed.

"Uh—no." Jody's voice tightened. "I forgot. It was—uh—well, I guess he forgot, too."

"Didn't mean to upset you."

"I'll pay him back tomorrow."

"I know you will." Harry's voice was warm. "Thanks for giving me your time. Oh, one more thing. I forgot to ask the others this. What do you, or did you, think of Mr. Fletcher's film department idea?"

" 'Today St. Elizabeth's, tomorrow Hollywood,' that's what he used to say. It was a great idea, but it'll never happen now."

"Thanks, Jody." Harry hung up the phone, returning to the sofa where she nestled in.

Mrs. Murphy crawled back in her lap. *"Now stay put."*

"Satisfied?" Fair asked.

"No, but I'm on the right track." She rested her hand on Mrs. Murphy's back. "I'm convinced. The real question is not who Roscoe offered candy to but who gave him candy. Rick Shaw must have come to the same conclusion." She tickled Murphy's ear. "He's not saying anything, though."

"Not to you."

"Mmm." Harry's mind drifted off. "Jody's upset over Sean. I guess they had a romance and I missed it."

"At that age you blink and they're off to a new thrill." He put his hands behind his head, stretching his upper body. Pewter didn't budge. "Everyone's upset. BoomBoom will be doubly upset." He exhaled, wishing he hadn't mentioned that name. "I'm surprised that you aren't more upset."

"I am upset. Two people are dead. Sean may well join them in the hereafter, and I can't figure it out. I hate secrets."

"That's what we pay the sheriff to do, to untie our filthy knots of passion, duplicity, and greed."

"Fair"—Harry smiled—"that's poetic."

He smiled back. "Go on."

"BoomBoom Craycroft." Harry simply repeated the name of Fair's former lover, then started laughing.

He smiled ruefully. "A brand-new BMW."

"She's such a flake. Pretty, I grant you that. I think I could have handled just about anyone else but BoomBoom." Harry took a sideswipe at Fair.

"That's not true, Harry, a betrayal is a betrayal, and it wouldn't have mattered who the woman was. You'd still feel like shit, and you'd say the same thing you're saying now but about her. I am rebuilding my whole life, my inner life. My outer life is okay." He paused. "I want to spend my life with you. Always did."

"Do you know why you ran around?"

"Fear."

"Of what?"

"Of being trapped. Of not living. When we married, I'd slept with three other women. I was a dutiful son. I studied hard. Kept my nose clean. Went to college. Went to vet school. Graduated and married you, the girl next door. I hit thirty and thought I was missing something. Had I married you at thirty, I would have gotten that out of my system." He softened his voice. "Haven't you ever worried that you're missing out?"

"Yeah, but then I watch the sunrise flooding the mountains with light and I think, 'Life is perfect.'"

"You aren't curious about other men?"

"What men?"

"Blair Bainbridge."

"Oh." She took her sweet time answering, thoroughly enjoying his discomfort. "Sometimes."

"How curious?"

"You just want to know if I'm sleeping with anyone, and that's my business. It's all about sex and possession, isn't it?"

"It's about love and responsibility. Sex is part of that."

"This is what I know: I like living alone. I like answering to no one but myself. I like not having to attend social functions as though we are joined at the hip. I like not having a knot in my stomach when you don't come home until two in the morning."

"I'm a vet."

She held up her hand. "With so many chances to jump ladies' bones, I can't even count them."

"I'm not doing that." He took her hand. "Our divorce was so painful, I didn't think I could live through it. I knew I was wrong. I didn't know how to make it right. Enough time has passed that I can be trusted, and I can be more sensitive to you."

"Don't push me."

"If I don't push you, you do nothing. If I ask anyone else to a party or the movies because I'd like to enjoy someone's companionship, you freeze me out for a week or more. I'm damned if I do and damned if I don't."

"He's right, Mom," Mrs. Murphy agreed with Fair.

"Yeah," Tucker echoed.

"They talk too much." Pewter, weary from her singing and all the spoon bread she'd stolen, wanted to sleep.

"Cheap revenge, I guess." Harry honestly assessed herself.

"Does it make you happy?"

"Actually, it does. Anyone who underestimates the joy of revenge has no emotions." She laughed. "But it doesn't get you what you want."

"Which is?"

"That's just it. I don't really know anymore."

"I love you. I've always loved you, and I always will love you." A burst of passion illuminated his handsome face.

She squeezed his hand. "I love you, too, but—"

"Can't we get back together? If you aren't ready for a commitment, we can date."

"We date now."

"*No,* we don't. It's hit or miss."

"You're not talking about dating. You're talking about sleeping together."

"Yes."

"I'll consider it."

"Harry, that's a gray reply."

"I didn't say no, nor did I say maybe. I have to think about it."

"But you know how I feel. You know what I've wanted."

"Not the same as a direct request—you just made a direct request, and I have to think about it."

"Do you love me at all?"

"The funny part of all this is that I do love you. I love you more now than when we married, but it's different. I just don't know if I can trust you. I'd like to, truly I would, because apart from Susan, Miranda, and my girlfriends, I know you better than anyone on the face of the earth, and I think you know me. I don't always like you. I'm sure I'm not likable at times, but it's odd how you can love someone and not like them." She hastened to add, "Most times I like you. Really, it's just when you start giving orders. I hate that."

"I'm working on that. Most women want to be told what to do."

"Some do, I know. Most don't. It's a big fake act they put on to make men feel intelligent and powerful. Then they laugh at you behind your back."

"You don't do that."

"No way."

"That's why I love you. One of the many reasons. You always stand up to me. I need that. I need you. You bring out the best in me, Harry."

"I'm glad to hear it," she replied dryly, "but I'm not on earth to bring out the best in you. I'm on earth to bring out the best in me."

"Wouldn't it be right if we could do that for each other? Isn't that what marriage is supposed to be?"

She waited a long time. "Yes. Marriage is probably more complicated than that, but I'm too tired to figure it out... if I ever could. And every marriage isn't the same. Our marriage was different from Miranda and George's, but theirs worked for them. I think you do bring out good things in me—after all, I wouldn't be having this conversation with anyone else, and that's a tribute to you. You know I loathe this emotional stuff."

He laughed. "Harry, I do love you."

She got up and kissed his cheek, disturbing a disgruntled Murphy one more time. "Let me think."

He mused. "I never knew love could be this complicated,

or even that I could be this complicated!" He laughed. "I always knew you were complicated."

"See—and I think I'm simple."

Mrs. Murphy settled down in front of the fireplace to stare into the flames. *"You know what worries me?"*

"What?" Pewter yawned.

"If Sean is part of Roscoe's murder, if he's in on this somehow, Mother was one of the last people to be with him. Only Cooper knows he didn't speak to her and Rick."

"So?" The gray cat fluttered her fur.

"So, Pewter, the killer might think he told Mother what's what."

Pewter's eyes opened wide as did Tucker's. They said in unison, *"I never thought of that."*

47

The antiseptic odor of hospitals turned Deputy Cooper's stomach. It stung her nostrils even though it wasn't as overpowering as, say, garbage. She wondered if the real offender was the associations she had concerning hospitals, or if truly she just hated the antiseptic.

Shorthanded though the department was, Rick was ferocious about maintaining vigilance over Sean. He'd broken half the bones in his body, his legs being the worst. His left arm was smashed in two places. His spleen was ruptured, and his left lung was punctured by his rib, which caved inward.

His right arm was fine. His skull was not crushed, but the force of the impact had created a severe concussion with some swelling in the brain. He had not regained consciousness, but his vital signs, though weak, had stabilized.

There was a good chance he'd live, although he'd never play football again. Sean's mother and father took turns watching over him. His grandparents flew in from Olathe, Kansas, to help.

Cynthia half dozed on the hard-backed chair. On the other side of the bed his mother slept in another chair, equally uncomfortable.

A low moan alerted Cynthia. Her eyes opened, as did Sean's.

He blinked strongly to make sense of where he was.

"Sean," Cynthia said in a clear low voice.

His mother awakened with a start and leaned over her son. "Honey, honey, it's Mom."

He blinked again, then whispered, "I'm a father." His lips moved but no more sound escaped. Then, as if he had never spoken, he shut his eyes again and lost consciousness.

48

A howitzer ripped through Harry's meticulously planned schedule. Each night before retiring she would take a sheet of tablet paper, eight by eleven inches, fold it in half, and number her chores in order of priority. She used to watch her mother do it, absorbing the habit.

Harry was an organized person. Her disorganization involved major life questions such as "Whither thou goest?" She told herself Americans put too much emphasis on direction, management, and material success instead of just jumping into life.

Awaking each morning between five thirty and six, she first drank a piping hot cup of tea, fed the horses, picked out the stalls, stripping them on Saturdays, turned the horses out, fed Mrs. Murphy, Tucker, and now Pewter. Then she usually walked the mile out to the road to get her paper. That woke her up. If she was running behind or the weather proved filthy, she'd drive out in the blue truck.

Thanks to BoomBoom, the blue truck reposed again at the service station. Fortunately, BoomBoom's insurance really did cover the damages. And she'd get a new BMW since Sean had destroyed hers. Harry's worry involved the ever-decreasing life span of the 1978 Ford. She had to get a new truck. Paying for it, even a decent used one, seemed impossible.

The morning, crisp and clear at 36° F, promised a glorious fall day ahead. She jogged back, never opening the newspaper. Reading it with her second cup of tea and breakfast rewarded her for finishing the farm chores before heading off to the post office. She adored these small rituals of pleasure. Another concept she'd learned from her mother.

She bit into a light biscuit...then stopped, the biscuit hanging from her mouth. As she opened her mouth, the biscuit dropped onto the plate.

She knocked the chair over calling Susan. "You up?"

"Barely."

"Open the paper."

"Mmm. Holy shit! What's going on around here?" Susan exploded.

On the front page of the newspaper ran the story of the high-speed car chase. Harry was quoted as saying, "Another ten seconds and he'd have been blown to bits."

But what caused Susan's eruption was a story in the next column concerning April Shively's release on twenty thousand dollars' bail. That was followed by April's declaring she would not release the papers she had taken from St. Elizabeth's until the board of governors audited the current accounting books in the possession of the temporary head-master, Sandy Brashiers. She all but accused him of financial misdeeds just this side of embezzlement.

As Harry and Susan excitedly talked in the background, Mrs. Murphy sat on the newspaper to read. Pewter joined her.

"Sean's not in the obit column, so we know he's still fighting." Murphy touched her nose to the paper.

"Going to be a hell of a day at the post office," Tucker predicted.

How right she was. A gathering place in the best and worst of times, it was packed with people.

Big Mim, hoisted up on the counter by the Reverend Jones, clapped her hands. "Order. Could I have some order, please?"

Accustomed to obeying the Queen of Crozet, they fell silent.

"Honeybun, we could move to city hall," her husband, the mayor, offered.

"We're here now, let's get on with it." Mim sat down and crossed her legs. Mrs. Murphy and Pewter flanked her. Tucker wandered among the crowd. The animals decided they would pay attention to faces and smells. Someone might give himself or herself away in a fashion a human couldn't comprehend.

Mim stared sternly at Karen, Jody, Brooks, and Roger. "Why aren't you in school?"

Karen answered for all of them. "Which school? We want to go back to St. Elizabeth's. Our parents won't let us."

"Then what are you doing here?" She pounded them like a schoolmarm.

"The post office is where everything happens, sort of," Brooks replied.

"Smart kid," Mrs. Murphy said.

Irene called out, "Marilyn, can you guarantee my child's safety?"

"Irene, no school can do that anymore, but within reason, yes." Marilyn Sanburne felt she spoke for the board.

Harry leaned across the counter. "Guys, I don't mind that you all meet here, but if someone comes in to get their mail, you have to clear a path for them. This is a federal building."

"The hell with Washington," Market Shiflett brazenly called out. "We had the right idea in 1861."

Cheers rose from many throats. Miranda laughed as did Harry. Those transplanted Yankees in the crowd would find this charming, anachronistic proof that Southerners are not only backward but incapable of forgetting the war.

What Southerners knew in their souls was that given half the chance, they'd leave the oppressive Union in a skinny minute. Let the Yankees tax themselves to death. Southerners had better things to do with their time and money, although it is doubtful those "better things" would be productive.

"Now we must remain calm, provoking as these hideous events have been." Mim turned to Harry. "Why don't you call Rick Shaw? He ought to be here."

"No." Herbie gently contradicted her. "If you'll forgive me, madam"—he often called Mim "madam"—"I think we'll all be more forthcoming without the law here."

"Yes." Other voices agreed.

Mim cast her flashing blue gaze over the crowd. "I don't know what's going on, I don't know why it's going on, but I think we must assume we know the person or persons responsible for Roscoe's demise as well as Maury's bizarre death. This community must organize to protect itself."

"How do we know the killer isn't in this room?" Dr. Larry Johnson asked.

Father Michael replied, "We don't."

"Well, Kendrick was found bending over Maury. Sorry, Irene, but it's true," Market said.

"Then we're telling the killer or killers our plans. How can we protect ourselves?" Lucinda Payne Coles, her brow furrowed, echoed what many others felt as well.

Harry raised her hand, a gesture left over from school.

"Harry." Mim nodded toward her.

"The question is not if the killer or killers could be in this room. The question is, why are people being killed? We'll worry ourselves into a fit if we think each of us is vulnerable."

"But we are!" Market exclaimed. "Two people are dead— and one seventeen-year-old boy who admitted planting the first obituary is in the hospital. Who or what next?"

Harry replied evenly, "Marilyn, I know you don't want to hear this, but everything points to St. Elizabeth's."

"Does that mean we're suspects?" Jody Miller joked.

Irene put her hand on her daughter's shoulder. "No one is suspecting students, dear." She cast a knowing look at Larry Johnson. She needed to talk to him. Jody was in the first trimester of her pregnancy. A major decision had to be made. On the other hand, she watched Father Michael and thought maybe she should talk to *him*. It didn't occur to her that Jody was the one who needed to do the talking.

Neither Sandy Brashiers nor any faculty members from the school were there to defend themselves or the institution.

They were holding back a tidal wave of questions, recriminations, and fear at their own faculty meeting. The reporters, like jackals, camped at the door.

"You must put aside April's absurd accusations," Marilyn said nervously, "and we will audit the books this week to lay her accusations to rest. She's only trying to divert our attention."

"It's true," Roger said in his quiet voice. "The problem is at St. E's."

Mim asked, "Do you have any idea, any idea at all, what is going on at your school? Is there a drug problem?"

"Mrs. Sanburne, drugs are everywhere. Not just at St. E's," Karen said solemnly.

"But you're rich kids. If you get in trouble, Daddy can bail you out." Samson Coles bluntly added his two cents even though many people shunned him.

"That's neither here nor there," Market said impatiently. "What are we going to do?"

"Can we afford more protection? A private police force?" Fair was pretty sure they couldn't.

"No." Jim, towering over everyone but Fair, answered that query. "We're on a shoestring."

"The rescue squad and other groups like the Firehouse gang could pitch in." Larry, getting warm, removed his glen plaid porkpie hat.

"Good idea, Larry." Mim turned to her husband. "Can we do that? Of course we can. You're the mayor."

"I'll put them on patrol. We can set up a cruise pattern. It's a start."

Mim went on. "While they're doing that, the rest of us can go over our contacts with Roscoe, April, Maury, and Sean. There may be a telling clue, something you know that seems unimportant but is really significant, the missing link, so to speak."

"Like, who gave Roscoe Fletcher candy at the car wash?" Miranda said innocently. "Harry thinks the killer was right there and gave him the poisoned candy right under everyone's nose."

"She just let the cat out of the bag." Murphy's eyes widened.

"What can we do?" Tucker cried.

"Pray the killer's not in this room," Mrs. Murphy said, knowing in her bones that the killer was looking her right in the face.

"But Rick Shaw and Cynthia must have figured out the same thing." Pewter tried to allay their fears.

"Of course they have, but until this moment the person who wiped out Roscoe didn't realize Mom had figured out most people were approaching Roscoe's murder backward. Now they'll wonder what else she's figured out."

"It's Kendrick Miller." Pewter licked her paw, rubbing her ear with it.

"If he is the one, he can get at Mom easily," Tucker responded. *"At least he's not here."*

"Don't worry, Irene will repeat every syllable of this meeting." Murphy's tail tip swayed back and forth, a sign of light agitation.

"We need to ask Fair to stay with Mom." Tucker rightly assumed that would help protect her.

"Fat chance." Murphy stood up, stretched, and called to her friends, *"Come on out back with me. Humans need to huff and puff. We've got work to do."*

Tucker resisted. *"We ought to stay here and observe."*

"The damage is done. We need to hotfoot it. Come on."

Tucker threaded her way through the many feet and

dashed through the animal door. Once outside she said, *"Where are we going?"*

"St. Elizabeth's."

"Murphy, that's too far." Pewter envisioned the trek.

"Do you want to help, or do you want to be a wuss?"

"I'm not a wuss." Pewter defiantly swatted at the tiger cat.

"Then let's go."

Within forty-five minutes they reached the football and soccer fields. Tired, they sat down for a minute.

"Stick together. We're going to work room to room."

"What are we looking for?"

"I'm not sure yet. If April took other books, they're truly cooked now. But none of these people thought they were going to be killed. They must have left unfinished business somewhere, and if the offices are clean as a whistle, then it means April knows the story—the whole story, doesn't it?"

49

Eerie quiet greeted the animals as they padded down the hall-way of the Old Main Building, the administration building. The faculty meeting was heating up in the auditorium across the quad. Not one soul was in Old Main, not even a recep-tionist.

"Think the cafeteria is in Old Main?" Pewter inquired plaintively.

"No. Besides, I bet no one is working in the cafeteria." Tucker was anxious to get in and get out of the place before the post office closed. If Harry couldn't find them, she'd pitch a fit.

"Perfect." Mrs. Murphy read HEADMASTER in gold letters on the heavy oak door, slightly ajar. The cat checked the door

width using her whiskers, knew she could make it, and squeezed through. Fatty behind her squeezed a little harder.

Tucker wedged her long nose in the door. Mrs. Murphy turned around and couldn't resist batting Tucker.

"No fair."

"Where's your sense of humor? Pewter, help me with the door."

The two cats pulled with their front paws as Tucker pushed with her nose. Finally the heavy door opened wide enough for the corgi to slip through. Everything had been moved out except for the majestic partner's desk and the rich red Persian carpet resting in front of the desk.

"Tucker, sniff the walls, the bottom of the desk, the bookcases, everything. Pewter, you check along the edge of the bookcases. Maybe there's a hidden door or something."

"What are you going to do?" Pewter dived into the emptied bookshelves.

"Open these drawers."

"That's hard work."

"Not for me. I learned to do this at home because Harry used to hide the fresh catnip in the right-hand drawer of her desk . . . until she found out I could open it."

"Where does she hide it now?" Pewter eagerly asked.

"Top of the kitchen cabinet, inside."

"Damn." Pewter rarely swore.

"Let's get to work." Mrs. Murphy flopped on her side, putting her paw through the burnished brass handle. Using her hind feet she pushed forward. The long center drawer creaked a bit, then rolled right out. Pens, pencils, and an avalanche of paper clips and engraved St. Elizabeth's stationery filled the drawer. She stuck her paws to the very back of the drawer. Mrs. Murphy shivered. She wanted so badly to throw the paper on the floor, then plunge into it headfirst. A paper bag

was fun enough but expensive, lush, engraved laid bond—
that was heaven. She disciplined herself, hopping on the floor
to pull out the right-hand bottom drawer. The contents
proved even more disappointing than the center drawer's: a
hand squeezer to strengthen the hand muscles, a few floppy
discs even though no computer was in the room, and one old
jump rope.

"Anything?" She pulled on the left-hand drawer.

Tucker lifted her head. *"Too many people in here. I smell
mice. But then that's not surprising. They like buildings where
people go home at night—less interference."*

"Nothing on the bookshelves. No hidden buttons."

Murphy, frustrated at not finding anything, jumped into
the drawer, wiggling toward the back. Murphy's pupils, big
from the darkness at the back of the drawer, quickly retracted
to smaller circles as she jumped out. She noticed a small ad-
hesive mailing label, ends curled, which must have fallen off a
package. *"Here's an old mailing label. Neptune Film Laboratory,
Brooklyn, New York—and three chewed pencils, the erasers
chewed off. This room has been picked cleaner than a chicken
bone."*

*"We could go over to where Maury McKinchie was killed, in
the hall outside the gymnasium,"* Tucker suggested.

"Good idea." Mrs. Murphy hurried out the door.

"She could at least wait for us. She can be so rude." Pewter
followed.

The cavernous gymnasium echoed with silence. The click
of Tucker's unretractable claws reverberated like tin drums.

"Know what hall?"

"No," Mrs. Murphy answered Tucker, *"but there's only one
possibility. The two side halls go to the locker rooms. I don't think
Maury was heading that way. He probably went through the*

double doors, which lead to the trophy hall and the big front door."

"Then why did we come in the backdoor?" Pewter grumbled.

"Because our senses are sharper. We could pick up something in the lockers that a human couldn't. Not just dirty socks but cocaine lets off a sharp rancid odor, and marijuana is so easy a puppy could pick it up."

"I resent that. A hound puppy is born with a golden nose."

"Tucker, I hate to tell you this but you're a corgi."

"I know that perfectly well, smart-ass." Ready to fight, she stopped in front of a battered light green locker. "Wait a minute." She sniffed around the base of the locker, putting her nose next to the vent. "Sugary, sticky."

"Hey, look at that." Pewter involuntarily lifted her paw, taking a step back.

"Dead." Mrs. Murphy noted the line of dead ants going into the locker. She glanced up. "Number one fourteen."

"How do we get in there? I mean, if we want to?" Pewter gingerly leapt over the ants.

"We don't." Tucker indicated the big combination lock hanging on the locker door.

"Why go to school if you have to lock away your possessions? Kids stealing from kids. It's not right."

"It's not right, but it's real," Mrs. Murphy answered pragmatically. "We aren't going to get anyone into this locker. Even the janitor has burnt rubber."

"He rides a bicycle," Tucker said laconically, picturing Powder Hadly, thirties and simpleminded. He was so simpleminded he couldn't pass the written part of the driving test although he could drive just fine.

"You get my drift." The tiger bumped into the corgi. Tucker bumped back, which made the cat stumble.

"*Twit.*"

"*It's all right if you do it. If I do anything you bitch and moan and scratch.*"

"*What are you doing then?*"

"*Describing your behavior. Flat facts.*"

"*The flat facts are, we can't do diddly.*" She halted. "*Well, there is one trick if we could get everyone to open their lockers. Not that the dead-ant locker has poison in it. That would be pretty stupid, wouldn't it? But who knows what's stashed in these things.*"

"*Do the faculty have lockers?*" Pewter asked.

"*Sure.*"

"*How do you know the faculty lockers from the kids'?*"

"*I don't know. We're on the girls' side. Maybe there's a small room we've missed that's set aside for the teachers.*"

They scampered down the hall and found a locker room for the female faculty. But there was nothing of interest except a bottle of Ambush perfume that had been left on the makeup counter. The men's locker room was equally barren of clues.

"*This was a wasted trip, and I'm famished.*"

"*Not so wasted.*" Murphy trotted back toward the post office.

"*I'd like to know why. Roscoe's office was bare. We passed through April's office, nothing there. The sheriff has crawled over everything, fouling the scent. The gym is a tomb. And my pads are cold.*"

"*We found out that the killer had to have left the gym before Maury McKinchie to wait outside the front doors. They're glass so he could see Maury come out, or he waited behind one of the doors leading to the boys' locker room or the girls'. He dashed out*" *and stabbed Maury and then either ran outside or he ran back into the gym. In costume, remember. He knew this setup."*

"Ah." Tucker appreciated Mrs. Murphy's reasoning. *"I see that, but if the killer had been outside, more people would have seen him because he was in costume—unless he changed it. No time for that, I think."* Tucker canceled her own idea.

"He was a Musketeer, if Kendrick is telling the truth. My hunch is he came from the side. From out of the locker rooms. No one had reason to go back there unless they wanted to smoke or drink, and they could easily do that outside without some chaperon or bush patrol. No, I'm sure he ran out the locker-room side."

"You don't believe Kendrick did it?" Pewter asked, knowing the answer but wanting to hear her friend's reasons.

"No."

"But what if Maury was sleeping with Irene?" Tucker logically thought that was reason enough for some men to murder.

"Kendrick wouldn't give a damn. A business deal gone bust, or some kind of financial betrayal might provoke him to kill, but he'd be cold-blooded about it. He'd plan. This was slapdash. Not Kendrick's style."

"No wonder Irene mopes around," Pewter thought out loud. *"If my husband thought money was more important than me, I'd want a divorce, too."*

"Could Maury have been killed by a jilted lover?"

"Sure. So could Roscoe. But it doesn't fit. Not two of them back-to-back. And April Shively wouldn't have vacuumed out the school documents if it was that."

They reached the post office, glad to rush inside for warmth and crunchies.

"Where have you characters been?" Harry counted out change.

"Deeper into this riddle, that's where we've been." Mrs. Murphy watched Pewter stick her face into the crunchies shaped like little fish. She didn't feel hungry herself. *"What's driving me crazy is that I'm missing something obvious."*

"Murphy, I don't see how we've overlooked anything." Tucker was tired of thinking.

"No, it's obvious, but whatever it is, our minds don't want to see it." The tiger dropped her ears for a moment, then pricked them back up.

"Doesn't make sense," Pewter, thrilled to be eating, said between garbled mouthfuls.

"What is going on is too repulsive for our minds to accept. We're blanking out. It's right under our noses."

50

The uneasiness of Crozet's residents found expression in the memorial service for Maury McKinchie.

There was a full choir and a swelling organ but precious few people in Reverend Jones's church. Darla had indeed flown the body back to Los Angeles, so no exorbitantly expensive casket rested in front of the altar. Miranda, asked to sing a solo, chose "A Mighty Fortress Is Our God" because she was in a Lutheran church and because no one knew enough about Maury's spiritual life to select a more personal hymn. BoomBoom Craycroft wept in the front left row. Ed Sugarman comforted her, a full-time job. Naomi Fletcher, in mourning for Roscoe, sat next to Sandy Brashiers in the front right row. Harry, Susan, and Ned also attended. Other than

that tiny crew, the church was bare. Had Darla shown her famous and famously kept face, the church would have been
overflowing.

Back at the post office Harry thought about what constituted a life well lived.

At five o'clock, she gathered up April Shively's mail.

"Do you think she'll let you in?"

Harry raised her eyebrows. "Miranda, I don't much care. If
not, I'll put it by her backdoor. Need anything while I'm out
there? I'll pass Critzer's Nurseries."

"No, thanks. I've put in all my spring bulbs," came the
slightly smug reply.

"Okay then—see you tomorrow."

Ten minutes later Harry pulled into a long country lane
winding up at a neat two-story frame colonial. Blair Bainbridge had lent Harry his truck until hers was fixed. When
she knocked on the door, there was no answer. She waited a
few minutes, then placed the mail by the backdoor. As she
turned to leave, the upstairs window opened.

"I'm not afraid to come in and get my mail."

"Your box was overflowing. Thought I'd save you a trip."

"Anybody know if Sean's going to make it?"

"No. The hospital won't give out information, and they
won't allow anyone to visit. That's all I know."

"Boy doesn't have a brain in his head. Have you seen
Sandy Brashiers or Naomi?" April half laughed. Her tone was
snide.

Harry sighed impatiently. "I doubt they want to see you
any more than you want to see them. Marilyn's not your
biggest fan now either."

"Who cares about her?" April waved her hand flippantly.
"She's a bad imitation of a bad mother."

"Big Mim's okay. You have to take her on her own terms."

"Think we can get inside?" Tucker asked.

"No," Murphy replied. *"She's not budging from that window."*

"What are they saying about me?" April demanded.

"Oh—that you hate Sandy, loved Roscoe, and you're accusing Sandy to cover your own tracks. If there's missing money, you've got it or know where it is."

"Ha!"

"But you do know something, April. I know you do," Murphy meowed loudly.

"That cat's got a big mouth."

"So's your old lady," Murphy sassed her.

"Yeah!" Pewter chimed in.

"April, I wish you'd get things right." Harry zipped up her jacket. "The school's like a tomb. Whatever you feel about Sandy—is it worth destroying St. Elizabeth's and everything Roscoe worked so hard to build?"

"Good one, Mom." Tucker knew Harry had struck a raw nerve.

"Me destroy St. Elizabeth's! If you want to talk destruction, let's talk about Sandy Brashiers, who wants us to commit our energies and resources to a nineteenth-century program. He's indifferent to computer education, hostile to the film-course idea, and he only tolerates athletics because he has to—if he takes over, you watch, those athletic budgets will get trimmed and trimmed each year. He'll take it slow at first, but I know him! The two-bit sneak."

"Then come back."

"They fired me!"

"If you give back the papers—"

"Never. Not to Brashiers."

Harry held up her hands. "Give them to Sheriff Shaw."

"Fat lot of good that will do. He'll turn them over to St. Elizabeth's."

"He can impound them as evidence."

"Are you that dumb, or do you think I am?" April yelled. "Little Mim will whine, and Mommy will light the fires of hell under Rick Shaw's butt. Those papers will go to the Sanburne house if not St. Elizabeth's."

"How else can you clear your name?"

"When the time comes, I will. You just wait and see."

"I guess I'll have to." Harry gave up, walking back to the truck. She heard the window slam shut.

"Time has a funny way of running out," Mrs. Murphy noted dryly.

51

Driving back into Crozet, Harry stopped and cajoled Mrs. Hogendobber to drive her through the car wash in her Falcon. Pewter, hysterical at the thought, hid under the seat. Harry filled Miranda in on the conversation with April, a belligerent April.

As they pulled right off Route 29, coasting past the Texaco station, Harry observed the distance between the gas pumps and the port of the car wash. It was a quick sprint away, perhaps fifty yards at the most. The Texaco station building blocked the view of the car wash.

"Go slow."

"I am." Miranda scanned the setup, then coasted to a stop before the port.

Jimbo Anson rolled out, the collar of his jacket turned up against the wind. "Welcome, Mrs. Hogendobber. I don't believe you've ever been here."

"No, I haven't. I wash the car by hand. It's small enough that I can do it, but Harry wants me to become modern." She smiled as Harry reached across her and paid the rate for "the works."

"Come forward...there you go." He watched as Miranda's left wheel rolled onto the track. "Put her in neutral, and no radio." Jimbo punched the big button hanging on a thick electrical cord, and the car rolled into the mists.

A buzzer sounded, the yellow neon light flashed, and Miranda exclaimed, "My word."

Harry carefully noted the time it took to complete the cycle as well as how the machinery swung out from the side or dropped from above. The last bump of the track alerted them to put the car in drive. Harry mumbled, "No way."

"No way what?"

"I was thinking maybe the killer came into the car wash, gave Roscoe the poisoned candy, and ran out. I know it's loony, but the sight of someone soaking wet in the car wash, someone he knew, would make him roll down the window or open a door if he could. It was a thought. If you run up here from the Texaco station, which takes less than a minute, no one could see you if you ducked in the car wash exit. But it's impossible. And besides, nobody noticed anyone being all wet."

"'Cain said to Abel, his brother, "Let us go out to the field." And when they were in the field, Cain rose up against his brother Abel, and killed him. Then the Lord said to Cain, "Where is Abel your brother?" He said, "I do not know; am I my brother's keeper?" And the Lord said, "What have you done? The voice of your brother's blood is crying to me from the ground." '" Mrs. Hogendobber quoted Genesis. "The first murder of all time. Cain didn't get away with it. Neither will this murderer."

"Rick Shaw is working overtime to tie Kendrick to both murders. Cynthia called me last night. She said it's like trying to stick a square peg in a round hole. It's not working, and Rick is tearing his hair out."

"He can ill afford that." Mrs. Hogendobber turned south on Route 29.

"I keep coming back to cowardice. Poison is the coward's tool."

"Whoever killed McKinchie wasn't a coward. A bold run-through with a sword shows imagination."

"McKinchie was unarmed, though," Harry said. "The killer jumped out and skewered him. Imagination, yes, but cowardice, yes. It's one thing to plan a murder and carry it out, a kind of cold brilliance, if you will. It's another thing to sneak up on people."

"It is possible that these deaths are unrelated," Miranda said tentatively. "But I don't think so; that's what worries me." She braked for a red light.

She couldn't have been more worried than Father Michael, who, dozing in the confession booth, was awakened by the murmur of that familiar muffled voice, taking pains to disguise itself.

"Father, I have sinned."

"Go on, my child."

"I have killed more than once. I like killing, Father. It makes me feel powerful."

A hard lump lodged in Father Michael's thin throat. "All power belongs to God, my child." His voice grew stronger. "And who did you kill?"

"Rats." The disguised voice burst into laughter.

He heard the swish of the heavy black fabric, the light, quick footfall. He bolted out of the other side of the confession booth in time to see a swirl of black, a cloak, at the side door, which quickly closed. He ran to the door and flung it open. No one was there, only a blue jay squawking on the head of the Avenging Angel.

52

"Nobody?"

Lucinda Payne Coles, her heavy skirt draped around her legs to ward off the persistent draft in the old office room, said again, "Nobody. I'm at the back of the church, Sheriff. The only way I'll see who comes in and out of the front is if I walk out there or they park back here."

Cynthia, also feeling the chill, moved closer to the silver-painted radiator. "Have you noticed anyone visiting Father Michael lately, anyone unusual?"

"No. If anything it's quieter than normal for this time of year."

"Thanks, Mrs. Coles. Call me any time of the day or night if anything occurs to you."

Rick and Cynthia walked outside. A clammy mist enshrouded them in the graveyard. They bent down at the side door. Depressions on leaves could be seen, a slight smear on the moisture that they tracked into the cemetery.

"Smart enough to cover his tracks," Cynthia said.

"Or hers. That applies to every country person in the county," Rick replied. "Or anyone who's watched a lot of crime shows." He sat on a tombstone for a moment. "Any ideas?"

"Nope."

"Me neither."

"We know one thing. The killer likes to confess."

"No, Coop, the killer likes to brag. We've got exactly one hope in hell."

"Which is?" She told herself she wasn't really a smoker as she reached into her pocket for a pack.

"I'll take one of those." Rick reached out.

They lit up, inhaling.

"Wonder how many people buried here died of emphysema?"

"Don't know." He laughed. "I might be one of them someday."

"What's your one hope, boss?"

"Pride goeth before a fall."

53

Rick Shaw set up a temporary command post in April Shively's office. Little Mim and Sandy Brashiers requested over the radio and in the newspaper that students return to St. Elizabeth's for questioning.

Every hand Rick could spare was placed at the school. Little Mim organized and Sandy assisted.

"—the year started out great. Practice started out great—" Karen Jensen smiled at the sheriff. "Our class had a special film week. We wrote a story, broke it down into shots, and then Friday, we filmed it. Mr. McKinchie and Miss Thalman from New York directed us. That was great. I can't think of anything weird."

"Sean?"

"Oh, you know Sean, he likes playing the bad boy, but he seemed okay." She was relaxed, wanting to be helpful.

"If you think of anything, come on back or give me a call." Rick smiled reflexively. When Karen had left, he said to Cooper, "No running nose, no red eyes or dilated pupils or pupils the size of a pin. No signs of drug abuse. We're halfway through the class—if only Sean would regain consciousness."

"If he is going to be a father, that explains a lot."

"Not enough," Rick grumbled.

Cynthia flipped through her notes. "He used to run errands for April Shively. Jody Miller said Sean had a permanent pink pass." She flipped the notebook shut.

A bark outside the door confused them for a moment, then Cynthia opened the door.

Fur ruffled, Tucker bounded in. *"We can help!"*

With less obvious enthusiasm Mrs. Murphy and Pewter followed.

"Where's Harry?"

As if to answer Coop's question, Harry walked through the door carrying a white square plastic container overflowing with mail. "Roscoe's and Maury's mail." She plopped the box on the table. "I put Naomi's mail in her mailbox."

"Anything unusual?" Rick inquired.

"No. Personal letters and bills, no Jiffy bags or anything suspicious."

"Has she been coming to pick up her mail?"

"Naomi comes in each day. But not today. At least not before I left."

Cynthia asked, "Does she ever say anything at all?"

"She's downcast. We exchange pleasantries and that's it."

"Good of Blair to lend you his Dually." Coop hoped her severe crush on the handsome man wouldn't show. It did.

"He's a good neighbor." Harry smiled. "Little Mim's pegged him for every social occasion between now and Christmas, I swear."

"He doesn't seem to mind."

"What choice does he have? Piss off a Sanburne?" Her eyebrows rose.

"Point taken." Cynthia nodded, feeling better already.

"When you girls stop chewing the fat, I'd be tickled pink to get back to business."

"Yes, boss."

"Spoilsport," Harry teased him. "If we take our minds off the problem, we usually find the answer."

"That's the biggest bunch of bull I've heard since 'Read my lips: No new taxes,'" Rick snorted.

"Read my lips: Come to the locker room." The tiger cat let out a hoot.

"Was that a hiccup?" Cynthia bent down to pat Mrs. Murphy.

"Let's try the old run away–run back routine." Tucker ripped out of the room and ran halfway down the hall, her claws clicking on the wooden floor, then raced back.

"Let's all do it." Mrs. Murphy followed the dog. Pewter spun out so fast her hind legs slipped away from her.

"Nuts." Rick watched, shaking his head.

"Playful." Coop checked the mail. There wasn't anything that caught her eye as odd.

Halfway down the hall the animals screeched to a halt, bumping into one another.

"Idiots." Mrs. Murphy puffed her tail. The fur on the back of her neck stood up.

"We could try again." Tucker felt that repetition was the key with humans.

"No. I'll crawl up Mother's leg. That gets her attention."

"Doesn't mean she'll follow us," Pewter replied pragmatically.

"Have you got a better idea?" The tiger whirled on the gray cat.

"No, Your Highness."

The silent animals reentered the room. Mrs. Murphy walked over to Harry, rubbed against her leg, and purred.

"Sweetie, we'll go in a minute."

That fast Murphy climbed up Harry's legs. The jeans blunted the claws, yet enough of those sharp daggers pierced the material to make Harry yelp.

"Follow me!" She dropped off Harry's leg and ran to the door, stopping to turn a somersault.

"Show-off," Pewter muttered under her breath.

"You can't do a somersault," Murphy taunted her.

"Oh, yes, I can." Pewter ran to the door and leapt into the air. Her somersault was a little wobbly and lopsided, but it was a somersault.

"You know, every now and then they get like this," Harry explained sheepishly. "Maybe I'll see what's up."

"I'll go with you."

"You're both loose as ashes." Rick grabbed the mail.

As Harry and Cynthia followed the animals, they noticed a few classrooms back in use.

"That's good, I guess," Cynthia remarked.

"Well, once you-all decided to work out of the school to question students, some of the parents figured it would be safe to send the kids back." Harry giggled. "Easier than having them at home, no matter what."

"Are we on a hike?" Cynthia noticed the three animals had stopped at the backdoor to the main building and were staring at the humans with upturned faces.

When Harry opened the door, they shot out, galloping across the quad. "All right, you guys, this is a con!"

"No, it isn't." The tiger trotted back to reassure the two wavering humans. *"Come on. We've got an idea. It's more than any of you have."*

"I could use some fresh air." Cynthia felt the first snowflake of winter alight on her nose.

"Me, too. Miranda will have to wait."

They crossed the quad, the snowflakes making a light tapping sound as they hit tree branches. The walkway was slick but not white yet. In the distance between the main building and the gymnasium, the snow thickened.

"Hurry up. It's cold," Pewter exhorted them.

The humans reached the front door of the gym and opened it. The animals dashed inside.

Mrs. Murphy glanced over her shoulder to see if they were behind her. She ran to the girls' gym door at one corner of the trophy hall. The other two animals marched behind her.

"This is a wild-goose chase." Cynthia laughed.

"Who knows, but it gives you a break from Rick. He's just seething up there."

"He gets like that until he cracks a case. He blames himself for everything."

They walked into the locker room. All three animals sat in front of 114. The line of dead ants was still there.

Since each locker wore a combination lock like a ring hanging from a bull's nose, they couldn't get into the locker.

But it gave Cynthia an idea. She found Coach Hallvard, who checked her list. Number 114 belonged to Jody Miller. Cynthia requested that the coach call her girls in to open their lockers.

An hour later, Coach Hallvard, an engine of energy, had

each field hockey player, lacrosse, basketball, track and field, anyone on junior varsity or varsity standing in front of her locker.

Harry, back at work, missed the fireworks. When 114 was opened, an open can of Coca-Cola was the source of the ant patrol. However, 117 contained a Musketeer costume. The locker belonged to Karen Jensen.

54

Rick paced, his hands behind his back. Karen sobbed that she knew nothing about the costume, which was an expensive one.

"Ask anybody. I was Artemis, and I never left the dance," she protested. She was also feeling low because a small amount of marijuana had been found in her gym bag.

Rick got a court order to open lockers, cutting locks off if necessary. He had found a virtual pharmacy at St. Elizabeth's. These kids raided Mom and Dad's medicine chest with regularity or they had a good supplier. Valium, Percodan, Quaaludes, speed, amyl nitrate, a touch of cocaine, and a good amount of marijuana competed with handfuls of anabolic steroids in the boys' varsity lockers.

Hardened though he was, he was unprepared for the extent of drug use at the school. When he pressured one of the football players, he heard the standard argument: if you're playing football against guys who use steroids and you don't, you get creamed. If a boy wants to excel at certain sports, he's got to get into drugs sooner or later. The drug of choice was human growth hormone, but none of the kids could find it, and it was outrageously expensive. Steroids were a lot easier to cop.

The next shocker came when Cynthia checked the rental of the Musketeer costume using a label sewn into the neck of the tunic. She reached an outfitter in Washington, D.C. They reported they were missing a Musketeer costume, high quality.

It had been rented by Maury McKinchie using his MasterCard.

$$55$$

The snow swirled, obscuring Yellow Mountain. Harry trudged to the barn, knowing that no matter how deep the snow fell, it wouldn't last. The hard snows arrived punctually after Christmas. Occasionally a whopper would hit before the holidays, but most residents of central Virginia could count on real winter socking them January through March.

The winds, stiff, blew the fall foliage clean off the trees. Overnight the riotous color of fall gave way to the spare monochrome of winter.

A rumble sent Tucker out into the white. Fair pulled up. He clapped his cowboy hat on his head as he dashed for the barn.

"Harry, I need your help."

"What happened?"

"BoomBoom is pitching a royal hissy. She says she has to talk to someone she can trust. She has a heavy heart. You should hear it."

"No, I shouldn't."

"What should I do?" He fidgeted. "She sounded really distressed."

Harry leaned against a stall door. Gin Fizz poked his white nose over the top of the Dutch doors, feed falling from his mouth as he chewed. Usually he'd stick his head out and chat. Today he was too hungry and the feed was too delicious.

"Mom, go along. That will give BoomBoom cardiac arrest." Murphy laughed.

"I'll tell you exactly what I think. She was sleeping with Maury McKinchie."

"You don't know that for a fact." He removed his hat and shook his head.

"Woman's instinct. Anyway, if you don't want to hear what I have to say, I'll go back to work and you can do whatever."

"I want to know."

"The more I think about the horrible events around here, the more it points to the battle between Roscoe and Sandy Brashiers over the future direction of St. Elizabeth's." She held up her hand. "I know. Doesn't take a genius to figure that out."

"Well, I hadn't thought about it that way."

"Comfort BoomBoom—within reason. She might have a piece of the puzzle and not know it. Or she may be in danger. On the other hand, BoomBoom won't miss a chance to emote extravagantly." She smiled. "And, of course, you'll tell me everything."

56

What was working on BoomBoom was her mouth. She confessed to Fair that she had been having an affair with Maury McKinchie. She had broken it off when she discovered he was having affairs with other women or at least with one important woman. He wouldn't tell her who it was.

She thought that the Other Woman, not his wife, of course, might have killed him.

"What a fool I was to believe him." Her expressive gray-blue eyes spilled over with salty tears.

Fair wanted to hug her, console her, but his mistrust of her ran deep enough for him to throttle his best impulses. One hug from him and she'd be telling everyone they had engaged in deep, meaningful discussions. Gossip would take it from there.

"Did he promise to divorce Darla?"

"No. She was his meal ticket."

"Ah, then what was there to believe? I'm missing a beat here. I don't mean to be dense."

"You're not dense, Fair, darling, you're just a man." She forgot her misery long enough to puff up his ego. "Men don't look below the surface. Believe? I believed him when he said he loved me." She renewed her sobs and no amount of light sea kelp essence could dispel her gloom.

"Maybe he did love you."

"Then how could he carry on with another woman? It was bad enough he had a wife!"

"You don't know for certain—do you?"

"Oh, yes, I do." She wiped her eyes with her handkerchief. "I ransacked his car when he was 'taking a meeting,' as he used to say, with Roscoe. He kept everything important in that car. Here." She reached into her silk robe, a luscious lavender, and pulled out a handful of envelopes, which she thrust into his hands. "See for yourself."

Fair held the light gray envelopes, Tiffany paper, wrapped in a white ribbon. He untied the ribbon. "Shouldn't you give these to Rick Shaw?"

"I should do a lot of things; that's why I need to talk to you. How do I know Rick will keep this out of the papers?"

"He will." Fair read the first letter rapidly. Love stuff only interested him if it was his love stuff. His mood changed considerably when he reached the signature at the bottom of the next page. In lovely cursive handwriting the name of "Your Naomi" appeared. "Oh, shit."

"Killed him."

"You think Naomi killed him?"

"She could parade around in a Musketeer costume as easily as the rest of us."

"Finding that costume in Karen Jensen's locker sure was lucky for Kendrick." Fair raised an eyebrow. "I wouldn't let him off the hook yet myself. That guy's got serious problems."

"Heartless. Not cruel, mind you, just devoid of feeling unless there's a dollar sign somewhere in the exchange." BoomBoom tapped a long fingernail in the palm of her other hand. "Think how easy it would have been for Naomi to dump that costume in a kid's locker. Piece of cake."

"Maybe." Fair handed the envelopes back to BoomBoom.

"You aren't going to read the rest of them? They sizzle."

"It's none of my business. You should hand them over to Rick. Especially if you think Naomi killed McKinchie."

"That's just it. She must have found out about me and let him have it after offing Roscoe. Ha. She thought she was free and clear, and then she finds out there's another woman. I give him credit for energy. A wife and two lovers." She smirked, her deep dimple, so alluring, drawing deeper.

"I guess it's possible. Anything's possible. But then again, who's to say you didn't kill Maury McKinchie?" Fair, usually indirect in such circumstances, bluntly stated the obvious.

"Me? *Me?* I couldn't kill anyone. I want to heal people, bind their inner wounds. I wouldn't hurt anyone."

"I'm telling you how it looks to a—"

"A scumbag! Anyone who knows me knows I wouldn't kill, and most emphatically not over love."

"Sex? Or love?"

"I thought you'd be on my side!"

"I am on your side." He leveled his gaze at the distressed

woman, beautiful even in her foolishness. "That's why I'm asking you questions."

"I thought I loved Maury. Now I'm not so sure. He used me. He even gave me a screen test."

"From a sheriff's point of view, I'd say you had a motive."

"Well, I didn't have a motive to kill Roscoe Fletcher!"

"No, it would appear not. Did anyone have it in for Roscoe? Anyone you know?"

"Naomi. That's what I'm telling you."

"We don't know that he was cheating on her."

"He gathered his rosebuds while he may. Don't all you men do that—I mean, given the opportunity, you're all whores."

"I was." His jaw locked on him.

"Oh, Fair, I didn't mean you. You and Harry weren't suited for each other. The marriage would have come apart sooner or later. You know I cherish every moment we shared, and that's why, in my hour of need, I called you."

How could he have ever slept with this woman? Was he that blinded by beauty? A wave of disgust rose up from his stomach. He fought it down. Why be angry at her? She was what she was. She hadn't changed. He had.

"Fair?" She questioned the silence between them.

"If you truly believe that Naomi Fletcher killed her husband because she wanted to be with Maury McKinchie and then killed him in a fit of passion because she found out about you, you must go to the sheriff. Turn over those letters."

"I can't. It's too awful."

He changed his tack. "BoomBoom, what if she comes after you—assuming your hypothesis is correct."

"No!" Genuine alarm spread over her face.

"What about April Shively?" he pressed on.

"A good foundation base would have changed her life. That and rose petals in her bathwater." BoomBoom's facial muscles were taut; the veins in her neck stood out. "O-o-o, I'm cramping up. A charley horse. Rub it out for me."

"Your calf is fine. Don't start that stuff with me."

"What stuff?" She flared her nostrils.

"You know. Now I'm calling the sheriff. You can't withhold evidence like this."

"Don't!"

"BoomBoom, for once put your vanity aside for the public good. A murderer is out there. It may be Naomi, as you've said, but"—he shrugged—"if news leaks out that you had a fling with Maury, it's not the end of the world."

"Easy for you to say."

"I thought the man was a perfect ass."

"He made me laugh. And I can act as well as half of those people you see on television."

"I would never argue that point." He paused a moment, a flicker, a jolt to the brain. "BoomBoom, have you ever watched any of Maury's movies?"

"Sure. Every one."

"Did you like them? I mean, can you tell me something about them?"

"He used hot, hot leading ladies. He gave Darla her big break, you know."

"Hot? As in sex?"

"Oh"—she flipped her fingers downward, a lightning-fast gesture, half dismissal—"everything Maury did was about sex: the liberating power of sex and how we are transformed by it. The true self is revealed in the act. I mean, the stories could be about the Manhattan district attorney's office or about a Vietnamese immigrant in Los Angeles—that's my favorite, *Rice Sky*—but sex takes over sooner or later."

"Huh." He walked over to the phone.

"Don't leave me."

"I'm not." He called Harry first. "Honey, I'm waiting for Rick Shaw. I'll explain when I get to your place. Is your video machine working? Good. I'm bringing some movies. We're going to eat a lot of popcorn." Then he dialed Rick.

In fifteen minutes Rick and Cynthia arrived, picked up the envelopes, and left after commanding BoomBoom not to leave town.

When she begged Fair not to leave, he replied, not unkindly, "You need to learn to be alone."

"Not tonight! I'm scared."

"Call someone else."

"You're going back to Harry."

"I'm going to watch movies with her."

"Don't do it. It's a big mistake."

"Do what?"

"Fall in love with her."

"I never fell out of love with her. I lost me first, then I lost my wife. Sorry, BoomBoom."

57

"Girl, you'd better have a good explanation." Kendrick's eyes, bloodshot with rage, bored into his daughter.

"I told you. I paid with Grandpa's legacy."

"I checked the bank. You're a minor, so they gave me the information. Your account is not missing forty-one thousand dollars, which is what that damned BMW cost!"

"The check hasn't cleared yet," she replied coolly.

"Pegasus Motor Cars says you paid with a certified check. Who gave you the money!"

"Grandpa!" She sat on the edge of the sofa, knees together like a proper young lady.

"Don't lie to me." He stepped toward her, fists clenched.

"Dad, don't you dare hit me, I'm pregnant."

He stopped in his tracks. "WHAT?"

"I . . . am . . . pregnant."

"Does your mother know?"

"Yes."

If Irene had appeared at that moment, Kendrick might have killed her. Luckily she was grocery shopping. He transferred his rage to the man responsible.

"Who did this to you?"

"None of your business."

"It is my business. Whoever he is, he's going to make good on this deal. He'll marry you."

"I don't want to get married."

"Oh, you don't?" Venom dripped from his voice. "Well, what you want is irrelevant. You got into this mess by following your wants. My God, Jody, what's happened to you?" He sat down with a thud, the anger draining into fear and confusion.

"Don't be mad at Mom. She did what a mother is supposed to do. She went to the doctor with me—once I knew. We were going to tell you, Dad, but with everything that's happened to you—we put it off."

"Who is the father?"

"I'm not sure."

"How many boys have you slept with?" His voice cracked.

"A couple."

"Well, who do you think it is?"

"Sean Hallahan—maybe."

"Oh, shit."

58

"Don't lie to me." Susan hovered over Brooks.

"I'm not. I don't do drugs, Mom."

"You hang out with someone who does."

"Jensen's not a druggie. She had one joint in her bag. Chill out."

Ned stepped in. "I think it's time we all went to bed."

"Danny's already in bed." Brooks envied her brother, off the hook on this one.

"Now look, daughter, if you are hiding something, you'd better come clean. Whatever you're doing, we'll deal with it."

"I'm not doing anything."

"Susan." Ned rubbed his forehead. A headache nibbled at his temples.

"I want to get to the bottom of this. Sheriff Shaw asked each of you questions after the marijuana was found and after that costume showed up. I can't believe it. It's too preposterous. Karen Jensen."

"Mom, Karen didn't kill Mr. McKinchie. Really. It's nuts."

"How do you suppose the costume got in her locker?"

"Easy. Everyone on the team knows everyone else's combination. We're always borrowing stuff."

Susan hovered over Brooks. "What do you know about Karen Jensen that we don't?"

"Karen's okay. She's not a druggie. The only thing I know about Karen is that she was dating an older guy from UVA this summer and got a little too close. Really. She's okay."

Susan put her arm around her daughter's shoulders. "I hope you are, too."

Later Susan called Harry, relaying the conversation with Brooks. Harry treated her to a synopsis of *Rice Sky*.

"Sounds boring."

"Made a lot of money. I think the real reason Roscoe was pushing the film-department idea was to punch up Maury. He was so overshadowed by Darla. Roscoe was smart. Cater to Maury and good things would follow."

"Money. Tons of money."

"Sure. They'd name the department after Maury. He'd donate all his scripts, round up old equipment; the whole thing would be an ego trip."

"How much do you think an ego trip like that would cost?"

"It would take at least a million-dollar endowment, I'd think. Probably more." Harry scribbled on a brown paper bag. "I'm not too good at knowing what it would be worth, really, but it would have to be a lot."

"What's Fair think?"

"Millions," he called out.

"Sandy Brashiers can't be that stupid," Harry said. "For a couple of million dollars even he would cave in on the film-department idea."

"I doubt Roscoe put it in dollars and cents."

"Yeah. Maybe it's in April's books."

"Susan, if that's all that's in there, what's to hide?"

"Damned if I know. We called about Sean, by the way. No change."

"I called, too."

"That kid has to know something. Larry Johnson said he'd heard the main swelling was diminishing. Maybe he'll snap out of the coma once the swelling is down."

"He's lucky to be alive."

59

"Why don't you just tell me the truth?" Rick rapped his fingers on the highly polished table.

"You have no right to push me like this." Naomi Fletcher had her back up.

"You know more than you're telling me." He remained cool and professional.

"No, I don't. And I resent you badgering me when I'm in mourning."

Wordlessly, Cynthia Cooper slid the packet of envelopes, retied with a neat bow, across the table to Naomi. Her face bled bone white.

"How—?"

"The 'how' doesn't matter, Naomi. If you are in on these

murders, come clean." Cynthia sounded sympathetic "Maybe we can work a deal."

"I didn't kill anyone."

"You didn't kill Roscoe to clear the way for McKinchie to marry you?" Rick pressured her.

"Marry Maury McKinchie? I'd sooner have a root canal." Her even features contorted in scorn.

"You liked him enough to sleep with him." Cynthia fel: the intimate information should best come from her, no Rick.

"That doesn't mean I wanted to spend my life with him Maury was a good-time Charlie, and that's all he was. He wasn't marriage material."

"Apparently, neither was Roscoe."

She shrugged. "He was in the beginning, but mer change."

"So do women." Cynthia pointed to the envelopes.

"What's good for the gander was good for the goose, ir this instance. The marriage vows are quite lovely, and one would hope to live up to them, but they are exceedingly unre alistic. I didn't do anything wrong. I didn't kill anyone. played with Maury McKinchie. You can't arrest me for that."

"Played with him and then killed him when you learned he wasn't serious about you and he was sleeping with anothe: woman."

"BoomBoom." She waved her hand in the air as though a an irritating gnat. "I'd hardly worry about her."

"Plenty of other women have." Cynthia bluntly stated the truth.

"BoomBoom was too self-centered for Maury. One wa never really in danger of a rival because he loved himself to much, if you know what I mean." She smiled coldly.

"You were at the car wash the day your husband died. You spoke to him. You could have easily given him poisoned candy."

"I could have, but I didn't."

"You're tough," Rick said, half admiringly.

"I'm not tough, I'm innocent."

"If I had a dollar for every killer who said that, I'd be a rich man." Rick felt in his coat pocket for his cigarettes. "Mind if I smoke?"

"I most certainly do. The whole house will stink when you leave, which I hope is soon."

Cynthia and Rick shared a secret acknowledgment. No Southern lady would have said that.

"How well did you know Darla?"

"A nodding acquaintance. She was rarely here."

"If you didn't kill Roscoe, do you know who did?"

"No."

"How does withholding evidence sound to you, Mrs. Fletcher?" Rick hunched forward.

"Like a bluff."

"For chrissake, Naomi, two men are dead!" Cynthia couldn't contain her disgust. Then she quickly fired a question. "Was your husband sleeping with April Shively?"

"God, no," Naomi hooted. "Roscoe thought April was pretty but deadly dull." Naomi had to admit to herself that dullness didn't keep men from sleeping with women. However, she wasn't going to admit that to Shaw and Cooper.

"Do you think Kendrick killed Maury?" Rick switched his bait.

"Unlikely." She closed her eyes, as if worn-out.

Cooper interjected. "Why?"

Naomi perked up. "Kendrick doesn't have the balls."

"Did you love your husband?" Rick asked.

She grew sober, sad even. "You live with a man for eighteen years, you tend to know him. Roscoe might wander off the reservation from time to time. He could indulge in little cruelties—his treatment of Sandy Brashiers being a case in point. He kept Sandy in the dark about everything." She paused. "Did I love him? I was accustomed to him, but I did love him. Yes, I did."

Cynthia mustered a smile. "Why?"

Naomi shrugged. "Habit."

"What did Roscoe have against Sandy Brashiers?"

"Roscoe always had it in for Harvard men. He said the arrogance of their red robes infuriated him. You know, during academic ceremonies only Harvard wears the crimson robe."

"Do you have any feeling about the false obituaries?" Cynthia prodded.

"Those?" Naomi wrinkled her brow. "Kids' prank. Sean apologized."

"Do you think he was also responsible for the second one?"

"No. I think it was a copycat. Sean got the luxury of being a bad dude. Very seductive at that age. Another boy wanted the glory. Is it that important?"

"It might be." Rick reached for his hat.

"Have you searched April Shively's house?" Naomi asked.

"House, car, office, even her storage unit. Nothing."

Naomi stood up to usher them out. "She doesn't live high on the hog. I don't think she embezzled funds."

"She could be covering up for someone else." Cynthia reached the door first.

"You mean Roscoe, of course." Naomi didn't miss a beat.

"Why not? He's dead. He can be accused of anything. You have to find criminals in order to keep your jobs, don't you?"

Rick halted at the door as Naomi's hand reached the knob. "You work well with Sandy, don't you? Under the circumstances?"

"Yes."

"Did you know that Sandy got a student pregnant at White Academy, the school he worked at before St. Elizabeth's?"

Cooper struck next. "Roscoe knew."

"You two have been very busy." Her lips tightened.

"Like you said, Mrs. Fletcher, we have to find criminals in order to keep our jobs." Rick half smiled.

She grimaced and closed the door.

60

Mrs. Murphy leaned against the pillow on the sofa. She stretched her right hind leg out straight and held it there. Then she unsheathed her claws and stared at her toes. What stupendously perfect toes. She repeated the process with the left hind leg. Then she reached with her front paws together, a kitty aerobic exercise. Satisfied, she lay back on the pillow, happily staring into the fire. She reviewed in her mind recent events.

Harry dusted her library shelves, a slow process since she'd take a book off the shelf, read passages, and then replace it. A light snow fell outside, which made her all the happier to be inside.

Tucker snored in front of the fire. Pewter, curled in a ball at the other end of the sofa, dreamed of tiny mice singing her praise. *"O Mighty Pewter, Queen of Cats."*

"Lord of the Flies." Harry pulled the old paperback off the shelf. "Had to read it in college, but I hated it." She dropped to the next shelf. "Fielding, love him. Austen." She turned to Mrs. Murphy. "Literature is about sensibility. Really, Murphy, John Milton is one of the greatest poets who ever lived, but he bores me silly. I have trouble liking any art form trying to beat a program into my head. I suppose it's the difference between the hedgehog and the fox."

"Isaiah Berlin." Mrs. Murphy recalled the important work of criticism dividing writers into hedgehogs or foxes, hedgehogs being fixed on one grand idea or worldview whereas foxes ran through the territory; life was life with no special agenda. That was how she thought of it anyway.

"What I mean is, Murphy, readers are hedgehogs or foxes. Some people read to remember. Some read to forget. Some read to be challenged. Others want their prejudices confirmed."

"Why do you read, Mother?" the cat asked.

"I read," Harry said, knowing exactly what her cat had asked her, "for the sheer exultant pleasure of the English language."

"Ah, me, too." The tiger purred. Harry couldn't open a book without Mrs. Murphy sitting on her shoulder or in her lap.

Sometimes Pewter would read, but she favored mysteries or thrillers. Pewter couldn't raise her sights above genre fiction.

Mrs. Murphy thought the gray cat might read some diet books as well. She stretched and walked over to Harry. She jumped on a shelf to be closer to Harry's face. She scanned the book spines, picking out her favorites. She enjoyed biographies more than Harry did. She stopped at Michael Powell's *My Life in the Movies*.

She blinked and leapt off the shelf, cuffing Tucker awake. *"Come on, Tucker, come on."*

"I'm so comfortable."

"Just follow me." She skidded out the animal door, Tucker on her heels.

"What in God's name gets into her?" Harry held *The Iliad*.

Forty-five minutes later both animals, winded, pulled up at Bowden's pond where the Camry and the grisly remains still sat, undiscovered by humans.

"Tucker, you cover the east side of the pond. I'll cover the west. Look for a video or a can of film."

Both animals searched through the snow, which was beginning to cover the ground; still the shapes would have been obvious.

An hour later they gave up.

"Nothing," Tucker reported.

"Me either."

A growl made their hair stand on end.

"The bobcat!" Mrs. Murphy charged up the slippery farm road, leaping the ruts. Tucker, fast as grease, ran beside her.

They reached the cutover hayfields, wide open with no place to hide.

"She's gaining on us." Tucker's tongue hung out.

And she was, a compact, powerful creature, tufts on the ends of her ears.

"This is my fault." The cat ached from running so hard.

"Save your breath." Tucker whirled to confront the foe, her long fangs bared.

The bobcat stopped for a moment. She wanted dinner, but she didn't want to get hurt. She loped around Tucker, deciding Murphy was the better chance. Tucker followed the bobcat.

"Run, Murphy, run. I'll keep her busy."

"You domesticated worm," the bobcat spat.

Seeing her friend in danger, Murphy stopped panting. She puffed up, turning to face the enemy. Together she and Tucker flanked the bobcat about twenty yards from her.

The bobcat crouched, moving low toward Mrs. Murphy, who jumped sideways. The bobcat ran and flung herself in the air. Murphy sidestepped her. The big cat whirled and charged just as Tucker hurtled toward her. The dog hit the bobcat in the legs as she was ready to pounce on Murphy. The bobcat rolled, then sprang to her feet. Both friends were side to side now, fangs bared.

"In here!" a voice called from the copse of trees a spring away.

"Let's back toward it," Murphy gasped.

"Where are we going?" Tucker whispered.

"To the trees."

"She's more dangerous there than in the open."

"It's our only hope."

"You two are worthless." The bobcat stalked them, savoring the moment.

"That's your opinion." Mrs. Murphy growled deep in her throat.

"You're the hors d'oeuvre, your canine sidekick is the main meal."

"Don't count your chickens." Murphy spun around and flew over the snow.

Tucker did likewise, the bobcat closing in on her. She heard breathing behind her and then saw Mrs. Murphy dive into a foxhole. Tucker spun around and snapped at the bobcat's forelegs, which caught her completely by surprise. It gave Tucker the split second she needed to dive into the foxhole after her friend.

"I can wait all night," the bobcat muttered.

"Don't waste time over spilt milk," Mrs. Murphy taunted.

"I'm glad some of you are big foxes." Tucker panted on the floor of the den. *"I'd have never gotten into your earth otherwise."*

The slight red vixen said to Murphy, *"You told me once to stay in the shed during a bad storm. I owe you one."*

"You've more than repaid me." Murphy listened as the bobcat prowled around, unwilling to give up.

"What were you two doing out here tonight?"

"Looking for a film or a video back where the dead human in the car is," Tucker said.

"Nobody will find that human until deer-hunting season starts, and that's two weeks away," the vixen noted wisely.

"Did you-all see anything?"

"No, although when we first found her at the end of September she'd only been dead a few weeks."

"September! I think the killer threw the evidence in the pond." Murphy was a figuring cat.

"How do you know?" Tucker knew that the feline was usually a few steps ahead of her.

"Because the murders are about film and Roscoe's film depart-

ment. It was right in front of my face, but I didn't see it. Whoever is in that car is the missing link."

"Murphy," Tucker softly said, *"have you figured out what's going on?"*

"Yes, I think I have, but not in time—not in time."

61

Kendrick and Jody sat on a bench outside the intensive-care unit. An officer guarded Sean inside. His grandfather was there, too.

Kendrick stopped Dr. Hayden McIntire when he came out of the room. "How is he?"

"We're guardedly optimistic." He looked at Jody. "Quite a few of his friends have stopped by. He's a popular boy."

"Has Karen Jensen been here?" Jody asked.

"Yes. So were Brooks Tucker, Roger Davis, and the whole football team, of course. They can't go in, but it was good that they came."

"Well, that's nice." Kendrick smiled unconvincingly.

After Hayden left, Kendrick took his daughter by the elbow. "Come on, he isn't going to rise up and walk just because you're here."

She stared at the closed doors. "I wish he would."

"I'll attend to Sean in good time."

"Dad, you can't make anybody do anything. One mistake isn't cured by making a bigger one."

They walked down the hall. "That's a mature statement."

"Maybe I'm learning something."

"Well, learn this. I'm not having bastards in my house, so you're going to marry somebody."

"It's my body."

He grabbed her arm hard. "There is no other option."

"Let me go or I'll scream bloody murder right here at University of Virginia Hospital. And you're in enough trouble." She said this without rancor.

"Yes." He unhanded her.

"Did you kill Maury McKinchie?"

"What?" He was shocked that she asked.

"Did you kill Maury McKinchie?"

"No."

62

Neither Mrs. Murphy nor Tucker returned home all night. Harry had called and called. Finally she fed the horses and, last of all, Pewter.

Walking down to get the paper, she heard Tucker bark. *"We're safe!"*

"Yahoo!" Mrs. Murphy sped beside the dog, stopping from time to time to jump for joy, straight in the air, the snow flying up and catching the sunlight, making thousands of tiny rainbows.

"Where have you two been?" Harry hunched down to gather them both in her arms. "I was worried sick about you." She sniffed. "You smell like a fox."

"We spent the night with our hosts," Murphy said.

Tucker, turning in excited circles, interrupted. *"We think there's evidence in Bowden's pond, and then we stayed too late and the bobcat tracked us. Oh, it was a close call."*

"Tucker was brave!"

"You, too."

"Such talk." Harry laughed at their unintelligible chatter. "You must be starving. Come on. We've got to hurry or I'll be late for work."

Driving Blair's Dually into Crozet, Harry noticed the snow lying blue in the deep hollows.

The three rushed into the post office, nearly getting stuck in the animal door. Mrs. Hogendobber, who usually greeted them, was so excited, she barely noticed their entry.

"Hi, Miranda—"

"Where have you been?" Miranda clapped her hands in anticipation of telling her the news.

"What is the matter?"

"Kendrick Miller confessed to Rick Shaw that he had killed Maury McKinchie and Roscoe Fletcher. He had made up the story about the Musketeer because he remembered the Musketeer was wearing a sword. The costume hanging in Jensen's locker was irrelevant to the case. He confessed last night at midnight."

"I don't believe it," Mrs. Murphy exclaimed.

63

A crowd had gathered at Mim's . . . a good thing, since she put them to work stuffing and hand-addressing envelopes for the Multiple Sclerosis Foundation in which she was typically active.

Brooks, Roger, and Karen were relieved now that St. Elizabeth's could return to normal. Sandy Brashiers, at the head of the envelope line, told them to pipe down.

Gretchen, Mim's cook, served drinks.

When Cynthia walked through the door, everyone cheered. Accorded center stage, she endured question after question.

"One at a time." Cynthia laughed.

"Why did he do it?" Sandy Brashiers asked.

Cynthia waited a moment, then said, "These were crimes of passion, in a sense. I don't want to offend anyone but—"

"*Murder* is the offense," Sandy said. "We can handle his reasons."

"Well—Roscoe was carrying on an affair with Irene Miller and Kendrick blew up."

"*Roscoe?* What about Maury?" Fair Haristeen, tired from a day in the operating room, sat in a chair. Enough people were folding and stuffing. He needed a break.

"Kendrick has identified the poison used. He said Maury was on to him, knew he'd killed Roscoe, and was going to prove it. He killed him to shut him up."

Harry listened with interest. She felt such relief even as she felt sorrow for Irene and Jody. Irene had had an affair. No cheers for that, but to have a husband snap and go on a killing spree had to be dreadful. No wonder Jody had beaned Maury McKinchie at the hockey game. The tension in the Miller household must have been unbearable. *"Nouveau riche,"* Mim cried.

"I'd rather be *nouveau riche* than not *riche* at all," Fair rejoined, and since Mim adored her vet, he could get away with it.

Everyone truly laughed this time.

"How did Kendrick get such powerful poison?" Reverend Herb Jones wondered.

"The nursery and gardening business needs pesticides."

Harry noticed BoomBoom's unusual reticence. "Aren't you relieved?"

"Uh—yes," said the baffled beauty. She'd had no idea about Roscoe and Irene. Why didn't Maury tell her? He'd relished sexual tidbits.

Sandy Brashiers put his hands on his hips. "This still

doesn't get April Shively off the hook. After all, she is withholding papers relevant to school operation."

"Maybe she will come forward now," Little Mim hoped out loud.

"How do you know for sure it was Mr. Miller?" Karen said to everyone's amazement.

Cynthia answered, "A detailed confession is about as close to a lock as you can get."

"Why'd he tell?" Harry wondered aloud.

Cynthia winked at her. "Couldn't live with the guilt. Said he confessed to Father Michael first, and over time realized he had to give himself up."

"Well, it's over. Let's praise the Lord for our deliverance," Miranda instructed them.

"Amen," Herb agreed and the others joined in.

"You know, I keep thinking about Irene and Jody sitting home alone. They must be wretched. We should extend our sympathy." Miranda folded her hands as if in prayer.

Everyone looked at Mrs. Hogendobber, thought for a moment, and then agreed that she had a point. It might not be fun to go over to the Millers', but it was the right thing to do.

After the work party, Harry, Fair, Big Mim, Little Mim, Herb Jones, Miranda, and Susan Tucker drove over. The kids piled into Roger's old car. Father Michael had been with the family since Kendrick gave himself up late that afternoon. It was the priest who answered the door. Surprised to see so many people, he asked Irene if she would be willing to see her neighbors. She burst into tears and nodded "yes."

The first person Irene greeted was Big Mim, who after the formalities offered them a sojourn in one of her farm dependencies if they should need privacy from the press.

Irene thanked her and began crying again.

Miranda put her arm around her. "There, there, Irene. This is too strange to contemplate. You must be feeling confused and terrible."

"Bizarre," Jody said forthrightly. "I can't believe he lost it like that."

Irene, not ready to give up on her husband, sputtered, "He's no murderer!"

"He confessed," Jody said flatly.

"We're your friends, no matter what." Softhearted Roger couldn't bear to see Jody's mother cry.

"Mom, I want to go back to school. I know this won't go away, but something in our lives has to be normal."

"Jody, that only puts more pressure on you." Irene worried about the reaction of the other students.

"Hey, I'm not responsible for Dad. I need my friends."

"We'll see."

"Mom, I'm going."

"We'll watch over her," Karen volunteered.

As this issue was hashed out, Father Michael and Herb Jones huddled in a corner. Father Michael, secure in the company of another cleric, whispered to him that he was tremendously relieved that Kendrick was behind bars. After all, he himself was likely to be the next victim.

"Bragging?"

"Not exactly. The first confession was straightforward. The second one, he said he liked killing. He liked the power. I can't say I ever recognized his voice."

"Was there a sense of vindication?" Herb inclined his head close to Father Michael's.

"I couldn't say."

"A touch dramatic."

"The entire episode was certainly that."

Later that evening Harry told Mrs. Murphy, Tucker, and Pewter all that had transpired at Big Mim's and then over at Irene Miller's. Angry though they were at not being included, they listened as she babbled while doing her chores.

"They're so far away from the truth it hurts," Tucker said and Pewter agreed, since Mrs. Murphy had briefed them on what she felt was truly going on.

"It's going to hurt a whole lot more." Mrs. Murphy stared out the window into the black night. Try as she might, she couldn't think of what to do.

64

Typical of central Virginia in late November, a rush of warm wind rolled up from the Gulf of Mexico. Temperatures soared into the low sixties.

Students were now back at St. Elizabeth's, thanks to Kendrick's midnight confession.

Harry and Miranda shoveled through the landslide of mail.

Jody Miller and Karen Jensen pulled in front of Market Shiflett's store.

"Things are finally settling down." Miranda watched the girls, smiling, enter the grocery store.

"Thank God." Harry tossed a catalog into the Tucker post box. "Now if my truck would just get fixed! I'm getting spoiled driving Blair's Dually and I don't want to wear out my welcome."

"*Think of all the string and rubber bands they have to remove,*" Pewter quipped sarcastically. "*What are Jody and Karen doing out of school?*"

"*Hookey,*" Tucker thought out loud.

Mrs. Murphy said, "*There's a big field hockey game after school today, and a huge football game Friday. Maybe their coach got them out of class.*"

"*Wish we'd get out of work early.*" Pewter rubbed the plastic comb Harry had just installed on the corner of the post boxes. It was advertised as a cat-grooming aid.

"*'Course St. E's won't be worth squat—they lost too much practice time, but Crozet High ought to have a good game.*" The tiger enjoyed sports.

"*St. E's practiced,*" Tucker said. "*Of course, how well they practiced with all the uproar is anyone's guess.*"

Jody and Karen came out of the store, placed a big carton in the back of Karen's old car, and drove off.

Susan zoomed into the post office through the backdoor. "Good news!"

"*What?*" came the animal and human chorus.

"Sean Hallahan has regained consciousness." She beamed. "He's not out of the woods yet, but he knows his name, where he is, he recognizes his parents. He's still in intensive care. Still no visitors."

"That's great news." Harry smiled.

"Once he's really clear, off some of the painkillers, he'll have other pains to deal with . . . still, isn't it wonderful?"

65

The deep golden rays of the late-afternoon sun slanted over the manicured field hockey pitch. The high winds and snow of the previous week had stripped the trees of their leaves, but the mild temperature balanced the starkness of early winter.

Knowing how rapidly the mercury could fall, Harry tossed four blankets over her shoulder.

As she made her way to the bleachers, the Reverend Herb Jones called out, "You opening a trading post?"

"Four beaver pelts for one heavy blanket." She draped a royal-blue buffalo plaid blanket over her arm as if to display her wares.

Miranda, warm in her MacLeod tartan kilt with a matching tam-o'-shanter, soon joined them. She carried two hot thermoses, one of tea, the other of chocolate.

"You come sit by me." Herb patted the hard wooden bleacher seat next to him.

Sandy Brashiers, beaming, shook the hands of parents, telling each of them how grateful he was that St. Elizabeth's frightful ordeal was behind them. He thanked everyone for their support, and he promised the best for the remainder of the semester.

Coach Hallvard, about to face the formidable St. Catherine's team from Richmond, had not a second to glad-hand anyone.

Mim accompanied her daughter, which put Little Mim's nose out of joint because she wanted to be accompanied by Blair Bainbridge. He, however, had been roped into setting up the hot dog stand since his Dually, the newest in town, could pull the structure. Not only did Blair's Dually have a setup for a gooseneck trailer, he also had a Reese hitch welded to the frame.

"Mother, why don't you sit with the girls?" Little Mim waved broadly at Miranda in MacLeod tartan splendor.

Mim, sotto voce, replied, "Trying to get rid of me?"

"Why, Mother, whatever gave you such a silly idea?"

"Humph. You need me to extract money out of these tightwads, Marilyn. You haven't been a raging success."

"Considering all that's happened here, I've done pretty damn well, Mother. And I don't need you to advertise my shortcomings. I'm conversant with them."

"Well, aren't we testy."

"Yes, we are." Little Mim gave her a sickeningly sweet smile.

These last two years Little Mim had found some backbone. Her mother enjoyed friction on the odd occasion, although she wasn't accustomed to receiving it from her formerly obsequious daughter. However, it did spice up the day.

"Mimsy," Miranda called out, knowing Mim hated "Mimsy." She felt devilish. "Sit with us."

Mim, throwing her alpaca shawl, deep raspberry, over her wildly overpriced Wathne coat, paraded grandly to the bleachers, leaving Little Mim to scoot to the hot dog stand where she found, to her dismay, Cynthia Cooper helping Blair set up shop.

The home team trotted across the field as the rhythm section of the band beat the drums.

Karen Jensen ran with Brooks. "Toni Freeman has moves like a snake," Karen said about the opponent who would be covering Brooks.

"I'll be a mongoose."

"This is going to be a tough game." Karen grew increasingly fierce before the game.

"Zone. You'll be in the zone."

"Yeah. There's Rog."

Brooks waved back at Roger.

"Tossed salad." Karen laughed, meaning Roger had flipped over Brooks.

Jody loped up from behind. "Let's skin 'em alive, pound 'em senseless! *Yes!*" She moved by them.

As the team approached the bench, the stands erupted in a roar. St. Catherine's also shouted. The entire senior class had trekked out from Richmond. This was a grudge match because St. Catherine's had edged out St. E's in the semifinals at last year's state tournament.

The three animal friends sat with the humans on the bleachers.

Pewter hated the crowd noises. *"I'm going back to the car."*

"Miranda closed up the Falcon; you can't get in," Mrs. Murphy told her.

"Then I'll go to the hot dog stand." Pewter's eyes glistened.

"Stay with us," Murphy told her loudly.

"Will you two stop fussing at each other!" Harry commanded.

"She started it." Pewter oozed innocence.

A phone rang in Herb's pocket.

"What on earth?" Miranda exclaimed when he pulled a fold-up cellular out of his Norfolk jacket.

"The modern age, Miranda, the modern age." He pulled out the antenna, hit a button, and said, "Hello."

Susan answered, "Herb, tell the gang I'm on my way. Oh, and tell Harry I dropped off BoomBoom to pick up her truck. It's ready."

"Okay. Anything else?"

"No. Be there in ten minutes."

"Fine. 'Bye." He pressed the green button again, sliding the aerial down. "Harry, Susan will be here in ten minutes, and BoomBoom is bringing your truck. Susan dropped her off."

"BoomBoom? Great. Now I have to be terminally grateful."

"No, you don't. After all, she wrecked your truck in the first place."

"Given the way she drives, she'll wreck it again."

"Mother, you're irrational about BoomBoom." Mrs. Murphy scratched her neck.

"No, she won't," Herb answered. "Here we go!"

The game started with St. Catherine's racing downfield, taking a shot on goal, saved.

"Jeez, that was fast." Harry hoped St. Elizabeth's defense would kick in soon.

"May I see that?"

"Sure." Herb handed Miranda the cellular phone.

She slipped the aerial out and held it to her ear. "It's so light."

"I'll pick up my messages; listen to how clear it is." He punched in what must have been seventeen or more numbers and held the phone to Miranda's ear.

"Amazing." Suddenly her face changed. "Herbie, look."

Parading in front of the bleachers was April Shively wearing a St. Elizabeth's jacket. She was carrying three closed cartons that she dumped at Sandy Brashiers's feet.

Blair noticed this from the hot dog stand. Cynthia hurried over, Little Mim at her heels.

"Deputy Cooper." A surprised Sandy put his hand on the boxes. "Marilyn."

"I'll take those." Little Mim bent over and picked up a rather heavy carton.

"No." Sandy smiled falsely.

April, her grin widening, turned on her heel and left. "Ta-ta!"

"Damn her," Sandy said under his breath.

"Cynthia, you can't have these." Little Mim squared her shoulders.

"Why don't we examine them together? It will only help St. Elizabeth's if everything is aboveboard from the start." Cynthia made a strong argument.

"As headmaster, I'll take charge of those documents."

"Down in front!" a fan, oblivious to the drama, yelled at them.

"Without me you won't be headmaster for long." Little Mim clipped her words, then smiled at the deputy as she changed course. "Come on, Cynthia. You're absolutely right. We should do this together."

As they hauled off the cartons, the announcer blared over the loudspeaker, "We are happy to announce that St. Elizabeth's own Sean Hallahan has regained consciousness, and we know all your prayers have helped."

A huge cheer went up from the stands.

66

After the game, won by St. Elizabeth's, Jody, who'd played brilliantly, drove alone to the University of Virginia Hospital.

Sean, removed to a private room, no longer had a guard since Kendrick had confessed. His father was sitting with him when Jody, wearing a visitor's pass, lightly knocked on the door.

"May I come in?"

Sean turned his head toward her, stared blankly for a moment, then focused. "Sure."

"Hello, Mr. Hallahan."

"Hello, Jody. I'm sorry this is such a troubling time for you."

"It can't be as bad as what you're going through." She walked over to Sean. "Hey."

"Hey." He turned his head to address his father. "Dad, could we be alone?"

In that moment Mr. Hallahan knew Jody was the girl in question, for his wife had told him Sean's words during his first, brief moment of lucidity when Cynthia Cooper was on guard.

"I'll be just down the hall if you need me."

When he had left, Jody leaned over, kissing Sean on the cheek. "I'm sorry, I'm really sorry."

"I was stupid. It wasn't your fault."

"Yes, it was. I told you—well, the news—when I was pissed off at you and the world."

"I'll marry you if you like," he gallantly offered.

"No. Sean, I was angry because you were paying attention to Karen. I wanted to hurt you."

"You mean you aren't pregnant?" His eyes brightened.

"No, I am."

"Oh." He dropped his head back on the pillow. "Jody, you can't face this alone. Lying here has given me a lot of time to think."

"Do you love Karen?"

"No. I haven't even gone out with her."

"But you want to."

He drew a long breath. "Yeah. But that was then. This is now."

"Will you walk again?"

"Yes." He spoke with determination. "The doctors say I'll never play football again . . . but they don't know me. I don't care what it takes. I will."

"Everyone's back at school. My dad confessed to the murders."

"Mom told me." He didn't know what to say. "I wish I could be at Homecoming."

"Team won't be worth squat without you."

"Paul Briscoe will do okay. He's just a sophomore, but he'll be good."

"Do you hate me?" Her eyes, misty, implored him.

"No. I hate myself."

"Did you tell anyone—"

"Of course not."

"Don't."

"What are you going to do?"

"Get rid of it."

He breathed hard, remaining quiet for a long time. "I wish you wouldn't do that."

"Sean, the truth is—I'm not ready to be a mother. You're not ready to be a father, either, and besides—it may not be yours."

"But you said—"

"I wanted to hurt you. It may be yours and it may not. So just forget it. Forget everything. My dad's in jail. Just remember—my dad's in jail."

"Why would he kill Mr. Fletcher and Mr. McKinchie?"

"I don't know."

His pain medication was wearing off. Sweat beaded on Sean's forehead. "We were having such a good time." He pushed the button for the nurse. "Jody, I need a shot."

"I'll go. Don't worry. You're sure you didn't tell anyone anything?"

"I didn't."

"I'll see you later." She passed Mr. Hallahan, who walked back into Sean's room the minute she left.

"She's the one."

"No." Grimacing, Sean pleaded, "Dad, get the nurse, will you? I really hurt."

67

That same night Cynthia Cooper and Little Mim sifted through papers at Little Mim's beautiful cottage on her mother's vast estate.

"Why do you think April finally changed her mind?" Little Mim said.

"Had to be that she heard about Roscoe's affair with Irene," Coop answered. "Her hero suddenly had feet of clay."

The minutes from the various committee meetings provided no surprises.

Roscoe's record book containing handwritten notes made after informal meetings or calls on possible donors did pack some punch.

After a meeting with Kendrick Miller, Roscoe had scrawled, "Discussed women's athletics, especially a new training room for the girls. Whirlpool bath. Won't give a penny. Cheap bastard."

On Father Michael's long prayers during assembly: "A simple 'Bless us, dear Lord' would suffice."

After a particularly bruising staff meeting where a small but well-organized contingent opposed athletic expansion and a film department, he wrote concerning Sandy Brashiers, "Judas."

As Little Mim occasionally read pungent passages aloud, Cynthia, using a pocket calculator, went through the accounting books.

"I had no idea it cost so much money to run St. E's." She double-checked the figures.

"What hurts most is maintenance. The older buildings suck up money."

"Guess they were built before insulation."

"Old Main was put up in 1834."

Cynthia picked up the last book, a green clothbound book, longer than it was wide. She opened it to the figures page without checking the front. As she merrily clicked in numbers, she hummed. "Do you remember what cost five thousand dollars the first week of September? It says 'W.T.' " She pointed to the ledger.

"Doesn't ring a bell."

Cynthia punched in more numbers.

"Hey, here's a good one." Little Mim laughed, reading out loud. " 'Big Mim suggested I butter up Darla McKinchie and get her to pry money out of Kendrick. I told her Darla has no interest in St. Elizabeth's, in her husband's career and, as best

I can tell, no affection for the state of Virginia. She replied, "How common!" ' "

Little Mim shook her head. "Leave it to Mother. She can't ever let me have something for myself. I'm on the board, she isn't."

"She's trying to help."

Marilyn's hazel eyes clouded. "Help? My mother wants to run every committee, organization, potential campaign. She's indefatigable."

"What cost forty-one thousand dollars?"

Little Mim put down Roscoe's record book to look at the ledger. "Forty-one thousand dollars October twenty-eighth. Roscoe was dead by then." She grabbed the ledger, flipping back to the front. "Slush fund. What the hell is this?"

Coop couldn't believe she'd heard Little Mim swear. "I suppose most organizations have a kitty, although this is quite a large one."

"I'll say." Little Mim glanced over the incoming sums. "We'll get to the bottom of this." She reached for the phone, punching numbers as she exhaled loudly. "April, it's Marilyn Sanburne." She pressed the "speaker" button so that Coop could hear as well.

"Are you enjoying yourself?"

"Actually, I am," came the curt reply. "Roscoe's record book is priceless. What is this green ledger?"

"I have no idea."

"April, don't expect me to believe you. Why else would you remove these papers and accounting books? You must have known about the slush fund."

"First of all, given everyone's temper these days, a public reading of Roscoe's record book is not a good idea. Second, I have no idea what the slush fund was. Roscoe never once mentioned it to me. I found that book in his desk."

"Could Maury have started giving St. Elizabeth's an endowment?"

"Without fanfare? He was going to give, all right, but we were going to have to kiss his ass in Macy's window."

Little Mim bit her lip. "April, I've misjudged you."

"Is that a formal apology?" April asked.

"Yes."

"I accept."

"Sandy Brashiers couldn't have handled this," Little Mim admitted.

"He'd have fumbled the ball. All we need is for the papers to get wind of this before we know what it's all about," April said.

"You have no idea?" Little Mim pressed.

"No. But you'll notice the incoming sums are large and regular. Usually between the tenth and fifteenth of each month."

"Let me see that." Coop snatched the green book out of Little Mim's hands. "Damn!"

"What?" Little Mim said.

Cynthia grabbed the phone. "April, seventy-five thousand dollars came in the week after Roscoe died. It's not reflected in the ledger, but there is a red dot by October tenth. For the other deposits, there's a red dot with a black line through it."

"Primitive but effective bookkeeping," April said.

"Did you know a Jiffy bag with seventy-five thousand dollars arrived in Roscoe's mailbox at Crozet on October"—she figured a moment—"twelfth? I'm pretty sure it was the twelfth."

"I didn't know a thing about it."

"But sometimes you would pick up Roscoe's personal mail for him?"

"Infrequently . . . but yes."

"Do you remember other Jiffy bags?"

"Cooper, most books are sent in bags like that."

"Do you swear to me you don't know what this money represents?"

"I swear, but I know it represents something not right. That's why I cleaned everything out. I didn't mind sitting in jail. I felt safe."

"One last question."

"Shoot."

"Do you believe that Kendrick Miller killed Roscoe and Maury?"

"Roscoe loathed him. But, no, I don't."

"He says he blew up in a rage."

"Show him the ledger."

"I'm going to do just that. One more question. I promise this is the last one. Do you think Naomi knows about the ledger?"

A pause. "If she did, we'd see the money. Even if just a pair of expensive earrings."

"Thanks, April."

"Are you going to prosecute me for obstructing justice?"

"I'm not the legal eagle, but I'll do what I can."

"Okay." April hung up, satisfied.

"Marilyn, I need this ledger. I won't publicize it, but I need to show it to Kendrick and Naomi. This is starting to look like money-laundering. Question is, was Kendrick Miller involved in it?"

The next day Kendrick examined the figures closely but said nothing. Cynthia could have bashed him.

Naomi appeared genuinely shocked by the secret book-keeping.

All Rick Shaw said when he read through the book was, "Dammit to hell!"

68

"Stick Vicks VapoRub up your nose." Rick handed over the small blue glass jar to Cynthia Cooper as they cut the motor to the squad car.

She fished out a big dab, smoothing it inside each nostril. The tears sprang from her eyes.

"Ready?"

"Yep." She noticed that the photographer was already there. The rescue squad would soon follow. "Boy, George Bowden looks rough."

"Probably puked his guts out. Natural reaction."

"George." Rick walked over, leaves crunching underfoot. "Feel up to some questions?"

"Uh-huh." He nodded.

"What time did you discover the body?"

"Well, now, let me see. I set the alarm for four o'clock 'cause I wanted to be at the edge of the oat fields just on my way down to the hayfields. Good year for grouse, I can tell you. Anyway, uh"—he rubbed his back pockets in an upward motion—"got here about four forty-five, thereabouts. The kids set up a ruckus. Followed them." He indicated his hunting dogs as the kids.

Cynthia carefully walked around the car. The Vicks killed the stench but couldn't do much about the sight. She dusted each door handle. As she was quietly doing her job, another member of the department, Tom Kline, arrived. He gagged.

"Vicks." She pointed to the squad car.

He jammed the stuff up his nose, then returned, carefully investigating the car.

"Guys, I'm going to open the door. It'll be a real hit even with the Vicks. We need to dust the inside door handles, the glove compartment, just hope we're lucky. We aren't going to get anything off the body."

When the door was opened, George, although twenty yards away, stepped backward. "My God."

"Walk on back here with me." Rick led him out of olfactory range. "It's overpowering. The carbon cycle."

"What?"

"Carbon. The breakdown of flesh." Since George wasn't getting it, Rick switched back to business. "Did you notice anything unusual apart from the corpse? Footprints?"

"Sheriff, that thing's been out here so long, any footprints would be washed out."

"A month to six weeks. 'Course, we've had some cold spells. Bill Moscowitz can pinpoint the time for us. Bad as it is, the corpse would be torn apart if it had been out of the car. The fact that it's relatively intact may help us."

"Tire tracks washed out, too. I mean, I would have noticed tire tracks before. Would have come on down."

"You haven't been over here?"

"Been up on the mountain fields, no reason to come down here. Hay's not worth cutting this year anyway. Forgot to fertilize. Mostly I've been working on the mountainside of the farm because of the apples. Good year."

"What about grapes?"

"Got them in 'fore the rains. Be real sweet 'cause of the light drought this summer."

"Do you recognize that corpse?"

"How would I?"

"Odd though it may seem, if that body belonged to someone you knew, you would probably recognize it even in its current condition. Nine times out of ten people do."

"You mean, you show people something like that?"

"Only if we can't make an identification by any other means. Naturally, you try to spare the family as much pain as possible."

"I don't know that"—he gesticulated—"don't know the car. Don't know why she came down this lane. Don't know nothing."

"George, I'm sorry this has happened to you. Why don't you go on home? If I need you, I'll call or come by."

"You gonna take that outta here, aren't you?"

"As soon as we finish dusting the car and taking photos."

"Something in the air, Sheriff."

"I beg pardon?" Rick leaned forward as if to draw closer to George's meaning.

"Evil. Something in the air. The headmaster fella at the

rich kids' school and then that Hollywood blowhard stabbed by Kendrick Miller. Sometimes I think a door to the underworld opens and bad spirits fly out."

"That's very interesting," said Rick, who thought George was slightly demented: nice but tilted.

"I was saying to Hilary the other day, evil flowing down the mountain with that cold wind. Life is an endless struggle between good and evil."

"I expect it is." Rick patted him on the back. "You go on home, now."

George nodded good-bye. The dogs tagged at his heels. George, not more than thirty-five, thought and acted like a man in his sixties.

"Boss, we're finished down here. You want a look before we wrap up?"

"Yeah." Rick ambled over. There were no weapons in the car or in the trunk, which ruled out a self-inflicted wound. There was no purse. Usually if someone committed suicide by drug overdose, the vial would be around. Given the body's state of decay, how she died would have to be determined by the coroner. "You satisfied?"

"Yes," Cooper replied, holding out the car registration. "Winifred Thalman."

"Okay." He nodded to the rescue squad.

Diana Robb moved forward with a net. When a body was decomposed, they placed a net around it to keep bones and disintegrating flesh together as much as possible.

"I'm going back to the office," Rick told Cynthia. "I'll call New York Department of Motor Vehicles and start from there. If there's a super at her address, I'll call him, too. I want you to make the rounds."

"You thinking what I'm thinking?"

"Yeah."

"She would have been killed close to the time of Roscoe's death."

He picked up a brittle leaf, pulling away the drying upper epidermis, exposing the veins. "Could have." He released the leaf to fall dizzily back to earth. "It's the why."

They looked at each other a long time. "Boss, how we gonna prove it?"

He shrugged. "Wait for a mistake."

69

The drive back from Richmond, hypnotic in its boredom, found Irene and Jody silent. Irene swung onto the exit at Manakin-Sabot.

"Why are you getting off Sixty-four?"

"I'll stay more alert on Two-fifty. More to see."

"Oh." Jody slumped back in her seat.

"Do you feel all right?"

"Tired."

"That's natural after what your body has just been through."

"Mom, did you ever have an abortion?"

Irene cleared her throat. "No."

"Would you?"

"I don't know. I was never in your position. Your father thinks it's murder." Her brow furrowed. "How are you going to break this to him?"

"He should talk."

"Don't start, today. He's a flawed man but he's not a killer. Now, I'm going to tell him you had a miscarriage. Leave it to me."

"We're lucky he's in jail." Jody smiled weakly, adding, "If he was home he'd kill us!"

"Jody!"

"I'm sorry, but, Mom, he's confused. People do have secret lives, and Dad is weird."

Irene raised her voice. "You think he did it, don't you? You think he killed Roscoe and McKinchie. I don't know why. You ought to give your father more support."

"Dad's got an evil temper."

"Not that evil."

"You were going to divorce him. All of a sudden he's this great guy. He's not so great. Even in jail he's not much different from when he was out of jail."

A strangled silence followed. Then Irene said, "Everyone can change and learn. I know your pregnancy shocked him into looking at himself. He can't change the past, but he can certainly improve the future."

"Not if he gets convicted, he can't."

"Jody, shut up. I don't want to hear another word about your father getting convicted."

"It's better to be prepared for the worst."

"I'm taking this a day at a time. I can't handle any more than I'm handling now, and you aren't helping. You know your father is innocent."

"I almost don't care." Jody sat up straight. "Just let me have what's left of this year, Mom, please."

Irene considered what her daughter said. Jody could seem so controlled on the outside, like her father, but her moods could also shift violently and quickly. Her outburst at the field hockey game, which now seemed years away, was proof of how unhappy Jody had been. She hadn't seen her daughter's problems because she was too wrapped up in her own. A wave of guilt engulfed her. A tear trickled down Irene's pale cheek.

Jody noticed. "We'll be okay."

"Yes, but we'll never be the same."

"Good."

Irene breathed in deeply. "I guess things were worse than I realized. The lack of affection at home sent you looking for it from other people . . . Sean in particular."

"It was nice being"—she considered the next word—"important."

They swooped right into the Crozet exit. As they decelerated to the stop sign, Irene asked, "Did you tell anyone else you were pregnant?"

"No!"

"I don't believe you. You can't resist talking to your girlfriends."

"And you never talk to anyone."

"Not about family secrets."

"Maybe you should have, Mother. What's the big deal about keeping up appearances? It didn't work, did it?"

"Did you tell anyone?"

"No."

"You told Karen Jensen."

"I did not."

"You two are as thick as thieves."

"She hangs out with Brooks Tucker as much as she hangs out with me." A thin edge of jealousy lined Jody's voice. "Mom, hang it up."

Irene burst into tears. "This will come back to haunt you. You'll feel so guilty."

"It was the right thing to do."

"It violates everything we've been taught. Oh, why did I agree to this? I am so ashamed of myself."

"Mother, get a grip." Icy control and icy fury were in Jody's young face. "Dad's accused of murder. You're going to run the business. I'm going to college so I can come home and run the business. You can't take care of a baby. I can't take care of a baby."

"You should have thought of that in the first place," Irene, a hard edge now in her voice, too, shot back.

"Maybe you should have thought about your actions, too." Jody's glacial tone frosted the interior of the car.

"What do you mean?" Irene paused. "That silly idea you had that I was sleeping with Samson Coles. Where do you get those ideas? And then to accuse the poor man in the post office."

"To cover your ass."

"What!" Irene's eyes bugged out of her head.

"You heard what I said—to cover your ass. You'd been sleeping with Roscoe. You thought I didn't know."

Irene sputtered, her hands gripping the steering wheel until her knuckles were white. "How dare you."

"Save it, Mom. I know because he told me."

"The bastard!"

"Got that right."

Irene calmed down a moment. "Why would he tell you?"

She still hadn't admitted to Jody the veracity of the accusation.

"Because I was sleeping with him, too."

"Oh, my God." Irene's foot dropped heavier on the gas pedal.

"So don't tell me right from wrong." Jody half smiled.

"I'm glad he's dead."

Jody smiled fully. "He didn't tell me, really—I figured it out for myself."

"You—" Irene sputtered.

"It doesn't matter." Jody shrugged.

"The hell it doesn't." She slowed down a bit since the red speedometer needle had surged past eighty. "*Did* you sleep with him?"

"Yes. Each year Roscoe picked his chosen one. My turn, I guess."

"Why?" Irene moaned.

"Because he'd give me anything I wanted and because I'd get into whatever school I wanted. Roscoe would fix it."

"Jody, I'm having a hard time taking all this in." Irene's lower lip trembled.

"Stop," Jody commanded.

"Stop what?"

"The car!"

"Why?"

"We need to pick up the mail."

"I'm too shook up to see people."

"Well, I'm not. So stop the damned car and I'll get the mail."

Irene parked at the post office, while Jody got out. Then she worried about what her daughter would say to Harry and Miranda, so she followed her inside.

Harry called out, "In the nick of time."

Miranda, busy cleaning, called out a hello.

"Irene, you look peaked. Come on back here and sit down. I'll make you a cup of tea."

Irene burst into tears at Miranda's kindness. "Everything is so awful. I want my husband out of jail."

"Mom, come on." Jody tugged at her, smiling weakly at Miranda and Harry.

"Poor Irene." Tucker hated to see humans cry.

"She's better off without him," Pewter stated matter-of-factly.

Two squad cars roared by the post office, sirens wailing, followed by the rescue squad. Cynthia trailed in her squad car. But she pulled away and stopped at the post office. She opened the door and saw Irene and Jody.

"What's going on?" Miranda asked.

"A corpse was found at Bowden's farm." She cleared her throat. "The car is registered to Winifred Thalman of New York City."

"I wonder who—" Miranda never finished her sentence.

"Mom, I'm really tired."

"Okay, honey." Irene wiped her eyes. "You can't accuse Kendrick of this one! He's in jail."

Cooper quietly replied, "I don't know about that, Mrs. Miller, she's been dead quite some time."

Tears of frustration and rage flooded Irene's cheeks. She slapped Cynthia hard.

"Mom!" Jody pulled her mother out of there.

"Striking an officer is a serious offense, isn't it?" Harry asked.

"Under the circumstances, let's just forget it."

"They finally found the body." Tucker sighed.

"*Yes.*" The tiger squinted as the dying sun sparked off Irene's windshield as she pulled away from the post office. "*They're getting closer to the truth.*"

"*What is the truth?*" Pewter said philosophically.

"*Oh, shut up.*" Mrs. Murphy cuffed her friend's ears.

"*I couldn't resist.*" The gray cat giggled.

"*We might as well laugh now,*" Tucker said. "*We aren't going to laugh later.*"

70

Mrs. Murphy worked feverishly catching field mice, moles, shrews, and one sickly baby bunny, which she quickly put out of its misery. Pewter opened the kitchen cabinets while Harry slept. She had a knack for flipping open cabinet doors. She'd grab the knob and then fall back. She rooted around the shelf until she found a bottle of catsup. Fortunately, the bottle was plastic because she knocked it out of the cabinet, shoving it onto the floor for Tucker to pick up.

The corgi's jaws were strong enough to carry the oddly shaped object out to the truck.

"I can put all the kill here in the bed," Mrs. Murphy directed the other two. *"If you'll help me, Pewter."*

"Harry's going to find all this."

"Not if Tucker can drag out the old barn towel."

"How are we going to get it up in the bed of the truck?"

"Pewter, let me do the thinking. Just help me, will you?"

"What do you want me to do with this bottle of catsup?"

"Put it behind the front wheel of the truck. When Harry opens the door for us, pick it up and jump in the truck. Pewter and I will distract her. You can drop it and kick it under the seat. Remember, gang, she's not looking for this stuff. She won't notice."

Tucker hid the catsup behind the front wheel, then strolled into the barn and yanked the towel off the tack trunk with Harry's maiden initials on it, MM. She tripped over the towel as she walked to the truck, so she dragged it sideways.

Murphy and Pewter placed the small dead prey at the back corner of the truck bed.

"Pewter, perch on the bumper step."

"You'd better do it. You're thinner." Pewter hated to admit that she was overweight.

"All right." Murphy jumped down on the back bumper step while Pewter hoisted herself over the side of the tailgate. Tucker sat patiently, the towel in her mouth.

Simon, returning home in the early dawn from foraging, stopped to wonder at this activity. *"What are you-all doing?"*

"Trying to get the towel into the bed of the truck. It's too big to put in my mouth and jump in," Mrs. Murphy informed him. *"Okay, Tucker, stand on your hind legs and see if you can reach Pewter."*

Tucker put her paws on the bumper, her nose edging over the top.

Mrs. Murphy leaned down, grabbing the towel with her left paw. *"Got it."*

Pewter, half hanging over the tailgate, quickly snatched the towel before Murphy dropped it—it was heavy. With Pewter pulling and Mrs. Murphy pushing, the two cats dumped the towel into the truck bed. Mrs. Murphy gaily leapt in, and the two of them placed the towel over the kill, bunching it up to avoid its looking obvious.

"*I'll be,*" Simon said admiringly.

"*Teamwork,*" Mrs. Murphy triumphantly replied.

"*What are you going to do with those bodies?*" Simon giggled.

"*Lay a trail to the killer. Mom's going over to St. Elizabeth's today, so I think we can get the job done.*"

The possum scoffed. "*The humans won't notice, or, if they do, they'll discount it.*"

The tiger and the gray cat peeped over the side of the truck. "*You might be right, but the killer will notice. That's what we want.*"

"*I don't know.*" Simon shook his head.

"*Anything is better than nothing,*" Murphy said forcefully. "*And if this doesn't work, we'll find something else.*"

"*Why are you so worried?*" Simon's furry nose twitched.

"*Because Mother will eventually figure out who the murderer really is.*"

"*Oh.*" The possum pondered. "*We can't let anything happen to Harry.*" He didn't want to sound soft on any human. "*Who else will feed me marshmallows?*"

71

The animals, exhausted from running back and forth across the playing fields, sacked out immediately after eating.

Pewter and Mrs. Murphy curled up on either side of Tucker on the sofa in front of the fire. Pewter snored, a tiny little nasal gurgle.

Fair brought Chinese food. Harry, good with chopsticks, greedily shoved pork chow mein into her mouth. A light knock on the door was followed by Cynthia Cooper, sticking her head in. She pulled up a chair and joined them.

"Where are the critters?"

"Knocked out. Every time I called them, they were running across the football field today. Having their own Homecoming game, I guess. Can I get you anything else?"

"Catsup." She pointed at her plate. "My noodles."

"You're kidding me." Harry thought of catsup on noodles as she opened her cabinet. "Damn, I had a brand-new bottle of catsup, and it walked away."

"Catsup ghost." Fair bit into a succulent egg roll, the tiny shrimp bits assaulting his taste buds.

"What were you doing at St. E's?"

"Like a fool, I agreed to help Renee Hallvard referee the field hockey games if she can't find anyone else. She can't for the next game, so I went over to review the rules. I wish I'd never said yes."

"I have a hard time saying no, too. The year I agreed to coach Little League I lost twenty pounds"—Fair laughed— "from worrying about the kids, my work, getting to practice on time."

"Is this a social call, Cynthia? Come on," Harry teased her.

"Yes and no. The corpse, Winifred Thalman, was a free-lance cinematographer. I called April Shively before anyone else—after I stopped at the post office. She says Thalman was the person who shot the little movies the seniors made their first week back at school."

"Wouldn't someone have missed her in New York? Family?"

Cooper put down her egg roll. "She was estranged from her only brother. Parents dead. As a cinematographer, her neighbors were accustomed to her being absent for months at a time. No pets. No plants. No relationships. Rick tracked down the super in her building."

"You didn't stop at the post office to tell me the news first, did you?" Harry smiled.

"Saw Irene's car."

"Ah."

"Kendrick's got to be lying. Only reason we can come up with for him to do that is he's protecting his wife or his daughter."

"They killed Roscoe and Maury?" Fair was incredulous.

"We think one of them did. Rick's spent hours going over Kendrick's books and bank accounts, and there's just no evidence of any financial misdoing. Even if you buy the sexual-jealousy motive, why would he have killed this Thalman woman?"

"Well, why would Irene or Jody have done it?" Harry asked.

"If we knew that, we'd know everything." Cynthia broke the egg roll in two. "Irene will be at the field hockey game tomorrow. We'll have her covered by a plainclothesman from Waynesboro's department. You'll be on the field. Keep your eyes open."

"Irene or Jody stabbed Maury? Jeesh," Fair exclaimed. "Takes a lot of nerve to get that close at a public gathering."

"Wasn't that hard to do," Harry said. "Sometimes the easiest crimes are the ones committed in crowds."

"The killer confessed twice to Father Michael. Since Kendrick has confessed, Father Michael hasn't heard a peep. Nothing unusual about that—if you're a murderer and someone has taken the rap for you. Still, the impulse to confess is curious. Guilt?"

"Pride," Harry rejoined.

"Irene or Jody . . . I still can't get over it."

"Do you think they know? I mean, does one of them know the other is a killer?" Harry asked.

"I don't know. But I hope whoever it is gets sloppy or gets rattled."

"Guess this new murder will be on the eleven o'clock

news"—Harry checked the old wall clock—"and in the papers."

"Whole town will be talking." Cynthia poured half a carton of noodles on her plate. "Maybe that'll rattle our killer. I don't know, she's been cold as ice."

"Yeah, well, even ice has a melting point." Fair tinkled the ice in his water glass.

"Harry, because you're in the middle of the field, you're secure. If it is Jody, she can't stab you or poison you without revealing herself. Are you willing to bait her? If we're wrong, there will be plenty of time to apologize."

"I'll do it." She nodded her head. "Can you set a trap for Irene?"

"Fair?"

"Oh, hell!" He put down his glass.

72

The colored cars and trucks filling the St. Elizabeth's back parking lot looked like jelly beans. The St. Elizabeth's supporters flew pennants off their antennas. So did the Chatham Hall fans. When the wind picked up, it resembled a used-car parking lot. All that was missing were the prices in thick grease crayon on the windshields.

Harry, despite all, read and reread the rule book in the faculty locker room. She knew the hardest part of refereeing would be blowing the whistle. Once she grew confident, she'd overcome that. And she had to establish her authority early on because if the kids thought they could get away with fouling, some would.

Mrs. Murphy sat on the wooden bench next to her. Pewter

and Tucker guarded the door. Deputy Cooper waited in the hall.

The noise of a locker being pulled over, followed by shouting, reverberated down the hall.

"What the hell?" Harry ran out the door toward the commotion.

Cooper jerked her head in the direction of the noise. "It's World War Three in there, and the game hasn't even started."

"Well, it is the qualifier for state." Harry tucked her whistle in the whistle pocket.

Pewter giggled. *"She found it."*

The animals ran down the hall. Tucker, losing her hind footing on the slick waxed surface, spun around once. They reached the locker room and crept along the aisle.

"What a dirty trick! I'll kill whoever did this!" Jody kicked her locker again for good measure. Dead mice, moles, and shrews were scattered over the floor. A bottle of catsup, red stuff oozing out of the bite marks, splattered everywhere. Jody's stick had catsup on it, too.

"Gross." Karen Jensen jumped backward as the tiny dead animals spilled everywhere.

"You did this!" Jody lost her composure, accusing the last person who would do such a thing.

"You're crazy," Karen shot back.

Jody picked up her hockey stick and swung at Karen's head. Fortunately, Karen, the best player on the team and blessed with lightning reflexes, ducked. Brooks grabbed Jody from behind, but Jody, six inches taller, was hard to hold.

Coach Hallvard dashed into the room. "Cut it out!" She surveyed the mess. "All right. Out of here. Everyone out of here."

"Someone filled my locker with dead mice and catsup!" ody shrieked. "And it's your fault. You won't let us keep locks n our lockers anymore!"

"We'll solve this after the game." Coach put her hands on er hips. "It could have been someone from Chatham Hall. It ertainly would benefit them to rattle one of our best players nd set this team fighting among ourselves, wouldn't it?"

The girls drank in this motivating theory, none of which Hallvard believed. However, it provided a temporary solu- ion. She'd talk to Deputy Cooper after the game. Coach was ntelligent enough to know that anything out of the ordinary t St. Elizabeth's must be treated with the utmost suspicion, nd Cynthia had briefed her to be alert. She didn't identify ody as a possible suspect.

"You're right, Coach." Jensen, the natural leader of the eam, finally spoke. "Let's wipe them off the face of the arth!"

The girls cheered. As they grabbed their sticks and filed ut of the room, Brooks noticed Mrs. Murphy.

"Murphy, hi, kitty."

"Keep your cool, Brooks, this will be a hell of a game."

When the home team ran across the field to the benches, he home crowd roared.

Fair sat next to Irene, as he promised Cynthia he would. 'he plainclothes officer from Waynesboro sat behind her, retending to be a Chatham Hall supporter.

Miranda, also alerted, huddled with Mim in the center of he bleachers.

Cynthia stayed behind the Chatham Hall bench, which ave her a shorter sprint to the gym if need be. She knew rene was well covered, so she watched Jody.

Herb Jones joined Sandy Brashiers and some of the facult on the lower bench seats.

Harry met her co-official, Lily Norton, a former Al American, who drove over from Richmond.

"I'm a last minute fill-in, Miss Norton. Bear with me. Harry shook her hand.

"I was a freshman at Lee High the year you-all won state. She warmly returned the handshake. "You'll do fine, an please, call me Lily."

"Okay." Harry smiled.

They both synchronized their watches, then Lily put th whistle to her lips, blew, and the two captains trotted out the center of the field.

Mrs. Murphy, Pewter, and Tucker, on the gym side of th field, watched closely, too.

"*Tucker, stay on the center line on this side. You know wha to do?*"

"*Yes,*" Tucker answered forcefully.

"*Pewter, you hang out by the north goal. There's a maple tre about twenty yards back from the goal. If you get up in there, yo can see what's going on. If anything worries you, holler.*"

"*You-all won't be able to hear me because of the crowd noise.*"

"*Well*"—Mrs. Murphy thought a minute—"*about all yo can do is run down the tree. We'll keep glancing in your direc tion.*"

"*Why can't we stay on the edges of the field?*" Tucker said.

"*The referees will chase us off. Mom will put us in the truc We've got to work with what we have.*"

"*That field is a lot of territory to cover,*" Pewter, not th fastest cat in the world, noted.

"*We'll do what we can. I'll stay under the St. Elizabeth*

bench. If I get shooed away from there, I'll head down to the south goal. We clear?"

"Yes," they both said.

"Why can't Coop shoot if Jody or Irene goes nuts?"

"She can, but let's hope she doesn't need to do that." Murphy exhaled from her delicate nostrils. *"Good luck."*

The three animals fanned out to their places. Mrs. Murphy ducked feet and the squeals of the players who saw her. She scrunched up under the players' bench, listening intently.

The first quarter provided no fireworks but showed off each team's defensive skills. Jody blocked an onrushing Chatham Hall player but got knocked sideways in the process. She leapt up, ready to sock the girl, but Karen yelled at her, "Stay in your zone, Miller."

"Up yours," Jody shot back, but she obeyed.

The first half passed, back and forth but no real excitement.

Pewter wished she were under the bench because the wind was picking up. Her perch was getting colder and colder.

The second half opened with Brooks stealing a Chatham Hall pass and running like mad toward the goal where, at the last minute, now covered, she fired off a pinpoint pass to Karen Jensen, who blazed her shot past the goalic. A roar went up from the St. Elizabeth's bleachers.

Susan jumped up and down. Irene, too, was screaming. Even Sandy Brashiers, not especially interested in athletics, was caught up in the moment.

The big girl whom Jody had blocked took advantage of the run back to the center to tell Jody just what she thought of her. "Asshole."

"It's not my fault you're fat and slow," Jody needled her.

"Very funny. There's a lot of game left. You'd better watch out."

"Yeah, sure." Jody ignored her.

Chatham Hall grabbed the ball out of the knock-in. The big player, a midfielder, took the pass and barreled straight at Jody, who stepped out of the way, pretended to be hit, rolled, and flicked her stick out to catch the girl on the back of the leg.

Harry blew the whistle and called the foul.

Jody glared at Harry, and as Chatham Hall moved downfield, she brushed by Harry, close enough to make Harry step back and close enough for Harry to say, "Jody, you're the killer."

A hard shot on goal was saved by the St. Elizabeth's goalie. Another roar erupted on the sidelines. But the game became tougher, faster, and rougher. By the end of the third quarter both sides, drenched in sweat, settled in for a last quarter of attrition.

Whether by design or under the leadership of the big Chatham Hall midfielder, their team kept taking the ball down Jody's side. Jody, in excellent condition and built for running, couldn't be worn down, but they picked at her. Each time she'd lose her temper, they'd get the ball by her.

Finally Coach Hallvard took her off the field, substituting a talented but green sophomore, Biff Carstairs.

Jody paced in front of the bench, imploring Renee Hallvard, "Put me back in. Come on. Biff can't handle it."

True enough. As they flew down the right side of the field, Biff stayed with them, but she hadn't been in a game this good, this fast, or this physically punishing.

Chatham Hall scored on that series of plays, which made Jody scream at the top of her lungs. Finally, Hallvard, fearing another quick score, put Jody back in. The St. Elizabeth's side cheered anew.

Fair murmured in a low voice as the crowd cheered, "Irene, give yourself up. We all know it wasn't Kendrick."

She whirled around. "How dare you!"

A pair of hands behind her dropped to her shoulders so she couldn't move. The plainclothesman ordered, "Stay very still." He removed one hand and slipped it inside his coat to retrieve a badge.

"I didn't kill those people." Irene's anger ebbed.

"Okay, just sit tight," the plainclothesman said quietly.

Perhaps Jody felt an extra surge of adrenaline. Whatever, she could do no wrong. She checked her woman, she stole the ball, she cracked the ball right up to her forwards. She felt invincible. She really could do no wrong. With Jody playing all out at midfield and Karen and Brooks lethal up front, St. Elizabeth's crushed Chatham Hall in the last quarter. The final score was four to two. The crowd ran off the bleachers and spilled onto the field. Mrs. Murphy streaked down the sidelines to escape the feet. Pewter climbed down from the tree, relieved that nothing dangerous had happened. The animals rendezvoused at the far sideline at center with Tucker.

"I thought she'd whack at Mom with her stick. I thought we rattled her enough." Pewter was dejected that Jody had proved so self-possessed.

"Oh, well." Tucker sat down.

Mrs. Murphy scanned the wild celebration. Harry and Lily slowly walked off the field. Jody watched out of the corner of her eye even as she jumped all over her teammates.

"Nice to work with you." Lily shook Harry's hand. "You did a good job."

"Thanks. Aren't you going back to change?"

"No, I'd better get on the road." Lily headed toward the parking lot behind the gym.

As Harry entered the gym, Jody drifted away from the group. There was nothing unusual in a player heading back to the gym.

Cynthia, caught in the crowd, fought to get through the bodies when she saw Jody leave.

The three animals raced across the grass, little tufts of it floating up in the wind as it flew off their claws. They reached the door just as Harry opened it.

"Hi, guys." She was tired.

Within a minute Jody, stick in hand, was also in the gym. As Harry turned right down the hall toward the faculty changing room, Jody, on tiptoes now, moved down the hall, carefully listening for another footfall. Without speaking to one another, the animals ducked in doorways. Only Murphy stayed with Harry in case Tucker and Pewter failed.

Jody passed Pewter, who ran out and grabbed the back of her leg with her front claws. Jody howled, whirled around, and slapped at the cat, who let go just as Tucker emerged from the janitor's door. She ran hard at Jody, jumped up, and smashed into her knees. Dog and human collapsed in a heap, and the hockey stick clattered on the shiny floor.

"Goddammit!" Jody reached for her stick as Tucker grabbed the end of it.

They tugged from opposite ends. Tucker slid along the floor, but she wouldn't let go. Jody kicked at the dog, then twisted the stick to force her jaws loose. It didn't work. Pewter jumped on Jody's leg again as Harry, hearing the scramble, opened the locker room door and came back into the hall. Mrs. Murphy stuck with Harry.

"Good work," the tiger encouraged her pals.

Jody, seeing Harry, dropped her hockey stick, lunging for Harry's throat.

Harry raised her forearm to protect herself. She stumbled back against the concrete wall of the gym, which gave her support. She lifted up her knee, catching Jody in the crotch. It slowed Jody, but not enough. Pewter, still hanging on to Jody's right leg, was joined by Murphy on the left. They sank their fangs in as deep as they'd go.

Jody screamed, loosening her grip on Harry's neck. The enraged girl lurched for her hockey stick. Tucker was dragging it down the hallway, but the corgi couldn't go fast, she being small and the stick being large.

Jody yanked the stick hard out of the dog's jaws. Tucker jumped for the stick, but Jody held it over her head and ran for Harry, who crouched. The hallway was long and narrow. She would use the walls to her benefit. Harry, a good athlete, steadied for the attack.

Jody swung the stick at her head. Harry ducked lower and shifted her weight. The tip of the hockey stick grazed the wall. Harry moved closer to the wall. She prayed Jody would crack her stick on the wall.

Jody, oblivious to the damage the cats were doing to her legs, she was so obsessed, swung again. The stick splintered, and that fast Harry pushed off the wall and flung herself at Jody. The two went down hard on the floor as the cats let go of their quarry. Tucker ran alongside the fighting humans, waiting for an opening. Her fangs, longer than the cats', could do more damage.

Sounds down the hall stopped Jody for a split second. She wriggled from Harry's grasp and raced away from the noise. Tucker caught her quickly and grabbed her ankle. Jody stopped to beat off the dog just as Cynthia Cooper rounded the corner and dropped to one knee, gun out.

"Stop or I'll shoot."

Jody, eyes glazed, stared down the barrel of a .357, stared at the bloody fangs of Tucker, then held up her hands.

73

Because of their bravery, the animals were rewarded with filet mignon cooked by Miranda Hogendobber. Harry, Fair, Susan, Brooks, Cynthia, and the Reverend Jones joined them. The animals had place settings at the big dinner table. Miranda went all out.

"This is heaven," Pewter purred.

"I didn't know Pewter had it in her." Susan smiled at the plump kitty.

"There's a lion beneath that lard," Mrs. Murphy joked.

As the humans put together the pieces of the murderous puzzle, Tucker said, *"Murphy, how did you figure it out?"*

"Mother was on the right track when she said that whoever killed Roscoe Fletcher did it at the car wash. Any one of the

suspects could have done it, but not one person recalled anyone giving Roscoe candy, although he offered it to them. Jody walked past the Texaco station on her way to the deli. The station blocks the view from the car wash. She gave him the candy; no one saw her, and no car was behind Roscoe yet. She could have worked fast, then run back to the office. It would give her a good alibi. She was waiting for an opportunity. She was smart enough to know this was a good shot. Who knows how long she carried that candy around?"

"I don't know whether to pity Jody or hate her," Susan Tucker mused.

" 'Behold, these are the ungodly, who prosper in the world; they increase in riches!' Psalm Seventy-three, verse twelve," Miranda recited. "Roscoe and Maury did increase in riches, but they paid for it. As for Jody, she was very pretty and vulnerable. But so are many other young people. She participated in her own corruption."

"The slush fund ledger gave me part of the motive— money—but I couldn't find the slushers. Drugs weren't it." Cynthia folded her arms across her chest. "Never would I have thought of porno movies."

"It is ghastly." The Reverend Jones shuddered.

"What tipped you off?" Pewter asked Murphy.

"It took me a long time to figure it out. I think finding that address label at the bottom of Roscoe's desk was my first inkling. Neptune Film Lab. And wonderful though it might be to have a film department at a private secondary school—it seemed like a great expense even if Maury was supposedly going to make a huge contribution."

"Kendrick was more of a man than we've given him credit for," Susan said.

"He guessed Jody was the killer. He didn't know why."

Cynthia recalled the expression on his face when Jody confessed. "She'd told Irene and Kendrick that she was pregnant by Sean. It was actually Roscoe."

"I'd kill him myself." Fair's face flushed. "Sorry, Herb."

"Quite understandable under the circumstances."

"She had slept with Sean and told him he was the father of her child. That's when he stole the BMW. He was running away and asking for help at the same time," Cynthia continued. "But she now says the father might be Roscoe. And she said this is the second film made at St. Elizabeth's. Last year they used Courtney Frere. He'd pick one favorite girl for his films. We tracked her down at Tulane. Poor kid. That's what the sleeping pills were about, not low board scores. The film she was in was shot at Maury's house, but then Roscoe and Maury got bolder. They came up with the bright idea of setting up shop at St. Elizabeth's. It certainly gave them the opportunity to troll for victims."

"Monsters." Miranda shook her head.

"There have always been bad people." Brooks surprised everyone by speaking up. "Bad as Mr. Fletcher and Mr. McKinchie were, she didn't have to kill them."

"She snapped." Susan thought out loud. "All of a sudden she must have realized that one mistake—that movie—could ruin the rest of her life."

"Exactly." Cynthia confirmed this. "She drove out with Winifred Thalman, thinking she could get the footage back, but Winifred had already mailed the rough cut to Neptune Lab. She only had outtakes with her, so Jody killed her. She threw the outtakes in the pond."

"How," Harry asked, "did she kill her?"

"Blow to the head. Maybe used her hockey stick. She walked across the fields after dark and arrived home in time for supper. After that she was driven by revenge. She wanted power over the people she felt had humiliated her—even though she'd agreed to be in these movies for money."

"The slush fund?" Harry asked.

"Right. Forty-one thousand dollars withdrawn by Maury, as it turns out. Forty-one thousand dollars for her BMW ... it all added up. Imagine how Kendrick must have felt when he saw that figure in Roscoe's secret ledger. The deposits were from other films. Maury and Roscoe shot porno movies in New York, too. There they used professionals. Roscoe's fund-raising trips were successful on both counts," Cynthia said.

"How'd she kill Maury?" Brooks was curious.

"She slipped into the girls' locker room, put on the Musketeer outfit, and rejoined the party. She saw Maury start to leave and stabbed him, with plenty of time to get back to the locker and change into her skeleton costume. She may even have lured Maury out of the dance, but she says she didn't," Cynthia answered.

"Does she feel any remorse?" Miranda hoped she did.

"For killing three people? No, not a bit. But she feels terrible that she lied to Sean about being the father. About goading him into calling in the false obituary and about following Roger on his paper route and stuffing in the Maury obit. That's the extent of her remorse!"

"Do you believe she's crazy?" Fair said.

"No. And I am sick of that defense. She knows right from wrong. Revenge and power. She should be tried as an adult. The truth is: she enjoyed the killing." Cynthia stabbed her broccoli.

"*Why would a human pay to watch another human have sex?*" Pewter laughed.

"*Boredom.*" Tucker ate table scraps slipped her by Fair.

"I wouldn't pay to watch another cat, would you?" Pewter addressed Murphy.

"Of course not, but we're cats. We're superior to humans." She glanced at Tucker.

"I wouldn't do it, I'm superior, too," Tucker swiftly said, around a mouthful.

"Yes—but not quite as superior as we are." Mrs. Murphy laughed.

Dear Highly Intelligent Feline:

Tired of the same old ball of string? Well, I've developed my own line of catnip toys, all tested by Pewter and me. Not that I love for Pewter to play with my little sockies, but if I don't let her, she shreds my manuscripts. You see how that is!

Just so the humans won't feel left out, I've designed a T-shirt for them.

If you'd like to see how creative I am, write to me and I'll send you a brochure.

Sneaky Pie's Flea Market
c/o American Artists, Inc.
P.O. Box 4671
Charlottesville, VA 22905

In felinity,

SNEAKY PIE BROWN

P.S. Dogs, get a cat to write for you!

Don't miss the new mystery from

RITA MAE BROWN

and

SNEAKY PIE BROWN

Whisker of Evil

Now available in hardcover

from Bantam Books

Please read on for a preview . . .

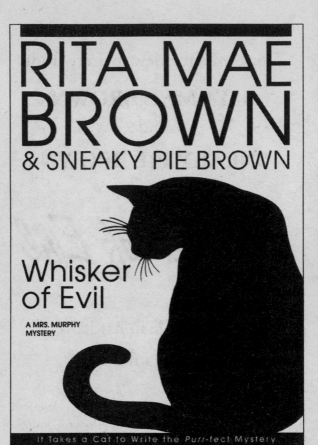

RITA MAE
BROWN
& SNEAKY PIE BROWN

Whisker
of Evil

A MRS. MURPHY
MYSTERY

It Takes a Cat to Write the *Purr-fect* Mystery

Whisker of Evil

on sale now

Barry Monteith was still breathing when Harry found him. His throat had been ripped out.

Tee Tucker, a corgi, racing ahead of Mary Minor Haristeen as well as the two cats, Mrs. Murphy and Pewter, found him first.

Barry was on his back, eyes open, gasping and gurgling, life ebbing with each spasm. He did not recognize Tucker nor Harry when they reached him.

"Barry, Barry." Harry tried to comfort him, hoping he could hear her. "It will be all right," she said, knowing perfectly well he was dying.

The tiger cat, Mrs. Murphy, watched the blood jet upward.

"Jugular," fat, gray Pewter succinctly commented.

Gently, Harry took the young man's hand and prayed, "Dear Lord, receive into thy bosom the soul of Barry Monteith, a good man." Tears welled in her eyes.

Barry jerked, then his suffering ended.

Death, often so shocking to city dwellers, was part of life here in the country. A hawk would swoop down to carry away the chick while the biddy screamed useless defiance. A bull would break his hip and need to be put down. And one day an old farmer would slowly walk to his tractor only to discover he couldn't climb into the seat. The Angel of Death placed his hand on the stooping shoulder.

It appeared the Angel had offered little peaceful deliverance to Barry Monteith, thirty-four, fit, handsome with brown curly hair, and fun-loving. Barry had started his own business, breeding thoroughbreds, a year ago, with a business partner, Sugar Thierry.

"Sweet Jesus." Harry wiped away the tears.

That Saturday morning, crisp, clear, and beautiful, had held the alluring promise of a perfect May 29. The promise had just curdled.

Harry had finished her early-morning chores and, despite a list of projects, decided to take a walk for an hour. She followed Potlicker Creek to see if the beavers had built any new dams. Barry was sprawled at the creek's edge on a dirt road two miles from her farm that wound up over the mountains into adjoining Augusta County. It edged the vast land holdings of Tally Urquhart, who, well into her nineties and spry, loathed traffic. Three cars constituted traffic in her mind. The only time the road saw much use was during deer-hunting season in the fall.

"Tucker, Mrs. Murphy, and Pewter, stay. I'm going to run to Tally's and phone the sheriff."

If Harry hit a steady lope, crossed the fields and one set of woods, she figured she could reach the phone in Tally's stable within fifteen minutes, though the pitch and roll of the land including one steep ravine would cost time.

As she left her animals, they inspected Barry.

"*What could rip his throat like that? A bear swipe?*" Pewter's pupils widened.

"*Perhaps.*" Mrs. Murphy, noncommittal, sniffed the gaping wound, as did Tucker.

The cat curled her upper lip to waft more scent into her nostrils. The dog, whose nose was much longer and nostrils larger, simply inhaled.

"*I don't smell bear,*" Tucker declared. "*That's an overpowering scent, and on a morning like this it would stick.*"

Pewter, who cherished luxury and beauty, found that Barry's corpse disturbed her equilibrium. "*Let's be grateful we found him today and not three days from now.*"

"*Stop jabbering, Pewter, and look around, will you? Look for tracks.*"

Grumbling, the gray cat daintily stepped down the dirt road. "*You mean like car tracks?*"

"*Yes, or animal tracks,*" Mrs. Murphy directed, then returned her attention to Tucker. "*Even though coyote scent isn't as strong as bear, we'd still smell a whiff. Bobcat? I don't smell anything like that. Or dog. There are wild dogs and wild pigs back in the mountains. The humans don't even realize they're there.*"

Tucker cocked her perfectly shaped head. "*No dirt around the wound. No saliva, either.*"

"*I don't see anything. Not even a birdie foot,*" Pewter, irritated, called out from a hundred yards down the road.

"*Well, go across the creek then and look over there.*" Mrs. Murphy's patience wore thin.

"*And get my paws wet?*" Pewter's voice rose.

"*It's a ford. Hop from rock to rock. Go on, Pewt, stop being a chicken.*"

Angrily, Pewter puffed up, tearing past them to launch

herself over the ford. She almost made it, but a splash indicated she'd gotten her hind paws wet.

If circumstances had been different, Mrs. Murphy and Tucker would have laughed. Instead, they returned to Barry.

"I can't identify the animal that tore him up." The tiger shook her head.

"Well, the wound is jagged but clean. Like I said, no dirt." Tucker studied the folds of flesh laid back.

"He was killed lying down," the cat sagely noted. *"If he was standing up, don't you think blood would be everywhere?"*

"Not necessarily," the dog replied, thinking how strong heartbeats sent blood straight out from the jugular. Tucker was puzzled by the odd calmness of the scene.

"Pewter, have you found anything on that side?"

"Deer tracks. Big deer tracks."

"Keep looking," Mrs. Murphy requested.

"I hate it when you're bossy." Nonetheless, Pewter moved down the dirt road heading west.

"Barry was such a nice man." Tucker mournfully looked at the square-jawed face, wide-open eyes staring at heaven.

Mrs. Murphy circled the body. *"Tucker, I'm climbing up that sycamore. If I look down maybe I'll see something."*

Her claws, razor sharp, dug into the thin surface of the tree, strips of darker outer bark peeling, exposing the whitish underbark. The odor of fresh water, of the tufted titmouse above her, all informed her. She scanned around for broken limbs, bent bushes, anything indicating Barry— or other humans or large animals—had traveled to this spot avoiding the dirt road.

"Pewter?"

"Big fat nothing." The gray kitty noted that her hind paws were wet. She was getting little clods of dirt stuck be-

tween her toes. This bothered her more than Barry did. After all, he was dead. Nothing she could do for him. But the hardening brown earth between her toes, that was discomfiting.

"*Well, come on back. We'll wait for Mom.*" Mrs. Murphy dropped her hind legs over the limb where she was sitting. Her hind paws reached for the trunk, the claws dug in, and she released her grip, swinging her front paws to the trunk. She backed down.

Tucker touched noses with Pewter, who had recrossed the creek more successfully this time.

Mrs. Murphy came up and sat beside them.

"*Hope his face doesn't change colors while we're waiting for the humans. I hate that. They get all mottled.*" Pewter wrinkled her nose.

"*I wouldn't worry.*" Tucker sighed.

In the distance they heard sirens.

"*Bet they won't know what to make of this, either,*" Tucker said.

"*It's peculiar.*" Mrs. Murphy turned her head in the direction of the sirens.

"*Weird and creepy.*" Pewter pronounced judgment as she picked at her hind toes, and she was right.

Welcome to the charming world of

MRS. MURPHY

Don't miss these earlier mysteries...

THE TAIL OF THE TIP-OFF

When winter hits Crozet, Virginia, it hits hard. That's nothing new to postmistress Mary Minor "Harry" Haristeen and her friends, who keep warm with hard work, hot toddies, and rabid rooting for the University of Virginia's women's basketball team. But post-game high spirits are laid low when contractor H.H. Donaldson drops dead in the parking lot. And soon word spreads that it wasn't a heart attack that did him in. It just doesn't sit right with Harry that one of her fellow fans is a murderer. And as tiger cat Mrs. Murphy knows, things that don't sit right with Harry lead her to poke her not-very-sensitive human nose into dangerous places. To make sure their intrepid mom lands on her feet, the feisty feline and her furry cohorts Pewter and corgi Tee Tucker are about to have their paws full helping Harry uncover a killer with no sense of fair play....

CATCH AS CAT CAN

Spring fever comes to the small town of Crozet, Virginia. As the annual Dogwood Festival approaches, postmistress Mary Minor "Harry" Haristeen feels her own mating instincts stir. As for tiger cat Mrs. Murphy, feline intuition tells her there's more in the air than just pheromones. It begins with a case of stolen hubcaps and proceeds to the mysterious death of a dissolute young mechanic over a sobering cup of coffee. Then another death and a shooting lead to the discovery of a half-million crisp, clean dollar bills that look to be very dirty. Now Harry is on the trail of a cold-blooded murderer. Mrs. Murphy already knows who it is— and who's next in line. She also knows that Harry, curious as a cat, does not have nine lives. And the one she does have is hanging by the thinnest of threads.

CLAWS AND EFFECT

Winter puts tiny Crozet, Virginia, in a deep freeze and everyone seems to be suffering from the winter blahs, including postmistress Mary Minor "Harry" Haristeen. So all are ripe for the juicy gossip coming out of Crozet Hospital—until the main source of that gossip turns up dead. It's not like Harry to resist a mystery, and she soon finds the hospital a hotbed of ego, jealousy, and illicit love. But it's tiger cat Mrs. Murphy, roaming the netherworld of Crozet Hospital, who sniffs out a secret that dates back to the Underground Railroad. Then Harry is attacked and a doctor is executed in cold blood. Soon only a quick-witted cat and her animal pals feline Pewter and corgi Tee Tucker stand between Harry and a coldly calculating killer with a prescription for murder.

"Reading a Mrs. Murphy mystery is like
eating a potato chip. You always go back for more....
Whimsical and enchanting...the latest expert tale
from a deserving bestselling series."
—*The Midwest Book Review*

PAWING THROUGH THE PAST

"You'll never get old." Each member of the class of 1980 has received the letter. Mary Minor "Harry" Haristeen, who is on the organizing committee for Crozet High's twentieth reunion, decides to take it as a compliment. Others think it's a joke. But Mrs. Murphy senses trouble. And the sly tiger cat is soon proven right...when the class womanizer turns up dead with a bullet between his eyes. Then another note followed by another murder makes it clear that someone has waited twenty years to take revenge. While Harry tries to piece together the puzzle, it's up to Mrs. Murphy and her animal pals to sniff out the truth.

And there isn't much time. Mrs. Murphy is the first to realize that Harry has been chosen Most Likely to Die, and if she doesn't hurry, Crozet High's twentieth reunion could be Harry's last.

> "This is a cat-lover's dream of a mystery.... 'Harry' is simply irresistible.... [Rita Mae] Brown once again proves herself 'Queen of Cat Crimes.'... Don't miss out on this lively series, for it's one of the best around."
> —*Old Book Barn Gazette*

CAT ON THE SCENT

Things have been pretty exciting lately in Crozet, Virginia—a little *too* exciting if you ask resident feline investigator Mrs. Murphy. Just as the town starts to buzz over its Civil War reenactment, a popular local man disappears. No one's seen Tommy Van Allen's single-engine plane, either—except for Mrs. Murphy, who spotted it during a foggy evening's mousing. Even Mrs. Murphy's favorite human, postmistress Mary Minor "Harry" Haristeen, can sense that something is amiss. But things really take an ugly turn when the town reenacts the battle of Oak Ridge—and a participant ends up with three very real bullets in his back. While the clever tiger cat and her friends sift through clues that just don't fit together, more than a few locals fear that the scandal will force well-hidden town secrets into the harsh light of day. And when Mrs. Murphy's relentless tracking places loved ones in danger, it takes more than a canny kitty and her team of animal sleuths to set things right again....

> "Told with spunk and plenty of whimsy, this is another delightful entry in a very popular series."
> —*Publishers Weekly*

MURDER ON THE PROWL

When a phony obituary appears in the local paper, the good people of Crozet, Virginia, are understandably upset. Who would stoop to such a tasteless act? Is it a sick joke—or a sinister warning? Only Mrs. Murphy, the canny tiger cat, senses true malice at work. And her instincts prove correct when a second fake obit appears, followed by a fiendish murder... and then another. People are dropping like flies in Crozet, and no one knows why. Yet even if Mrs. Murphy untangles the knot of passion and deceit that has sent someone into a killing frenzy, it won't be enough. Somehow the shrewd puss must guide her favorite human, postmistress "Harry" Haristeen, down a perilous trail to a deadly killer... and a killer of a climax. Or the next obit may be Harry's own.

> "Leave it to a cat to grasp the essence of the cozy mystery: murder among friends." —*The New York Times Book Review*

MURDER, SHE MEOWED

The annual steeplechase races are the high point in the social calendar of the horse-mad Virginians of cozy Crozet. But when one of the jockeys is found murdered in the main barn, Mary Minor "Harry" Haristeen finds herself in a desperate race of her own—to trap the killer. Luckily for her, she has an experienced ally: her sage tiger cat, Mrs. Murphy. Utilizing her feline genius to plumb the depths of human depravity, Mrs. Murphy finds herself on a trail that leads to the shocking truth behind the murder. But will her human companion catch on in time to beat the killer to the gruesome finish line?

"The intriguing characters in this much-loved series continue to entertain." —*The Nashville Banner*

PAY DIRT

The residents of tiny Crozet, Virginia, thrive on gossip, especially in the post office, where Mary Minor "Harry" Haristeen presides with her tiger cat, Mrs. Murphy. So when a belligerent Hell's Angel crashes Crozet, demanding to see his girlfriend, the leather-clad interloper quickly becomes the chief topic of conversation. Then the biker is found murdered, and everyone is baffled. Well, almost everyone... Mrs. Murphy and her friends Welsh corgi Tee Tucker and overweight feline Pewter haven't been slinking through alleys for nothing. But can they dig up the truth in time to save their human from a ruthless killer?

"If you must work with a collaborator, you want it to be someone with intelligence, wit, and an infinite capacity for subtlety—someone, in fact, very much like a cat. . . . It's always a pleasure to visit this cozy world. . . . There's no resisting Harry's droll sense of humor . . . or Mrs. Murphy's tart commentary." —*The New York Times Book Review*

MURDER AT MONTICELLO

The most popular citizen of Virginia has been dead for nearly 170 years. That hasn't stopped the good people of tiny Crozet, Virginia, from taking pride in every aspect of Thomas Jefferson's life. But when an archaeological dig of the slave quarters at Jefferson's home, Monticello, uncovers a shocking secret, emotions in Crozet run high—dangerously high. The stunning discovery at Monticello hints at hidden passions and age-old scandals. As postmistress Mary Minor "Harry" Haristeen and some of Crozet's Very Best People try to learn the identity of a centuries-old skeleton—and the reason behind the murder—Harry's tiger cat, Mrs. Murphy, and her canine and feline friends attempt to sniff out a modern-day killer. Mrs. Murphy and corgi Tee Tucker will stick their paws into the darker mysteries of human nature to solve murders old and new—before curiosity can kill the cat . . . and Harry Haristeen.

"You don't have to be a cat lover to love *Murder at Monticello*." —*The Indianapolis Star*

REST IN PIECES

Small towns don't take kindly to strangers—unless the stranger happens to be a drop-dead gorgeous and seemingly unattached male. When Blair Bainbridge comes to Crozet, Virginia, the local matchmakers lose no time in declaring him perfect for their newly divorced postmistress, Mary Minor "Harry" Haristeen. Even Harry's tiger cat, Mrs. Murphy, and her Welsh corgi, Tee Tucker, believe he smells

A-okay. Could his one little imperfection be that he's a killer? Blair becomes the most likely suspect when the pieces of a dismembered corpse begin turning up around Crozet. No one knows who the dead man is, but when a grisly clue makes a spectacular appearance in the middle of the fall festivities, more than an early winter snow begins chilling the blood of Crozet's Very Best People. That's when Mrs. Murphy, her friend Tucker, and her human companion Harry begin to sort through the clues ... only to find themselves a whisker away from becoming the killer's next victims.

"Skillfully plotted, properly gruesome ... and wise as well as wickedly funny." —*Booklist*

And don't miss the very first

MRS. MURPHY

mystery . . .

WISH YOU WERE HERE

Small towns are like families. Everyone lives very close together . . . and everyone keeps secrets. Crozet, Virginia, is a
typical small town—until its secrets explode into murder.
Crozet's thirty-something postmistress, Mary Minor
"Harry" Haristeen, has a tiger cat (Mrs. Murphy) and a
Welsh corgi (Tee Tucker), a pending divorce, and a bad
habit of reading postcards not addressed to her. When
Crozet's citizens start turning up murdered, Harry remem-
bers that each received a card with a tombstone on the front
and the message "wish you were here" on the back. Intent
on protecting their human friends, Mrs. Murphy and
Tucker begin to scent out clues. Meanwhile, Harry is con-
ducting her own investigation, unaware that her pets are
one step ahead of her. If only Mrs. Murphy could alert her
somehow, Harry could uncover the culprit before another
murder occurs—and before Harry finds herself on the
killer's mailing list.

"Charming . . . Ms. Brown writes with wise, disarming wit."
—*The New York Times Book Review*

RITA MAE BROWN

___56497-8	**VENUS ENVY**	$7.50/$10.99 in Canada
___38040-0	**BINGO**	$19.00/$28.00
___27888-6	**HIGH HEARTS**	$6.99/$9.99
___27573-9	**IN HER DAY**	$6.99/$9.99
___27886-X	**RUBYFRUIT JUNGLE**	$7.50/$10.99
___27446-5	**SOUTHERN DISCOMFORT**	$6.99/$9.99
___26930-5	**SUDDEN DEATH**	$6.99/$9.99
___38037-0	**SIX OF ONE**	$12.95/$19.95
___57224-5	**RIDING SHOTGUN**	$6.99/$9.99
___56949-X	**DOLLEY:** A NOVEL OF DOLLEY MADISON IN LOVE AND WAR	$6.50/$8.99
___34630-X	**STARTING FROM SCRATCH:** A DIFFERENT KIND OF WRITER'S MANUAL	$19.00/$28.00
___37826-0	**RITA WILL:** AN AUTOBIOGRAPHY	$14.95/$22.95

Please enclose check or money order only, no cash or CODs. Shipping & handling costs: $5.50 U.S. mail, $7.50 UPS. New York and Tennessee residents must remit applicable sales tax. Canadian residents must remit applicable GST and provincial taxes. Please allow 4 – 6 weeks for delivery. All orders are subject to availability. This offer subject to change without notice. Please call 1-800-726-0600 for further information.

Bantam Dell Publishing Group, Inc.
Attn: Customer Service
400 Hahn Road
Westminster, MD 21157

TOTAL AMT $_____
SHIPPING & HANDLING $_____
SALES TAX (NY, TN) $_____

TOTAL ENCLOSED $_____

Name _____

Address _____

City/State/Zip _____

Daytime Phone (_____) _____

RMB 4/04